W9-DHX-910

Korea

Nanking

Hankow

Shanghai

Canton

Hongkong

Borneo

Bali

THE ROUTE OF
Santha Rama Rau

0   100   200   300   400

APPROXIMATE SCALE OF MILES

East of Home

Books by Santha Rama Rau

EAST OF HOME

HOME TO INDIA

East of Home

by SANTHA RAMA RAU

HARPER & BROTHERS PUBLISHERS

New York

EAST OF HOME

Copyright, 1950, by Santha Rama Rau

Printed in the United States of America

FIRST EDITION

K-Z

Author's Note

During the journey through Asia which is recorded in this book I had innumerable occasions on which to be grateful to my traveling companions for their friendship, intelligence and energy in pursuing their divergent interests which gave me opportunities of seeing much that I would otherwise have missed. So my first thanks are due to them and especially to Marguerite Brown, whose modesty and request for anonymity have led me to omit her and her valuable contributions from the following pages, and to Faubion Bowers. Without his remarkable knowledge of languages (Japanese, Chinese, Russian, French and Malay—to mention only the ones we used) this journey would have been, if not impossible, at least unrewarding. His understanding of Asia and his quick adjustments to different societies gave us all access to information, friends and ways of life that would have taken far longer in the ordinary way.

My thanks are also due to the many people who were kind to us on this trip, in particular, Dr. S. Allagapan, Indian Consul-General in Batavia, and Mr. and Mrs. John Thivy, Representative of the Government of India in Singapore, for their help and hospitality; to Mr. and Mrs. Dayal of Bangkok, to Mr. and Mrs. Hans Snelleman of Den Pasar, Bali, Mr. Daan Hubrecht of Batavia, to Mr. and Mrs. William Anderson and Mr. D. Ruttonji of Hong Kong, and to Mr. and Mrs. James Nelson of Singapore for their assistance, generosity and the very pleasant times they gave us.

TO ASHA AND NIKHIL WAGLÉ

Contents

Japan

1 Someone in the plane to Japan wakes you soon after sunrise so that you will not miss the sight of Mount Fuji, pale, pretty and unreal at dawn. With this in your mind, if you haven't already seen the bombed cities and the destruction of Europe, the first impression of Tokyo is shocking. Driving in from the airport the desolation you see on each side of the street is given pathos—though that is too weak a word—by the little jerry-built shacks which mushroom out of the piles of rubble and the stricken spaces. Here and there, a concrete building freakishly untouched stands out in important isolation. In the industrial sections the blinded warehouses and factories are everywhere surrounded by the little clusters of wooden huts and their small patches of vegetable gardens. The few blocks which surround the Imperial palace are more or less intact. It is the center of town and there you can see that Tokyo must have been built on a gracious plan with its wide avenues, parks and gardens.

In the grilling heat of the summer of 1947, my father—who had just been appointed India's first ambassador to Japan—and I drove into town and gazed entranced at our first evidence of the Military Occupation. Tokyo's street names had been changed. Bright new signs indicated A Avenue or 15th Street; parks and movies were now called Doolittle Field or the Ernie Pyle Theatre; another notice pointed the way to Washington Heights, a housing settlement.

My father, who feels less need to talk than anyone I know, made one of his rare comments. "Americans," he said, "get homesick so easily."

"And I suppose we don't?" I said. "East is east and. . ."

"It's all very well," he told me, "to be flippant about it, but you

[3]

have traveled only in the West, and you know nothing about your own continent. Here you now feel a foreigner to the Japanese; soon you will feel increasingly foreign to the Americans and Europeans. After all," he said unemphatically, "you belong to Asia, you know, not just India."

"Yes," I said, not believing him, and concentrating much more on the rather theatrical arrival I had planned for us. We were to sweep up to the beautiful Indian Embassy house, I would nod in a kind and friendly way to the Japanese servants lined up on the front porch, order tea in the drawing room, and set about giving it those little touches that the magazines tell me make a house a home. Actually, however, after steaming hours of muddle in which we discovered that the overcrowding in Tokyo was so acute that it would be impossible for us to have a house just yet, we drove to the Imperial Hotel. There a worried American sergeant who looked at my wilted sari (simple but dignified, I had hoped) and could only consider it some unfortunate form of nightdress, told us that they could allot us two rooms on different floors. He didn't take us up by the service elevator, but he looked as if he would like to.

My mother had sent me off to be my father's official hostess, partly because she had too much of her own work at home, and partly, she said, "because it is only a matter of seeing that people don't get orange juice when they want a cocktail at your parties, and in any case I am too old and tired to start dealing with foreigners all over again." At which point she bustled energetically off to one of her endless welfare meetings.

Those first two weeks in Tokyo, among the strangest in my life, almost convinced me that Mother had meant her remarks quite seriously. We were plunged at once into the diplomatic round, and I had the dazed feeling that the foreigners did nothing in Japan except entertain and be entertained. One changed one's clothes half a dozen times a day, arrived breathless at cocktail parties where people were apt to ask in the same tone one uses for commenting on the weather, "And how do you think democratization is coming along?"

My father seemed relatively unimpressed by the curious Occupation dream world in which we saw the Japanese on the streets, re-quisitioned their houses, used their movies and clubs, but never met them. It was after a remark from a fellow guest at a dinner that I finally decided something must be done about it. I had said by way of conversation that I had never been to so many parties in such a short time. "Oh," she said, "just wait till the winter. That's when the Season starts, and really, I think you see as much jewelry and lavishness as you do at the Paris Opera."

On the way home I announced to my father with some despera-tion that I thought the whole point of coming to Japan was to get to know the Japanese, and that so far the only Japanese I had met were the room girls at the hotel. I asked him what he suggested I should do.

With his usual brevity, he said, "Anyone of intelligence would get a job."

"What sort of job?"

"Well, the extraordinary education they give you children these days doesn't really equip you to do anything. I suggest you teach English. I understand they are very short of teachers in Japanese schools just now."

"Yes," I said meekly.

"Not," he continued, "that I expect your unfortunate students to learn very much, but I think they should be able to teach you some-thing. The second thing that you might do is go to the theater. It is not, as you know, something that I particularly enjoy, but you will find that it is the quickest way of learning how a nation thinks. None of the Allied personnel is allowed to go to the Japanese theaters, but as a member of the Diplomatic Corps you can get an off-limits pass." He added in a mutter something that sounded like, "One of the few advantages. . . ." Overcome by this long speech, he relapsed into silence for the rest of the way home.

Just before we got out of the car, he said, "Tomorrow we lunch with General and Mrs. MacArthur. It seems to be the way one presents one's credentials here. After that we will take your problem in hand."

[5]

A few days later my father and I drove out to the Jiyu Gakuyen (Freedom School) which is in one of the Tokyo suburbs. The school grounds are fairly extensive, and scattered through them are the buildings, some Japanese in style, and some of a design I think of, for some reason, as Swedish—big plate-glass picture windows, some of which had been broken and replaced by rice-paper screens; blond wood furniture and walls; flat roofs and terraces. Because the school is not near the industrial section, its buildings were neither bombed nor burned, but there are still the remains of a couple of craters in the grounds.

Old Mrs. Hani, who with her husband runs the school, was waiting to receive us. One of the smallest women I have ever seen, she wore a plain gray kimono, and walked uncertainly down the path toward us. She is nearly blind, and her skin has crumpled, like tissue paper, into a tangle of tiny wrinkles. Her daughter and Mr. Hani walked beside her, watching and guiding her from time to time as though she were a favorite child taking her first steps. Miss Hani, speaking good English, translated her mother's little speech of welcome. We all bowed and smiled. Mrs. Hani raised a tiny trembling hand and touched my sari. In her rather incongruously harsh voice she said something in Japanese. Her daughter translated, "My mother says that she is honored to meet people from the country of Mahatma Gandhi. So late in her life she has not much expectation, but this wish, at least, has come true."

Feeling remarkably silly I replied that I was the one to feel privileged as I had heard a great deal about her valuable work in education in Japan. Then we were formally shown around the school.

Miss Hani, a young woman of considerable charm and a timid manner, told me a little of the history of the Jiyu Gakuyen as we went. Its story is one of great liberalism and equally great hardship. One of the few progressive schools in Japan, it was also the first to introduce co-education. "Of course we had to do that gradually," she said. "To us it is a very foreign idea to have boys and girls in the same school. Even now, they must be in separate

[6]

classrooms, and during meals they sit on opposite sides of the dining hall. We can only move as fast as our supporters will follow."

The difficulties the war years brought started with the name of the school. Great pressure was put on them by the Ministry of Education to change it because the word "Freedom" should not figure in the title of any institution. The Hanis refused to change the name, even though it meant that the Jiyu Gakuyen was not recognized as a school at all. Their graduates were not admitted to any universities, the boys were denied commissions in the army, and the girls—because they were not officially students—were recruited for duty in the wartime factories. The Hanis managed to circumvent this last ruling by moving the classes to the factory and instructing the girls during their lunch hour and in the evenings.

"But the saddest thing," Miss Hani said, "was that often when the students arrived at our little suburban station from their homes, the people of this district used to throw stones at them as they walked to school."

After class we sat in Mrs. Hani's room and had tea and biscuits. All the furnishings in the room had been made by the girls in the handwork classes. The biscuits had been baked by them as part of their training in cooking, and were served by two of the girls. "There are," said Miss Hani, "no servants in our school. You are an Asian so you will understand how strange that seems here."

Mrs. Hani croaked an interruption, "The only way to learn the pain and the value of labor is to labor yourself."

Out of the window I could see several of the boys working in a vegetable garden. "Food," Miss Hani explained, "is so scarce that we have had to dig up the playing fields and grow vegetables in them. Before the war we used to be very proud of our flowers, but now our girls have to learn to make their flower arrangements at home. It has become too expensive an art for us here."

Other things had to go, too. Benches and chairs were burned during the worst days as firewood for cooking. No longer could all the members of a class go on a field trip, so the one or two who

[7]

could manage such a luxury returned to lecture to the rest of their class on what they had learned.

As we were leaving I summoned up enough courage to say, "Miss Hani, I understand that Japanese schools are hard up for English teachers."

"Yes," she said sadly, "here I alone teach English, with one woman to help with the younger children."

"Would you like an assistant?" I asked, and then, most embarrassed at her bewilderment, I rushed on incoherently, "I mean I would love to come and teach here, but I haven't any experience and I went to school in England and college in America but I don't know whether that is a qualification or a disadvantage. And I don't speak Japanese."

"Oh dear!" said Miss Hani, laughing, "You do surprise me. I would be most grateful for any assistance. You could take the older girls. Most of them can read and write English a little and understand it fairly well, but they never hear it spoken. They need practice mostly in conversation, and to you they would *have* to speak in English." After a pause she said, "To an American I would speak about salary, but," smiling comfortably at me, "we understand each other, and I would not insult you with such a discussion."

2 The next week when I went to the Jiyu Gakuyen for my first lesson, I found that my students were to be girls ranging in age from fifteen to seventeen. They were divided into two sections, one slightly more advanced than the other. Miss Hani led me to the classroom and I saw outside the door neatly ranged rows of shoes and slippers. I was wondering whether I should take mine off, when Miss Hani swept me in, introduced me to the girls, and told them in English that I was to teach them conversational English. She added that the girls should feel fortunate because I could tell them about both my own country and the West.

With that remark whatever small degree of self-possession I had retained, vanished, and I said hysterically, "But I don't *know* anything either about India or the West—"

Miss Hani smiled as though she had expected just such Oriental humility from me, and closed the door behind her, leaving me with thirty bright-cheeked and solemn girls. They stood there in their ugly dark-blue uniforms, and followed my progress from door to platform in silence. When I sat down, they all sat, too, produced notebooks and pencils and diligently bent over their desks until all I could see were rows of shiny black heads. There was dead silence and I could think of nothing to say.

Finally I said in desperation, "Well, what do you usually do in this class?"

Nobody answered.

"You," I said, pointing to a girl at the back of the room. "You tell me."

She got obediently to her feet and said, "We study English," and sat down.

"Oh," I said, and stared at the rows of bare feet neatly together under the chairs. "What sort of English?" Then, thinking that that sounded unnecessarily idiotic, I amended it to, "I mean poetry or prose?"

Nobody answered.

"You," I said, pointing to another girl, "do you know any poetry?" This was really not at all the way I had planned the first lesson—or indeed any other lesson.

She stood up and recited without punctuation and in a completely flat voice, "I saw eternity the other night like a great ring of pure and endless light all calm as it was bright and down beneath it time in hours days years driven by the spheres like a great shadow moved in which the world and all her train were hurled." She stopped abruptly.

"Do you understand what that means?"

"Yes."

"Well, what *does* it mean?"

"I cannot explain it in English."

[9]

"Oh," I said with relief, "I can't either."

There was another pause, and some of the girls smiled uncertainly. I smiled back at them and wondered how long we could sit smiling at each other. Then to my intense gratitude, one of the students said, "If you please, with Miss Hani we were reading the *Canterbury Tales* by Chaucer, an English poet of the fourteen century."

Rather startled I asked, "In Middle English?"

"Please?"

"I mean," I said, and stopped, suddenly uncertain of how to define Middle English, and ended weakly, "is it in English?"

"Yes," she said, looking very puzzled.

"Well, then, if you will all get out your books we shall go on reading the *Canterbury Tales*."

They moved their chairs closer together because there was apparently only one book to every three girls. Before they started reading I said importantly, "If there is anything you don't understand, stop and ask me to explain," not at all certain that I would be able to.

One of them gave me a copy of the text, and I saw that it was a series of stories from the *Canterbury Tales* written in a curious stilted prose. In turns the girls laboriously read the even more laborious sentences, until we came to a paragraph in which someone was asked to swear on the Bible.

"Please," one of my students said, "what does this mean, to swear on the Bible?"

"It means that you put your hand on the Bible—the holy book of Christian countries—and after that you are supposed to tell the truth."

The class went into gales of giggles. I asked the girl who had been reading why she laughed.

"It is a strange," she flipped through the pages of her dictionary, "su–per–sti–tion," she said.

"Superstition?"

"Why should he tell the truth because he puts his hand on a book?"

"It is used as a sort of standard. If, after you swear on the Bible, you tell a lie, you are legally liable—I think."

She clearly didn't understand the last sentence, but she asked, "This is still the custom in English?"

After a little thought I said, "Yes, it is. In English courts you are asked to swear on the Bible."

With more giggles she said, "How superstition is the West!"

When both my classes were finished, I had lunch with Miss Hani in the small but very elegant house which she and her parents have on one side of the grounds. We discussed the classes and I asked her whether I could change the text, because I didn't think the girls would ever learn natural conversation if they spent their time reading such starchy English.

"Oh, I agree with you. We use this book because it is the only one with enough copies for the two classes. They were a present many years ago to the school. We cannot get textbooks now."

"How awful! How do you manage?"

"Well," she said, turning bright pink, "although my English is not good, I try to translate foreign books into Japanese. Then the students copy out the whole text longhand. We have to keep those very carefully, so that we can pass them on from class to class. During the war it was particularly necessary because, you see, all the textbooks in Japanese schools had been falsified to make our country appear greater. I have been in Europe and studied there, so I knew there were other books we should study. Those are the ones I brought back, and I still translate them. It takes a long time. But," she went on more briskly, "things will get better now. We get some encouragement from the Occupation people."

Miss Hani was one of the original twenty-six students for whom the school was started; the rest were children of friends who had been dissatisfied with the formal education for Japanese girls. "My mother wanted to make the school a 'family-society.' The first suggestion that we should have no servants came from one of the girls, not from my mother. But we were all interested and so we adopted the plan. I think," she said, "it has been fairly successful."

All the way home, through the shattered suburbs, I planned my

[11]

future clasess and wondered if my students would despise my ineptitude.

That evening my father and I were sitting and reading before dinner. "Would you," I asked him, "call swearing on the Bible a superstition?"

He rustled the evening paper indignantly. "Every nation considers the religious practices of another nation superstitious."

3   As the summer sharpened into autumn in Tokyo, most of my interest was taken up with the Jiyu Gakuyen and my students. The best way to teach them conversational English, I had decided, was to read modern plays aloud in class so that the girls could take different parts and have some feeling of sharing in a not wildly improbable conversation. After some thought I decided on Lillian Hellman's *Watch on the Rhine* as the first to be read, partly because of my great admiration for her as a playwright, partly because her language was not too hopelessly colloquial and slangy, and partly because I felt the play contained some sound democratic principles. After all, one of the aims of the Occupation was supposed to be to teach democracy to the conquered nation. I had copies of the play mimeographed to avoid the textbook problem.

Meanwhile, some other incidents helped me to see a little more of the Japanese. The Occupation personnel (though they were, of course, far from poor) were always with us. While my work at the Jiyu Gakuyen excused me from the ladies' lunches, the evening parties were unavoidable. One evening, however, following my father's advice, I went to the theater. The first play I saw was one of the rare performances given for the Allied personnel, and consequently the program notes were very full. They contained a translation of the play in English by Faubion Bowers, an American major who had been aide to General MacArthur and had given up that job to become the chief censor of the Japanese theater. From the notes I learned that the leading parts were to be played by Japan's most celebrated actors, Baigyoku and Kichiemon. Baigyoku, the last of the great onnagata (man-actress) was seventy-three years old, and in that play, Gappo Ga Tsuji, played the part of a girl of nineteen. Stylized, extraordinarily delicate and precise of gesture, Baigyoku was certainly the most beautiful and convincing nineteen-year-old I had ever seen on the stage.

The story was my first example of the highly involved morality of the Japanese stage, the incessant fight between love and duty, and—surprisingly—a passionate rebellion against the rigid cruelties which the old Japanese code forced on its people. Gappo, an old man who has renounced his life as a samurai to become a priest, has one daughter, Tamate Gozen. She is married to one of the ruling lords of the country, many years older than herself, and with two sons by his first wife. She discovers that one of the stepsons wants to usurp the power of the House by killing his brother, so to save the good stepson from death she gives him a magic potion which makes him appear to be leprous. She knows that in no other way can he be made to leave the house.

Meanwhile, she has allowed stories to be circulated which make it appear that she and her stepson have been lovers. Since such a love was considered incestuous by the Japanese it is one of the most terrible crimes she could have committed. She runs away to her father's place of retirement where her stepson, blind and disfigured, also seeks refuge.

Tamate deliberately lets her parents overhear a scene in which she confesses her love to her stepson. Horrified at her unnatural wickedness, Gappo rushes out and stabs her, shouting, "I who have not even killed a fly in twenty years, have killed my own flesh and blood, vile daughter! Now die."

In an infinitely moving last scene Tamate tells her parents and her stepson the whole story, that she had feigned the passion for her stepson because she knew she could drive her father to kill her for it, that the only cure for the stepson's leprosy is the lifeblood of a woman. She gives him the blood to drink, tells him the plot and returns him, miraculously cured, to his fiancée.

Told like that it sounds flat and melodramatic, but on the stage, like all great art, it has such power and beauty that the story scarcely

[13]

matters. It was a combination of music, dance and drama, costumed with great magnificence, brocades, cloth of gold and silks. A chorus, in the Greek sense, commented on and described the action, and little men in black costumes and black caps changed the props and arranged costumes on the stage for dramatic poses or speeches. After the first few minutes one was not conscious of them at all. The dancing and the acting had an assurance and polish which I had seen nowhere else in the world. I had certainly never thought of the Japanese as a theatrically minded people.

4   My father and I had called officially on Matsudaira, the president of the Upper House. His daughter then invited me to lunch a few days later at her mother's house. She phoned to ask if I would please come to her house first so that we could go on together and she could show the driver the way.

When I got there she came out carrying a shopping bag and dressed in a rather crumpled rayon crepe dress. She is a short, plumpish woman of about thirty to thirty-five with the usual short-legged, wide-hipped Japanese figure and no pretensions to beauty or even prettiness, but with a great grace of manner and a very appealing simplicity. The first thing she asked me was whether she could take her two daughters with us "because they love to visit my mother and they so seldom have a chance to ride in a car."

"How do you usually get about?"

"By bus—we cannot afford a car and my mother lives so far away that by bus it takes us an hour and a half and this is very tiring for the children."

On the drive she pointed out her children's school to me. It was in pretty bad repair and it had been used as a barracks during the war but the children were helping to reconstruct it and did not seem to mind too much. "Except in winter," she said, "it is very cold and then they have no heat in the school. Some of their classes are given while the children run around in the room to keep warm."

I asked her more about the school, having by now a professional interest. She told me that this used to be the school to which only the children of the aristocracy or people connected with the Imperial household could go. In those days before the war the girls were taught the things correct for the aristocracy to know—Japanese history, painting, music and ladylike arts. With the end of the war this school, along with the others was "democratized." Anyone can go there now. A change of heart was supposed to accompany a change of textbooks.

I asked her if she approved of the changes. She said carefully that it was too early to judge. "It is like having your entire adolescence crowded into two years. Luckily my children are still very young, only five and eight, so that they have not felt the change as badly. It is the sixteen-year-olds who suffer most for they have had some years of schooling under the old system and a couple under the new. They do not know how to adjust to the changes and they think it simply means that they can go out and generally defy their parents —all these things were strongly disapproved of in my day. I do not think they understand yet what it is all about. They are both too young and too old to be able to assimilate the new—is 'ideology' the word I want?" I could not decide whether she was being sarcastic. "I expect they will calm down after a while when the novelty has worn off but I do not know whether they will adjust to either world."

"Does that mean that you think there is a chance of the old order returning?"

She smiled. "I do not know about these things but I can tell you that for the next few years their parents will worry dreadfully because, like parents all over the world, I suppose, they will feel that their children have not the experience or the firm standards to find their way in the new world and, what is worse, have not the time to learn before they are adults and expected to assume the responsibility for that world. So far they have learned only the easy and superficial things—the impertinence and the dancing."

Her mother's house turned out to be a small wooden cottage, typically Japanese, some distance from the center of Tokyo, with a pocket handkerchief of a garden, all of it used for growing vege-

[15]

tables. The children ran in to their grandmother who was standing on the stairs and were promptly put into the hands of an amah and sent off to eat their lunch. The president's wife is a slender, extremely poised woman. As a girl she must have been beautiful and her face still has the clean lines and easy assurance of what one likes to call 'breeding.' She was wearing a dark-blue kimono with a gray silk obi. She bowed to me in greeting and then to her daughter, waited while we took off our shoes, and then welcomed us into her house.

The ground floor had one long room with a veranda opening onto the garden all along one side. Beyond that there was only a kitchen. The main room was divided into two with the usual light wooden Japanese partitions. It had tatami matting on the floor and parchment windowpanes.

The old lady began the conversation on a light diplomatic level, chatting in good, careful English about Europe and people. Her husband, as ambassador for the old government of Japan, and she had traveled over most of Europe and America, stationed first in London, later in Paris and still later in Washington. Her daughters went to school at Cheltenham and were presented at Court, of which she made rather an amusing story about the difficulty of keeping ostrich feathers in the straight, heavy Japanese hair.

I gathered that she and her family had been among the most powerful in prewar days, with several town and country houses and all the attendant luxury, but she made no reference to her change of circumstances. The whole conversation had a most unreal quality like a scene from one's childhood.

"I have often wanted to visit your country. My husband was there for a brief stay once."

"When conditions are a little easier I hope you will come."

She smiled as if I had said something rather witty. "Ah yes. Traveling these days is not very amusing. Everything must be in quadruplicate with fingerprints and photographs—and I photograph exceedingly badly."

Of course, we both knew that no Japanese was allowed to travel yet. She continued, "I feel that our two great countries have much

[16]

in common," and smiling so that I could decide for myself whether or not she meant it, "we both have a foreign conqueror to get rid of, for instance."

Feeling both flattered that she should say such a thing to me, and worried because, after all, I was a member of the Allied personnel, I changed the subject quickly and commented on the charm of the house. She looked around the room and suggested that it was rather incongruous. It was clear what she meant because, though this cheap little house had not much furniture in it, what there was must have cost more than the entire house.

She said, "We salvaged what we could from our home in the country—just a few pieces, that is." She looked around the room and pointed out two fat Japanese dolls in gaudy clothes. "Those two dolls in the corner have only a sentimental value, of course. When our town house was bombed, everything was burned to the ground but, curiously enough, these two escaped. They are the symbols of good fortune and long life."

I looked at her sharply to see if I could catch the irony in her expression because there was none in her tone, but she only smiled vaguely.

"It is stupid to get so attached to *things*," her daughter said, "yet when I visited our Tokyo house after the Americans had lived in it I could not help being sad at the wreck of all our beautiful things. You see, my mother and father spent a lifetime collecting the stuff for that house from every country they visited. Most of it was broken or scarred beyond repair—and the floors somehow saddened me most! Although the house had no purpose once the things in it were ruined—but the parquet and the marble—it was very depressing."

I thought, one cannot be sorry for them, think of the things *they* ruined and scarred.

Her sister-in-law who, owing to the housing shortage, was living there with her children, came in to tell us that lunch was ready. The old lady led the way into the other half of the room. This part was completely bare except for a rickety table and four chairs. In a recess at the far end of the room was a very beautiful arrangement

[17]

of flowers and beyond it, hanging on the wall, was a long scroll picture of trees and mountains. I asked about that and was told that it is customary in Japanese homes to have in the main room such a recess "where we place something beautiful and also a picture appropriate to the season of the year."

Lunch, served by a maidservant, was brought on separate little lacquer trays holding a bowl of rice, a glob of bean curd and a green vegetable that looked like spinach, four tiny pieces of very crisp fried fish, and chopsticks. For the first time the old lady looked uncomfortable.

"You must forgive the simplicity of the meal. My daughter assured me that you would prefer to eat what the family normally eats every day."

"Of course," I said, embarrassed by her embarrassment, "you must tell me what it all is. It is very exciting for me as I have never eaten Japanese food before."

"Ah yes," she said, "all of you have your food flown out from America or Australia, don't you?"

"Well," I said, a little on the defensive, "the idea is, that while there is still a food shortage in Japan we should not consume any of the country's supplies while we can be supplied from abroad."

"Indeed?" noncommittally.

The maid came in with four little bowls containing one onion each covered with a sort of meat sauce. I noticed that everybody finished everything on their trays so I did, too. No waste. We were not offered a second helping of anything and I hoped that I did not shorten the family's food supply too much by sharing their lunch. The old lady again apologized because there was no sweet. "Sugar is so hard to get that I usually reserve it for the children. We make a kind of sweet out of maize and sugar for them."

Unaccountably, all three of them began laughing. She said, "That is a sort of family joke. You see there was a time when we all believed that the only use for maize was to feed it to our pet birds. Now I tell the children that it is the most rare and most delicious food there is. That is why we offer it to them." She went on quickly, "Of course, this is nothing new. During the war it was the same and it has the advantage of keeping our figures slender, and for the children it is no hardship because they have never tasted real sweets and chocolate. The trouble with you girls," she said to her daughter, "was really that you had far too much of that kind of thing when you were children. I remember I had a shocking time with your complexions!"

Before we had finished lunch the maid came in and whispered something to the old lady. She said, "Excuse me," and got up. "Apparently, my other daughter has come to visit me today, too." There was a feeling of excitement. She went off and I heard voices in the hall and then they went upstairs.

We finished lunch and her daughter and I returned to the living room where I was shown some flower and landscape paintings, some done on fans, others on rice paper, and a couple on silk. She told me that they were her mother's work—her relaxation when she had some spare time. They were very pale and delicate, fugitive bamboos blowing across the ghosts of rivers, curly faded chrysanthemums against watery skies.

Soon the maid came down and asked if we would go upstairs. "Would you mind if we go and see my sister? We so seldom get a chance of seeing her."

The upstairs floor was arranged exactly like the living and dining rooms except that there was no furniture at all. I supposed the entire family slept there. As we got to the doorway my hostess made a very low ceremonial bow and waited till she was asked to come in. I rather stupidly held out my hand and said, "How do you do!" The sister looked surprised, but took it. The old lady said, "I wanted you to meet my other daughter, the Princess Chichibu."

We all waited for the princess to sit down on the floor and then we sat, too. They treated her with all the formality of royalty and none of the familiarity of a member of the family. She asked me if I minded sitting on the floor. I said, "No, it is our custom in India, too."

She said, "That gives us something in common."

There was a silence and I gathered that nobody spoke until the princess chose a subject. She was about the same height and build as her sister, with the same sort of figure, a prettier face, beautiful hands but less charm, and gracious rather than graceful. Her dress was light-green linen with no style, badly cut, and did not begin to fit her—she wore no make-up.

Finally, "How nice it is to be in Tokyo again!"

I said, "Do you live far from here?"

"We have to stay in our house at the foot of Mount Fuji. You must visit us there sometime. It is quite a pretty place."

"It is supposed to have the best view in Japan," said her sister.

"That sounds beautiful. Do you manage to come in often?—though I cannot imagine why you should want to leave a place like that."

"Not often, sometimes twice a month, traveling is so difficult these days."

"But I have heard it is a heavenly drive."

"We cannot drive," she said, amused. "We have no petrol for our car."

"But your trains," I said, not realizing that I was getting myself in deeper, "I have only been in them once but they were so comfortable and quick."

"Ah, you speak of the Allied Ltd. No, we may not travel on this. We must go by the regular day coach and that means waiting at the station for a ticket for three hours—there are no reservations as you know—and then the coaches are so crowded that we usually have to stand all the way, but everyone must travel that way nowadays."

Her mother joined in, "Last time my husband and I traveled it was quite funny. He is an old man and could not stand in line so I queued up for him: then we got our tickets and rushed for the train, but he is a little slow and got pushed to the outside of the crowd. I was jammed in the middle but managed to get on. Then I noticed that he was not there and had no hope of getting through the crowd around the door before the train started, so I shouted to him and he climbed in through one of the windows. People helped to push him in because he is an old man, but he got stuck in the window, which is small, and the train began to move. I was terrified. Eventually we pried him loose. The crowd was much amused."

I did not know what to say. Fortunately she continued, "That kind of thing is all right for us." And then, with her first sign of anger, and one which I did not think her capable of, "To treat royalty that way is inexcusable."

The princess said, "It is not always quite so bad. When people recognize me they usually clear a seat for me and leave one on each side free. That is not too bad."

Her mother repeated, "They may take away our cars, our houses, whatever they want to, but they should respect royalty. At first, you know, I refused to leave the house when I found that I must travel by bus and train, but how long can that feeling last? Now I do my own marketing with all the other housewives. I bargain at the bazaars along with my servants. For us it does not matter. But for the imperial family. . . . Only in Asia do they understand royalty, even in Europe it is gone."

Clearly the whole family was very proud when the Emperor's brother had chosen to marry one of their girls. Very few families of the aristocracy have the privilege of being so closely connected with the Imperial household.

I left soon after that. I said, "Good-bye, your Highness. It has been most pleasant."

She said, "It has been a long time since a stranger called me that. We shall look forward to entertaining you."

Her sister saw me to the door. As I was leaving I said, "May I phone you sometime? Perhaps we could drive out to the country with the children."

She said, "This is very kind of you but I will phone you. We are not allowed to be listed in the phone book."

The old lady said, "It has been an honor to have you here."

I said, "It has been an honor to be here."

The next day I sent my entire month's chocolate ration to the children because chocolates are such an important part of being eight years old, and since no Japanese was allowed in the hotel I had no other way of returning their hospitality. I felt rather silly about it afterward. They probably took a bite and thought, what strange tastes these foreigners have—maize flour and sugar is much nicer. . . .

5 I have always thought of autumn as a fading, misty time. Damp woods, the smell of dead leaves, the dying season. In Japan it has a flamboyance and a glory that seems to be vaguely improper, mourners in scarlet. We spent a week end at Nikko, driving there for hours between mountains flaming with autumn. It seemed strange to be surrounded by such extravagance of color; in Bombay, autumn is only a steamy, shabby month between the rains of summer and the equability of winter. In Nikko itself the famous temple came as another surprise—the ornate gold and red arches, the lacquered pavilions. It was extraordinary that the Japanese, who in their manners and their private homes display such elegance and restraint, should have a countryside theatrical to the point of vulgarity.

I said something of the sort to my father who turned and stared at me. "What astonishing things you come out with," he said. "All this talk of vulgarity and good taste. Is it something you have picked up in the West? It seems too elementary to tell you that standards in art, as in food, vary from country to country. The point at which you start to understand the Japanese will be the point at which you find the same things as they do beautiful. By which I do not mean simply *recognize* what they think beautiful but actually get the same esthetic pleasure from them although. . ." his sentence trailed off, "one has to select—an activity youth is congenitally incapable of. . . ."

Autumn at the Jiyu Gakuyen was beautiful, too, but in a quieter way than the mountains. I found my eyes turning continually to the copper and gold outside the classroom window. Through the paper screens the powdered sunlight slanted more acutely across the floor. The girls seemed interested in *Watch on the Rhine.* Reading the first act we came to the sentence, "On that day, I see twenty-seven murdered in a Nazi street fight." One of the girls asked, "What does this word mean—'murder'?"

I said, without thinking much, "To kill someone."

"Is it the same thing," the girl asked, "to kill and to murder?"

"Not exactly, murder implies a motive."

The girl did not quite understand that. "If you drive your car and a child runs across the street and is killed, is it murder?"

"No, that would be an accident. You do not wish to kill the child."

She said, "Ah so, a soldier in the war he sees an enemy coming to him he shoots and kills; he wishes very much that man dead, is it a killing?"

I did not quite know how to explain that and fell back on legalisms that I am not sure they understood. I said that would probably be considered manslaughter in a court of law, a killing in self-defense.

"Not in law," she said, "in morals?"

"I cannot tell you," I answered. "Some aspects of that problem are being considered in the War Crimes Tribunal in Tokyo. Why don't you go and listen sometime? Have any of you ever been?"

None of them had so I told them if they wanted to go I would give them study time off for it. Apparently some of them did go because after class one day one of the girls came up to me. She was a sturdy, quiet girl called Yoko who knew rather more English than the rest of the class because her father had been educated in America. She said, "I speak English badly but would like to ask some questions about the trial."

"Of course," I said, pleased.

She frowned, "Like this. You too are of Asia, otherwise I could not ask." She framed her sentences carefully as though she had been thinking them out. "Our leaders are accused of aggression and imperialism. Is that so?"

"Yes."

[23]

"Well, among the judges is a Dutchman, and do the Dutch not conquer and rule Indonesia?"

I nodded feebly.

"Also there is a Frenchman, his country rules Indo-China. The Englishman left your country only in August but stays in Burma and Malaya. The Chinese say they rule Tibet and Sinkiang who do not wish them there."

"Yes," I said, "but those are old conquests. One cannot go back through history righting wrongs—one must begin somewhere."

"The Russian," Yoko asked gently, "the conquests of his country in East Europe, they are old, too?"

"No, listen," I said, "I agree with you. Where conquests are so old that the people themselves have forgotten, one might as well leave those alone. But I think the principle should be that where a nation wants a foreign conqueror to leave their country and yet they remain, that should be remedied." I stopped suddenly wondering if that applied to the Occupation of Japan. "Besides," I said, trying to put myself right, "there were other things, atrocities and so on."

"Ah! those come in any war."

"Well, the Allies did not go around beheading captured airmen," I said on surer ground.

"Yes, those should be punished. But is it worse to behead a man than to shoot him or hang him or kill him with an atom bomb?"

"It seems barbaric to the West or rather," I said, thinking of the far worse atrocities that the West has been guilty of, their concentration camps, and torture chambers, "to the democracies." Then I amended that to, "to Americans," because of the atrocities of the democratic countries in their Asian colonies.

"It is," Yoko said thoughtfully, "the custom of the country. Some foreign customs seem barbaric to us, too." She apologized to me. "You said you wish us to understand these things. I do not criticize. There are many good things, but is confusing. Is it not so?"

[24]

6 Toward the end of October my father had to go on a tour of Kyoto, Osaka and Kobe to inspect the factory conditions and to confer with the Indian local community which has dwindled through war and the Occupation from thousands to a few business men and their families.

In Kobe and Osaka we were conducted by Japanese officials around the industrial and shipping areas. The Kobe docks were like something from one of those photographs of the surface of the moon. It was hard to believe that such destruction was possible. Here the structures had been of steel, stone and concrete. Some of the bombed areas in Japan looked less frightful because there was relatively little rubble. The wooden houses burned away to ash, and in the two years since the end of the war huts had grown up lining the roads and hiding the vast blank areas behind them. Here, too, they were rebuilding but still the scars were wide and humiliating.

We were staying for a few days in Kobe with a Japanese business-man who had had, before the war, extensive trade interests in India, and had been a millionaire in his own country. He had been com-pelled to sell his other houses and live in their little house in Tarumi which was originally intended as a seaside honeymoon house for their only daughter, Sakiko, and her husband.

It was the first time that I had stayed in a real Japanese home with a Japanese family, because without permission no Occupation personnel, including the Diplomatic Corps, were allowed to be in a Japanese house later than eleven o'clock at night. I took in every detail of this visit because I thought it might be my only one.

The Tarumi house was partly Japanese in style with tatami floors, sliding screens and paper windows, but a new wing was built on at the time of Sakiko's marriage. This was more Western in style with big picture windows on the sunny side of the house and mod-ern bathrooms. That was the reason the family now lived there— the heating problem was much lessened.

When we arrived we were taken into the Japanese part and sat formally on the floor, and drank the tea that was served. Old Mr. Kishimoto sat with us and equally formally offered us the hospitality of his house. He was a small thin man with enormous poise and a certain weariness of manner that foreigners might easily mistake for arrogance. He spoke some English but preferred to converse through an interpreter. Later, after I had been in Japan for some time, I discovered that many Japanese, particularly the older people, would rather work through an intermediary, or a go-between, whether it is with foreigners or with people of their own nationality, and whether it is to arrange an assignation or a business deal.

Once I asked my father what the reason was. "I dare say it seems evasive," he said, "and slightly dishonest to your generation, but I find that it saves much of the embarrassment and allows for a far clearer exposition of things than direct contact. The responsibility is taken off both parties, and if it is possible to quarrel in a civilized way, that must surely be it."

Mr. Kishimoto's daughter, who, to my bewilderment, was introduced as Mrs. Kishimoto, was very unlike him. She spoke fluent English because she had had an English governess as a child and felt much more at home in "modern" Japan than her parents did. She was a pretty, high-colored girl, short but with an athletic definiteness about her movements.

When she saw me to my room in the new wing, I was impressed first of all by the magnificent view of sea and rocks and garden from the window. It is the well-known Japanese genius for making the view of their country-side an essential part of their interior decoration. On the shelf over the bed was a picture of Sakiko in her wedding dress, standing with a good-looking Japanese man.

"Is that your husband?" I asked.

"Yes, that was taken on our wedding day."

"Is he also a Kishimoto?"

"No, that is a custom we have in this country. I was the only daughter, you see, and my parents wished for the Kishimoto name to continue, so my husband married into my family instead of the other way round. It is sometimes done that way but it would mean,

[26]

of course, that I could never marry the eldest son of another family. He would have to continue his father's name."

"And your daughter? Does she continue a Kishimoto?"

"Yes, all my children would continue with my name. In a way it is a pity that I have only a daughter because with the changing times it may not be possible to keep this custom up here."

I think that this was yet another proof of the importance of one's name in any country in Asia. It is a feeling that the West seems to be losing, but here it is very important for people to have the assurance of this continuity. The maid came in after a few minutes and showed me down to the bathroom—a sort of modern version of the Japanese bath. Here, unlike most Japanese baths, you could lock the door and have the place to yourself but you were still expected to wash on the little stool outside the bathtub and get into the bath only when you were already clean. Then you sit on the benches around the side of the tub to warm yourself and relax. Here, too, as in India the people consider an ordinary tub bath an extraordinarily dirty habit. The thought of sitting in one's own soiled water is altogether revolting to them. The maid waited about a bit to find out whether I wanted her to scrub my back for me. I think she thought I was rather lacking in elegance because I said, no, I could do it myself.

In the afternoon Sakiko and I went for a long walk into the beautiful hills behind Tarumi. We talked a lot about the war and she told me that she was married when she was nineteen and the war was still in its victorious stages. The next year the air raids started and her baby was born in the middle of one of the worst. "Those were dreadful days and nights after that—the bombing and the fires. Even now I can never listen to the sound of dried autumn leaves blowing along the roads because that was the sound the fires made in the wooden houses near the hospital." She stared down the hill at the gilded trees and the distant glitter of the sea. "After I came home with my baby I used to see very few people. In those days people were so harsh about any foreign ideas that even if I were to read one of my English books on the train, people might denounce me for being a spy. I used to turn the dust covers of

[27]

the books inside out and write Japanese titles on them so that people would not guess. You see I was already under suspicion because I had several foreign friends."

We sat on top of the hill in the warm autumn sunshine, looking out at the coast and the little boats. She suddenly sprang up, and smiled at me in a wide friendly way. "After all," she said, "in the end there is only this—the hills, the sea, and the lovely times of day."

When we got back to the house, Sakiko asked me to come to her room and showed me her magnificent kimonos, including her wedding ones which she had never worn since. There were dozens that came in her trousseau which she had not even unpacked from their original wrappings because during the war one did not wear bright-colored kimonos or display new ones. She poured them out on the floor—the oranges, greens and purples; the obis with golden flowers, the brocaded ones, and the brilliant, soft, silk petticoats. She told me that a kimono must always be patterned in some way, however insignificant. A plain-colored kimono is never worn. The younger you are, the brighter the colors you may wear. In fact it used to be possible to guess the age of a Japanese woman within a couple of years by looking only at the color and design of her dress. Nowadays, of course, with the shortage of materials, you wore whatever you could afford.

Sakiko called in her maid and said "Now we will put a kimono on you and you will see how it looks."

"Oh no," I protested, "you are so much shorter than I. How could I possibly fit into your clothes?"

She laughed and told me that all kimonos are the same size and have to be shortened to suit the individual figure. When Sakiko wears one it trails for several inches on the floor until it is taken up by the sashes that hold it in place.

First of all she made me wear a plain white cotton jacket next to my skin. Over that came a solid-colored silk kimono tied firmly around the hips with a sash. On top of that, several more of varying designs and colors—reds and greens decorated with plum blossom,

[28]

pine trees or geometrical patterns until there was the final formal kimono—the one that the outsider would see. You vary the number that you wear underneath according to the temperature of the day and even in winter you wear only silk, many layers of it, but never wool. The hem of the kimono should come to the ankle in front and a little lower behind. For the outside kimono, several silk sashes bind it firmly in place around your hips and waist, and over the whole lot the obi is tied. This is a long strip of stiff brocade nine inches to a foot wide which is pulled very tight over the sashes. The obi pushes your breasts in and extends to your hipbone, thus giving you the ideal Japanese figure which is a slender cylinder. I found it hard to breathe in an obi, but when I sat on the floor in the Japanese way, back on my heels, then it gave my back the support it needed.

In return I dressed Sakiko in one of my saris and she was amazed at the freedom a sari gives, the fact that it pulls nowhere and is tight nowhere. Used to the long trailing sleeves of the kimono, the management of which is a special art in itself, she found the bare arms and midriff that a sari leaves very disconcerting and embarrassing.

"Isn't it curious," she said, "how the customs of different countries can train you to think that this is seductive, or that is immodest. Here for instance, it is the back of a woman's neck which is considered most seductive. In China, I am told, it is the feet, and a woman will not expose them except in the most intimate times. How is it in India?"

"In some parts it is considered immodest to show your legs, but in other parts you drape your sari in such a way that the backs of your legs all the way to the knee are exposed. The orthodox Muslim women, of course, keep their faces veiled."

"Then there are some who find a woman's long hair most seductive. In America it is the breasts, is it not?"

"So one gathers," I said.

"And in France?"

"Well—" I began uncertainly.

"But the French, I hear, are very reasonable people," she interrupted, "perhaps it is by her character that they find a woman attractive?"

"Yes," I said quickly, "I'm sure that's right."

Sakiko wouldn't wear her sari to dinner, though. And we both went down in kimonos to the great amusement of both Mr. Kishimoto and my father. It was a Japanese dinner in the Japanese part of the house. Sakiko prepared sukiyaki for us because, she said, "It is the dish that foreigners like best in Japanese food."

With it she served a lot of saké and like a conventional Japanese woman went from guest to guest filling the wine cups and sipping them only when she was asked to. We all laughed a lot and sang and moved about the table drinking with each other.

My father who, I think, usually felt that chopsticks, raw fish and all this taking off and putting on of shoes was designed only to embarrass the foreigner, seemed interested and amused by a dinner party for the first time that I could remember. We drank to each other, to our respective countries. Sakiko kept filling up the little white porcelain wine cups. Altogether it seemed like the friendliest and easiest evening I had spent in Japan so far. There is a curious solidarity between Asians of which I had never been conscious until I went to Japan, and here I began to notice it in my own attitude, too. It is like having been at the same school with someone, however different your opinions may be. Finally Mr. Kishimoto, in his tired voice, said, "Let us drink to the prosperity and freedom of Asia." For that toast we all stood up.

7 The day before we left for Kyoto, the Kishimotos took us up to an enormous theatrical school outside Kobe where hundreds of girls are trained every year for musical comedy. It is called the Takarazuka School, a flourishing establishment, with several auditoriums of varying sizes where the girls put on their tremendously successful shows. The day we went there they performed a Japanese version of *Lilac Time*. They handled the Schubert music with ease

and precision and surprisingly little sentimentality, and had dressed it up with special choruses of their own, and dances in which rows of girls in sequins and tights, crinolines and garden hats performed with the symmetry and exactness that I had thought one could not find outside the Radio City Music Hall.

The Takarazuka Girls' Opera, with its lavish, flashy musicals, is unique in Japan, and extraordinary anywhere in the world. Sakiko told me that the theater was started before the war, and now employs about five hundred girls who are hired when they are about sixteen, and who are trained for four years in dancing, singing and acting—all Western in style. All the parts in the plays and the vaudeville shows are taken by girls, dressed up as men if necessary. They have become so popular that they have built their own special theaters for their shows in some of the major Japanese cities.

After the show, Sakiko took me to the stage entrance to see the crowds of schoolgirls who wait to ask their favorite Takarazuka stars for autographs, photographs, or simply to touch their dresses as they leave the theater. Some of the stars leave the Takarazuka Theater for the movies, some stay on as instructors, many marry and leave the stage completely.

It seemed very odd, after that glimpse of Broadway inside the theater, to stand in the Japanese evening afterward and watch the crowds hurry along in their kimonos and sandals to get home before dark.

We left Tarumi the next day and drove to Kyoto, taking Sakiko with us to spend a few days there before our return to Tokyo. It was with a feeling of unfamiliarity and almost surprise that I saw a city untouched by the war. No bomb damage, no burned houses, no wide untidy spaces in the city scene.

In our short holiday there we wandered around the palaces and the gardens and walked bare-footed along the corridors of the old shogun's palace where the highly polished floorboards were fitted in such a way that as you walked they squeaked against each other and produced the continuous sound of nightingales to accompany your footsteps.

We walked through the broad avenues and narrow alleys of the

[31]

city and I had never realized that wooden architecture could acquire such a glow and such distinction. One afternoon we drove to a place just outside the city where the river spreads out from its rapids into a more peaceful stream. Sakiko said, "Before the war it used to be wonderful to come here in the springtime. We used to get into flat-bottomed boats and shoot down the rapids to this bridge. The cherry blossom is all out at that time—can you imagine it?—rushing down the river with the flowers overhead almost meeting across the narrow parts of the rapids and the petals all about you in the water."

We leaned on the railing of the bridge and Sakiko told me some children's stories because I was collecting them to send back to my small niece. The first one she told me was a story about sparrows. "Once upon a time," she said, "there lived an old couple and they had a pet sparrow. One day the old man returned home to find the sparrow crying, and when he asked the reason the sparrow said that the old woman had cut his tongue off because he had eaten some of the starch she had made."

"But what a peculiar story," I said.

"Don't you like it?"

"Well it doesn't seem to have much point."

"What do you mean 'point'?"

"I mean it has no incident or climax."

She looked most surprised. "But how can you have more incident than the tragedy of that sparrow?"

"Well tell me another one, a happy one."

The next story, very like *Rip Van Winkle*, was about a fisherman who makes friends with an old tortoise and is taken by him to a luxurious palace under the sea. He stays there for a few days and returns to his home laden with presents, only to find that years have passed, his friends are dead and he himself is an old, old man.

8 Our Kyoto visit ended with a dinner given for us by Mr. Kaku, a business friend of my father, in one of the famous old restaurants of the city. It was an enthralling evening for me because it was the first time I had ever seen geishas. He had invited the best of the Kyoto geishas to entertain us and the small group of his friends that were there, too. None of the guests brought their wives so I was the only girl at dinner that night.

Until that time I had had the usual vague ill-informed idea of the geishas and their work. At dinner that evening I found that they were middle-aged women, not particularly beautiful but with a social assurance and dignity that was most unexpected. Mr. Kaku told me that the word "geisha" means literally an "art person." The old tradition of the courtesans from which the present geisha system evolved, placed the emphasis on the art and intelligence of the woman rather than on her sexual appeal. A trained geisha must be proficient in flower arranging, singing, dancing, conversation, the tea ceremony and writing, "which is the same as painting," said Mr. Kaku. "You will notice how often we hang a series of written characters on our walls for the same pleasure as we get from a picture." They received a formal education and sometimes became the valued, behind-the-scenes advisors of statesmen.

"There are subsidiary arts, too," Mr. Kaku explained. "Conversation with men, for instance, is considered a separate art. In the old days, flower, and autumn-leaf viewing was considered most important and indeed a special esthetic knowledge. Sometimes one would have moon-viewing parties and in that, too, a geisha should be proficient."

Since the geishas are mainly entertainers they can choose their lovers to the degree that they are valuable as artists. A very great singer, for instance, cannot be bought because her income from her music, from records, and public or private performances is great enough to give her complete independence. All the great women artists were trained from among the geishas until now. "The system

[33]

is decaying and so is much of the art," Mr. Kaku said. "It is a tragedy, do you not think? Can this democratic civilization be worth the loss of things that were great in our country? Even if democracy were suitable for Asians—and I am not sure that it is—it ought to be the kind of democracy that would help us to preserve the best in our culture rather than to accept the second-best in somebody else's culture."

During the war the geishas worked in factories, and their hands, famous for their softness and beauty of gesture, became rough and unattractive. They had to sell their hair, so in many cases the elaborate characteristic coiffure of the geishas, with its loops and wings of highly varnished hair, its combs and ornaments, is now replaced by either Western hair styles, by a knot at the nape of the neck, or if the geisha still attempts the traditional, a wig.

Besides the geishas there were four or five maikos brought in to entertain us. The maiko, literally "a dancing child," is twelve to fifteen in age, and there are now only thirty left in Kyoto. There used to be two hundred before the war. They are a sort of apprentice geisha and get their education and training in art in the geisha house and under the protection of the older geishas. It is a system which seems to the Western mind rather shocking, yet compared with what some children can expect should they stay with their very poor families or in the villages, it has its compensations.

In contrast with the simple sober-colored kimonos of the older geisha, the maiko wears brilliant silks with wide elaborate obis in gold and brocade. Her hair style is highly complicated. It takes several hours to dress, then it is decorated with little tinkling ornaments, with silver and tinsel; combs with twisting, flashing sequins dangling from them, little bells, tiny fans and paper flowers can all be used. As I came into the restaurant they giggled and whispered with excitement, and as soon as I sat down all the little girls ignored the men guests and crowded around me to examine my sari and ask whether the jewelry I was wearing was Indian and to find out whether the gold in my brocade choli was real; to open my evening bag and with no embarrassment to examine the contents in great

[34]

detail. They were called back to their work by the older geishas and, still chattering, picked up the bottles of saké and poured out the wine for the guests. During the evening I noticed that even the older geishas found opportunities to come to where I was sitting and asked me exactly the things that the maikos had wanted to know. "Only the Orient," one of them told me, "really understands materials."

The meal was a rather elaborate version of the usual Japanese dinner—raw fish (tuna fish this time), eels, *tempura*-style fried prawn, various sorts of pickles, fried mushrooms, two sorts of soup and rice. The geishas unobtrusively but most efficiently helped one to eat, saw that more was brought of any dish you particularly liked, took the bones out of the fish for you, kept your cup full of warmed wine, and made conversation on whatever subject you showed an interest in. Between courses they sang for us and danced the formal, slow-moving Japanese dances. The maikos did rather gayer dances than the geishas and seemed to enjoy themselves enormously. They didn't drink at all, and the geishas drank only if you insisted.

Near the end of the dinner some sweets were brought in wrapped in paper. Inside the paper little poems were written. I asked Mr. Kaku to translate one. He handed it to the geisha, saying that it must be read by a woman and interpreted as she read:

> I think of you all day,
> In the long hours of the night I dream of you,
> But when you come I cannot speak to you,
> I cannot even raise my eyes to yours.

I asked if that was a famous poem or an ordinary one, or simply the kind of jingle you get in party favors. He said that it was nothing special, simply a mediocre poem written to give you a chance to become sentimental if you feel like it.

One of the guests leaned across toward me and said, "You know Mr. Kaku is well known for his knowledge of Japanese poetry, specially in the haiku form."

We all insisted that he recite some to us and finally, rather red in the face, he turned to me and said, "First I must tell you what the haiku is. It is a short poem that must have exactly seventeen syllables. It must connect itself with one of the seasons of the year and usually it leaves suitable room for interpretation. There are no rhymes."

Then he recited a very famous haiku about a girl who walks to the well to fetch water only to find the morning-glory vine has wrapped itself around the rope that works the bucket, so rather than break the stem of the morning glory she borrows water from a neighbor. The seventeen syllables of the poem gave, as is usual, only the most fragmentary clues to the actual story. This haiku refers, of course, to summer because that is when the morning glory blooms. "Western poetry," he said, "seems so obvious to us, leaving no room for imagination or interpretation."

Later he really got into the spirit of the thing and recited several more, including "the most famous of all poems." The other guests and the geishas joined in that one. He translated it:

> May the reign of the Emperor continue
> For a thousand years and forever
> Until the pebbles gather together and become rocks
> And until moss grows over the rocks.

9 In the few days that we had been away from Tokyo, winter seemed to have arrived. Sodden piles of leaves in the parks, a sharper note to footsteps in the streets, a darkening of the clothes of the Japanese as they appeared more frequently in their worn winter coats and shawls. Gray afternoons and early evenings all brought the bitter Japanese winter suddenly to Tokyo. There is a curious decisiveness to the seasons of Japan: no mists or indeterminate days take you gradually from one to the other.

I stopped wearing saris to the Jiyu Gakuyen, and began to feel cold even in tweeds and sweaters. My students used to place a small charcoal burner near my desk so that I could keep my hands warm enough to be able to write on the blackboard.

A small incident rather impressed me about this time. Feeling that I knew the girls well enough to be able to say what I thought from time to time, I was quite irritated that they would never tell me when they did not understand something—a very ordinary exasperation among foreigners in Japan. One day I had explained to them some word that had come up in our reading and asked if there was anyone who had not understood. Nobody answered, and we continued. Later in the lesson it became clear that most of them had not the least idea what I had been talking about.

"Really," I said crossly, "why can't you tell me when you don't understand? I am not going to get angry with you for not knowing a word, but I can't hope to teach you anything when I don't know how much you are taking in."

After the class, Yoko, the girl who spoke fairly good English, came up rather timidly. "We could not answer yes or no clearly in past lesson. We will try to answer more frankly in the coming lesson because there is no reason to hesitate we see now."

"Well, that will be much easier."

"But it is not that we are afraid you will be angry with us for not knowing."

"Then what is the reason?"

"We do not wish you to think that your explanation is so bad that we do not understand—that would not be polite."

"I see," I said, left with no answer. "That is most considerate of you."

"Do not mention," Yoko said.

To give them some basis for contrast and some feeling for the construction of Western plays, I wanted them to read the translation of one of their own nō plays as well as *Watch on the Rhine*. Two Americans whom I knew in Japan—certainly among the most intelligent and constructive of the Allied personnel—Bruce Rogers and Meredith Weatherby, had made a beautiful translation of a nō play called *Birds of Sorrow*.

It concerns a legend about the utō bird which the Japanese hunt because it is supposed to be most delicious to eat. According to the legend the birds hide their young so carefully in the sand that they cannot later find them to take them food. To discover where

[37]

their young birds are the parents call "Utō . . . utō . . . ." The chicks reply, "Yasskata . . . ." They are therefore not hard to find: all the hunters have to do to catch both the birds and their young is to imitate the cries. But tradition says that "the parent birds weep tears of blood upon seeing their young taken, and that hunters must wear large hats and raincloaks to protect themselves from the falling tears, the touch of which causes sickness and death."

This play, acted on an entirely bare stage, first shows a monk journeying to the mountain Tateyama to practice religious austerities. He arrives at the wild volcanic site where he meets the ghost of a dead hunter who asks the monk to take a message to his wife and child "to offer up for me the cloak of straw and the sedge hat which are there." The monk asks for a token which will make the wife believe his story and the hunter rips off the sleeve of his kimono and gives it to him.

The chorus, which describes the scene, the emotions of the character, or makes comments in keeping with the mood of the play, says, "The footsteps of the monk lead away . . . , down through the flaming, budding trees of spring, far and far away. . . ."

When the monk reaches the fishing village which has been the home of the hunter, he finds the wife still grieving for her husband. He tells her his story and produces the sleeve for her inspection.

"Surely this is a dream," she cries. "And even as I listen, the tears are springing to my eyes. Nevertheless, it is too strange a thing, passing all belief. And, therefore, crude though it be and lowly as cloth woven of wisteria bark, I will bring out his kimono."

She unfolds the kimono. It has a sleeve missing. The monk matches the sleeve he is carrying and the proof is complete. They offer up the cloak of straw and the sedge hat to expiate the crime against the Buddhist teaching that one should not take life.

After an interval of music the hunter appears in a tragic mask and laments his sins and his fate, "still the burden of sins heaps high upon this flesh. . . . When may this soul find peace? . . . When can the birds find their stolen young? . . . O the killing!"

He walks slowly around the stage revisiting the scene of his earthly life. He sees his wife and child, "Alas!" he says, "in other days this was the wife of my bed and the child of my heart. But now we are estranged forever. Like the parent bird I cry 'Utō' and, waiting with beating heart, never hear the answering 'Yasskata' . . . and now when I long to stroke the hair of my son Chiyodo and say, 'Oh, how I have missed thee!' . . ." The hunter holds out his arms to his son and runs toward him but at each step the child retreats from his father.

The rest of the play is a long dreamlike sequence in which the hunter and the chorus review his past history of killing with the tragic refrain of, "There was only the coming of the day, the coming of the night—and the killing!" It ends with a climactic re-enactment in dance form of the slaughter of the birds, the tears of blood which fall in a scarlet rain, until eventually the hunter collapses to remain endlessly in pain. He begs the monk for help. . . .*

Apart from its merit as a piece of literature, the *Birds of Sorrow* suited my purpose perfectly because it was most conveniently printed with the original Japanese at one end of the book and the translation at the other. The publishers managed to obtain sixty copies of it to be distributed among my students. When I handed them out in class I asked if any of them had seen it—none had.

"Has anyone read it? No? Well has anyone ever seen any nō play? How about kabuki?" I discovered then that only one of the girls had ever been to a theater in her life. I, who had been to the theater quite frequently since that first Allied performance, had seen more of the Japanese stage than all the girls in school.

10 The office of the theatrical section of the Civil Censorship Detachment was large, rather messy, with posters and photographs on the walls, and windows at the far end. As I walked in, the girls—either Japanese or Nisei, from their looks—stopped typing and stared at me with the interested regard of psychoanalysts.

"Is this Mr. Bowers' office?" I asked nervously.

* All quotations are taken from Motokiyo Zeami, *Birds of Sorrow* (Obunsha, Tokyo, 1947), translated by Meredith Weatherby and Bruce Rogers.

One of the girls pointed to the desk in front of the window. Around, and on it, there were four men playing, as far as I could make out, a card game. Three of the men were Nisei in American army uniforms. As I came up to the desk, the fourth, a tall young American, stood up. It was blackjack that they were playing.

I said, "I came to ask you if you can get me sixty seats for a kabuki performance."

"What?" The entire office was listening spellbound.

I told him about my Jiyu Gakuyen students, explained that I hadn't enough yen to buy tickets, and asked whether it could somehow be arranged because it seemed too miserable for girls to grow up without ever going to the theater.

One of the Nisei said, "You ought to fix it, Faubion, they would be so much better in the audience than all these black-market people who are trying to Get Culture the easy way." He turned to me and explained, "The sad thing is that the people who really love kabuki and understand it, mostly can't afford to buy a ticket."

The girls, with Miss Hani in charge, arrived at the theater in considerable excitement a few days later. There was much subdued whispering and many comments among them. We took them up to their seats, and Faubion Bowers was introduced to Miss Hani. "Ah yes," she said, "I have heard about you. You have the reputation of knowing more about the Japanese theater than any foreigner has ever known. It is very seldom that people from outside learn about our great arts—usually it is only flower arrangements and little trees that interest them."

The three of us sat rather grandly in a box from which we could watch both the stage and the girls. Downstairs there was the usual crowd of the kabuki theater. The audience, composed largely of women at this time of the day, sat absorbed, or wandered quietly into the lobby to get cups of tea or simply to stretch their legs. Many of them had arrived at ten o'clock in the morning when the theater opened and would sit until the evening when their husbands came back from work. They brought their babies with them. It is said of

[40]

Japan that there the dogs do not bark, the flowers have no smell, and the children do not cry. Whenever a child in the audience got hungry, the mother opened up her kimono at once and fed him, without taking her eyes away from the stage.

The play that day was *Ishikiri Kajiwara*. It is an extraordinary story about a retainer, Kajiwara, who is asked to appraise a sword which his wicked lord wants to buy. Kajiwara examines it and sees that it has a marking on it which shows it belongs to the enemy side. It is a priceless and wonderful sword, one of the best in the world, but Kajiwara finds out that the old man who is selling it is doing so to raise funds for a rebellion against the wicked lord.

The claim made about the sword is that it can cut two people in half at one stroke. The wicked lord sends for two prisoners who have been condemned to death on whom Kajiwara is to test the sword. But there is only one such prisoner in the jail. So eager is the old man to get the money that in spite of the remonstrances of his daughter he offers himself as the second body.

He lies down, the prisoner is put on top of him and with a tremendous flourish Kajiwara brings the sword down—but only the prisoner is cut in two. The wicked lord laughs at the claims made for the sword, refuses to buy it, and leaves with the rest of his retainers.

The bewildered old man and Kajiwara remain. Kajiwara tells him that he knows the plans for the rebellion and wishes to join with them because theirs is the side of righteousness. He gives the old man the money for his sword, but the old man says that the money means nothing to him now because the honor and the reputation of his sword are gone. It can't do what he said it could.

Kajiwara laughs and says that the old man has underestimated his skill in cutting. He picks up the sword and cuts an enormous stone basin in two—an even greater feat than the two bodies would have been.

This play," Faubion told me, "has only recently been approved for performance. It was censored before that."

"But it seems to go against the old loyalty code business. Kajiwara comes out on the side of righteousness in spite of his fealty to the lord. I should have thought that would be in line with Occupation policy. Why did they ban it?"

"Because we are teaching the Japanese democracy, I suppose."

"No, but seriously?"

"Well, I suppose because a man is chopped in half. In the Western theatrical world you can show a man beaten up, tortured, shot, stabbed and so on, but for some reason if a dummy is cut in half and you see its insides painted red, that is undemocratic. The Japanese are not concerned with life in the same way as we are. Seeing it doesn't make them want to be cut in two, or to cut anyone else in two. It's a fact of life, and that is that."

The play, as all kabuki plays are, was superbly acted. Huge gestures, voices with all the authority in the world in them, emotion controlled by stylization, the plays always left me shaken and entranced. The actors are costumed with great magnificence, usually in the dress of the old samurai with the grotesquely wide shoulders, and the long trousers (about a yard longer than the legs of the actors) which make them look as though they were walking on their knees. The purpose of such trousers was to ensure that courtiers did not fight in the palace, and couldn't escape easily if they did. The onnagata (men who take women's parts) wear ceremonial kimonos with trains, and their hair dressed in the high, elaborate old style.

After the performance Faubion took me backstage to meet the leading actor, Kichiemon. He was one of Japan's four great classical actors. When we went into his dressing room he was sitting on the floor. On a low stool in front of him was a small shaving mirror. He had taken off the elaborate costume of Kajiwara and was wearing a plain, dark-green kimono. Two assistants stood near him. One was hanging up the costume he had just taken off and the other held a bowl and a small towel to help him remove his make-up.

Faubion stood at the door and made a very low bow to Kichiemon. I did not know how to bow, or how low to bow, so I gave him the Indian greeting of folded hands. He stared at me and his first words

[42]

were to ask me to drape my sari over my head. Then he said, "Now I see that India is really the mother of Asia."

I must have looked puzzled and a little worried, hoping that I did not look like a mother of anything, because by way of explanation he pointed to a picture on the wall of the Goddess of Mercy, Kwannon. Her draperies, old-fashioned and typical of Japan, were, in fact, close enough to the folds of the sari to be unmistakably the same in origin. Her hands were folded.

At the time I put down his remark to the sentimentality of an old man or at most to coincidence. It took me a year and a half of traveling through Asia to realize the truth and the meaning of his statement.

Kichiemon was sixty when I first met him, with a deeply lined, extremely sensitive face, straight back, eloquent hands, and one of the most powerful voices I have ever heard.

On the other side of the room sitting on the tatami was his daughter Seiko—the most beautiful woman I had seen so far in Japan. Tall for a Japanese, she had a flawless complexion and the kind of clarity of feature that is quite international in its appeal. She would be a beauty in any country. She was wearing a purple kimono with a hand-painted design of bamboos in the winter. Very delicately the bamboos curved from the weight of the snow on them, and there was a faint suggestion of snowy hills behind.

After the introductions were complete, Kichiemon asked me if we would excuse him for a moment while he took off his make-up. I said, "Please before you do, may I look at it more closely? It looked so impressive on the stage."

He turned his face full to me. Then he picked up the towel which his assistant was holding and very carefully placed it over his face. He pressed it gently over the lines of his make-up and peeled it off. He spread it on the table, called for a brush and ink and painted his signature in the corner.

"Now," he said, "you will always have something by which to remember Kajiwara." It was the traditional souvenir which great actors give their admirers.

Faubion told Kichiemon that we had brought the Jiyu Gakuyen

[43]

girls to see his performance. Kichiemon very solemnly said, "This is a great service that you do. For if the young people do not learn to appreciate kabuki, it will surely die."

In the course of conversation about the play I asked Kichiemon if the Japanese audience found the scene in which the man is chopped in half very gruesome to watch.

He looked puzzled and said, "But it is a comic scene."

"Comic?" I said foolishly.

"The prisoner," he said in a kindly, explanatory way, "is very comical, and is due to die in any case. Besides, he is a criminal. A *funny* one," making sure I saw the point.

"I see," I said, not seeing at all.

After that, he and Faubion plunged into the technicalities of the performance, rattling away in Japanese which I could not follow. Faubion was one of the few Americans in the Occupation who spoke perfect Japanese and it was largely because of it that he had held his previous job of aide to General MacArthur. I turned to Seiko, accustomed by now to the fact that anywhere in Asia women sit with, and talk to women, and the men to the men. Seiko spoke a little English and I understood a little Japanese so in our curious hybrid language we began a friendship which gave me perhaps more pleasure than any other in Japan. She was very excited and happy that day because her small son, five years old, had made his first appearance on the kabuki stage the day before.

"At least," she said, "that tradition will not die with our generation."

Eventually we all left and Seiko showed us to the door and put on her own silk coat over her kimono. This had an enormous stork painted across the back. It had the same exquisite line and detail that the paintings on her kimono had. When I admired it she said, "I am so glad that you like it. My husband painted it for me one day."

A few days later the Kichiemon family invited Faubion and me to dinner. We walked upstairs to the usual Japanese room, decorated this time with a celadon vase in the corner in front of a long *kakemono* (a scroll painting) of a winter scene in north Japan.

When I walked in, Kichiemon bustled up to me and said, "Since you are young enough to be my daughter there must be no formality." He rubbed my hands and found them cold. "Look," he said, "I have arranged for you to sit in this corner near the charcoal stove and here are some quilts which we shall wrap around you like this and now perhaps you will be warm enough. It must be terrible to come to our winter from your own warm country." He bundled me up in so many quilts that not only was I warm enough but I was unable to find my way out of the quilts to eat.

During the dinner, Kichiemon told me that he had wanted very much to meet somebody who was "truly Indian, because Buddhism, which is so important both in our lives and in our acting, came from India. It is impossible," Kichiemon told me "to be a good kabuki actor unless you have a religion."

"You mean it needs the same fervency?" I asked.

"No, no, I mean *religion*. You can have fervency about many things, frivolity or even evil, but to be an actor you must know God. It astonishes me that Western actors feel that they can learn their art after they are adults. To act well one should start from the time one is young so that one grows up in the knowledge and tradition of the theater. It is impossible to *learn* the parts. One must *be* a character so intensely that kabuki is the reality and the ordinary world is fantasy."

A little later I asked a small request of Kichiemon. He said "yes" in his beautiful, florid, actor's voice. Faubion explained that he had said it with the inflection used by a good man in the kabuki plays. A bad man would have said "yes" with a different inflection so that the audience would know he did not plan to carry out the order. Faubion turned to Kichiemon and asked him to demonstrate to me how a bad man in kabuki would have said it. Kichiemon said casually but with great sincerity, "I cannot do that; I am not a bad man."

After dinner Kichiemon said, "I have arranged for you to see the greatest artist in Japan." As I was about to interrupt he held up his hand and continued, "Ah, yes! You may think me great, but wait until you have seen Ohan-san."

Ohan-san, who is a geisha, is really a dancer's dancer. So subtle is her style, so light and full of suggestion are her movements, and so great is her precision that to the accomplished artist there is more beauty in her attenuated, interior sort of dancing than in all the fire and emotion of a dancer who has yet to prove his competence. The story of her dance was a simple one. Faubion translated it for me as, "I stand alone on Arashi Hill [in Kyoto] and watch the gaily colored autumn leaves fall as the moon slowly rises."

The entire dance took place at one end of the narrow room. I suppose she could have danced it in an area three feet square, so slight were her steps and gestures. Her expression didn't alter at all, yet after she had finished, Kichiemon turned to me with tears in his eyes and said, "Have you ever seen such an exquisite performance? Such intense emotion? The entire tragedy of a love-forsaken girl is there."

I met Kichiemon's wife for the first time that evening. I scarcely noticed her at first because she was so retiring and so unobtrusive in her movements that it was only when Faubion took me up to her and said, "You must bow very low. This is the great man's wife," that I realized she had been there ever since I came in. She had served the entire meal with occasional help from a couple of maidservants and from Seiko who spent part of the meal next to me so that I would not feel strange at being the only woman at table, and part of the meal seeing that everybody's saké cup remained full.

When it was time to leave, Kichiemon's last words to me were, "If you are really interested in learning about the Japanese theater you must come to the rehearsals. From those you will learn the principles of the art and not be carried away merely with the strength of the performance."

11 Throughout the winter in Tokyo I went to the kabuki theater a great deal and gradually I came to know the actors themselves and their families. It is an extraordinary society, rigid, insular, with a great tradition and an equal consciousness of it. Their distinction is enormous and so is their inability to compromise. With them, how low you bow, the phrasing of your sentences, the degree of your deference to your elders, and your respect for artistic attainment can make you welcome or ignored. Brought up in the theater, and with dramatic perfection as their highest purpose, they pattern their lives and thinking to a large extent on the convention, principles and old-fashioned behavior of the kabuki characters.

Kichiemon and his family adopted me and provided my introduction to the rest of the kabuki circle partly because they had met me through Faubion whom they had known since before the war and who, Kichiemon told me very seriously, "saved the Japanese theater from the ruin that would have befallen it under foreign governments and the inexplicable conditions in Japan today"; and partly, too, because he felt that as I was Indian, in some vague way I represented the religion which was so important in his life. With Seiko, Kichiemon and Faubion, who practically lived in the theater anyway, I used to sit for hours watching rehearsals. In the empty, unheated auditorium, shivering and wrapped in coats and blankets, I watched the young actors receive direction from their masters. During the performances Seiko and I sat together and saw the great men and their young protégés acting against the beautifully constructed scenery, in their fantastic and rich costumes.

Afterward Seiko would criticize or approve, and I would pretend to take in what she was saying, filled still with the magic of the performance.

One day, at rehearsal, Kichiemon said to me, "When you are with us you must have a Japanese name. What does your name mean?"

"Spring," I said, for once unembarrassed by how silly it sounded.

"That is good," he said. "Faubion tells me that in the West most names have no meaning. It is strange. How can you call a child without knowing what you are saying to her? Spring. We too have a spring among our names. We shall call you Haruko-san." Then he turned his attention back to the stage where Shoroku, a young actor, was rehearsing a dance.

I had learned by then just how important this business of names was—anywhere in Japan—but particularly among the kabuki people whose names have carried theatrical distinction for centuries. Each actor will perform under a lower grade name until his father or patron dies, then he will adopt that name, and must live up to its generations of glory. If a young actor is not worthy of his master's great name it will not be given to him, and may remain unused for generations before it is again given to an actor.

For another hour Shoroku danced, and eventually came to sit with us, still tense from the criticism and abuse his master, Kikugoro, had given him. He stretched his leg carefully into the aisle, and explained to Seiko, "I could not dance today. I hurt my knee playing baseball, and it was all swollen." The bandage had not shown underneath his kimono.

"Why on earth didn't you tell Kikugoro?" I asked

"Had I hurt it when I was dancing I could have told him and I would have been excused from rehearsals. Kikugoro would have been most considerate. But as I am a dancer, to hurt my knee playing baseball is no excuse."

"I must say," I announced indignantly, "I call that most inhuman."

Shoroku patted his injured knee and said, "In Kikugoro's time it was worse. He would have been beaten for hurting his knee, not just made to rehearse as though nothing had happened."

After the rehearsal we all followed Kichiemon, with his beautiful straight back and his dancer's walk, up to his dressing room for a cup of tea. There Baiko, another young actor, joined us, and we all discussed the rehearsal. Baiko was the actor I knew least well. He was a gentle, quiet young man, quite plain and wearing rimless

[48]

glasses. He specialized in women's parts and would become, eventually, one of the leading *onnagata* of his generation. On the stage he was ravishingly lovely with all the elegance in the world in his manner and his dancing.

Because his stage personality was essentially feminine, off stage, too, he rather deferred to the actors of male parts. Faubion and I told him about Shoroku's hurt knee, and Baiko answered, "He was lucky that it was an indoor scene. Once I was rehearsing the part of a woman who makes her first entrance onto the stage walking through snow. Over and over again I could not get the movement exactly enough to please my master. So in the first snowfall of the winter I had to practice outside for two hours in the bitter cold to learn how a woman walks through snow. Now," he said in his soft voice, "my technique is perfect."

Kichiemon who had overheard part of this, and could never bear to be left out of a conversation, tapped his fingers authoritatively on the low tea table, "Haruko-san," he ordered, "listen to me. There are many different ways of teaching but only one way of learning an art. Some people will tell you that you can only teach by kindness, others that harshness is the only way. My mother who believed that an artist must conquer in spite of everything, would never show me the good reviews of my performances, only the bad ones, so that I should learn humility and integrity to myself. Everywhere in Asia you will find that the artist's great seriousness and discipline in his art is the product of a way of learning—the product of the relationship between the teacher and the pupil, which like all human relationships must include the harshness, kindness, reason and eccentricity that go to make up a human personality. Your Sanskrit name for such a teacher is guru. He will have one or at the most two pupils. He is certain to be an old man because the study of art is a long and difficult one, and he must be a genuine master of his art. What do these children know about acting? Of course they must have respect and humility before their teacher, for the thing that they must learn—and it will take them all their lives—is that nothing can be more important to them than their art. Baseball?" he said, glaring at Shoroku, "is *that* a reason for a bad performance?"

[49]

12   In the early part of that December, whenever I saw the kabuki actors and Faubion, they were immersed in long discussions about the forthcoming performances of *Chushingura*, the most famous of the kabuki play cycles. It is the story of the forty-seven retainers, who decide to avenge the treachery that made their lord commit suicide. In its entirety the play takes two days to perform because various of the forty-seven retainers have to be followed through exile and conspiracy to kill the wicked noble who engineered the death of their lord. All the best actors of both the older and younger generations were to take part in it, even old Baigyoku, whom I had seen in my first kabuki play, was to come up from Osaka to act in *Chushingura*. He was ill, and Kichiemon was worried that the strain would be too much for him.

"You have seen him recently," he said to Faubion, "how is he? What is his acting like?"

"Outwardly he is as beautiful as ever. The detail and the precision of his acting haven't changed, but the emotion is at the lowest possible ebb. It is the acting of a ghost. He told me that while he was on the stage he felt no pain, but as soon as the play was over the closeness of death returns."

Kichiemon frowned and nodded, but made no further inquiries about Baigyoku's health. He immediately began to think of scenes that they would play together in *Chushingura*, and to plan with Faubion how he could tone down his own vigorous style of acting to match the remote and uncharged quiet of Baigyoku's present performances. The applause for the individual actor was not important. The production as a whole must be perfect.

Until that time, *Chushingura* had been banned by the Occupation authorities, and it was only after a struggle of months that Faubion had finally managed to get it approved. Occasionally, during that time, I would find him in Kichiemon's dressing room sitting back on his heels like a Japanese and lecturing furiously about the stupidity of the censorship policy. "The idiocy of it!" he would say. "Can you imagine?—they want to suppress it because it is a 'revenge play,' so it will give the Japanese ideas. Hamlet is a revenge play, too. Do you want to rush out and murder your uncle when you've seen it? But then," he added bitterly, "the British aren't a defeated nation, so I suppose it's all right for them to have undemocratic ideas."

"Calm yourself," Kichiemon said. "You present these arguments the wrong way. You should tell them that the principle is wrong; one should not interfere with a classic art. Let them," he waved his hand grandly, "censor the modern theater if they wish."

Faubion began to laugh. "Really, you are sweet. I can just see those army colonels worrying about classic art."

"One has," said Kichiemon as though Faubion hadn't spoken, "to know the history of Japan and of kabuki, the lines of the play, and one has to understand the minds of the Japanese seeing the play. Do any of the people making your policies know all that?"

"Of course not. Does any colonizer understand the people he tries to colonize? You can only be a successful colonist if you believe that your civilization, culture, religion, way of life—anything—are superior. The minute you start to understand the other people you are no longer sure."

"Exactly," Kichiemon said. "That is the paradox at the heart of this Occupation. So you see, my dear Faubion, you must explain it to them in their terms. These plays are a protest against bushido; there is always the cry against the samurai in kabuki. Remember, these plays were written by commoners whose enemies were the samurai. Of course they were fascinated by their lives; who is not interested in kings and queens and nobles? Before the war our government tried to forge kabuki into a weapon for their side by deleting lines and suppressing plays. Now, by doing the same things you show yourselves no better than the government which you claim were your enemies."

Apparently he had had enough of censorship because then he told us a rather funny story about the early days of the Occupation when all the swords of the Japanese had to be turned in, and even the heirlooms forfeited. "One over-enthusiastic young man in the provinces confiscated the wooden swords of a kabuki company. It ruined that night's performance." After a pause he said, "Faubion, do civilians in America carry guns?"

"No," Faubion said, rather startled. "Why?"

"I just wondered. I see them in the American movies. . ." he said vaguely.

However, after all the argument and exasperation, *Chushingura* was approved at last, and came on in the middle of December. Seiko and I went to the first performance. Seiko refused to go backstage. For once, she said, she was going to be only the audience. It must have been something of a relief to her because she occupied such a strange position in the kabuki circle. She was the only daughter of her famous father, and this at first was a great disappointment to him; there was no son to carry on Kichiemon's name. But it was not long before he was so devoted to Seiko that he could not bear her to be out of his sight. She went to the theater with him, learned his parts with him, came to understand the finest details of his technique. Now she mixed freely and independently with the actors; her scholarship and knowledge were respected by even the great old men themselves.

Inevitably she fell in love with an actor, Somegoro, the son of Koshiro, another of the big four in kabuki. Kichiemon was furious. The thought of losing his beloved daughter was more than he could stand, and he forbade her to see Somegoro. "Of course," she told me once, "if he had persisted in his opposition, I could not have married. But for three days I cried and didn't eat, and in the end he relented." For all his dominance Kichiemon is as soft as butter.

Eventually Seiko's two sons became the pride of his life. One would take Kichiemon's name in deference to his greatness. The other would take his father's name.

The children, already happier playing with grease paint than with toys, were backstage in the middle of the excitement. But Seiko was determined to let no technical worries disturb her enjoyment of *Chushingura*. We arrived at the theater at noon and stayed until

[52]

ten in the evening watching the magnificent story, partly tragic, partly comic, work itself out.

The theater was packed more tightly than I had ever seen it, and the aisles were crowded with people on campstools and crouching or standing, as they could best accomodate themselves. As famous moments of the play came up, members of the audience shouted out to the actors, "*Matte imashita!*" (I have waited for that!")

I had often heard these shouts during various kabuki plays, but never given with the enthusiasm—almost ecstasy of the *Chushin-gura* audience. In the acting parts Kichiemon's reverberating voice put the audience into a frenzy of shouting, and when Kikugoro danced the house rocked again. There was never such a play for a display of virtuosity.

Seiko sat in a kind of dream throughout the performance. After the last act, and Kichiemon's last tremendous speech, which took thirty minutes by itself, she turned to me with tears streaming down her beautiful face and said, "I am so happy—so happy to be my father's daughter—"

13 The days narrowed with astonishing speed to Christmas. The winter weeks brought us to the end of the term at the Jiyu Gakuyen. Just before the short winter holidays the school gave a Christmas party to which my father and I were invited. The girls gave a concert and afterward we all had Christmas dinner together. My students had collaborated on little gifts for me which they had made themselves and which were far more moving than if they had collected their coppers and bought something. There were two paintings, one of a chrysanthemum and one of plum blossom. Some of the girls had made me bamboo baskets, some had woven a tablecloth with wool embroidery on the edges, one of them had carved three wooden buttons, and there were several decorated fans. I was impressed, not for the first time, with the artistic competence of any Japanese child or adult. Some of the painting was mediocre

of course and some was very good, but at least any one of them could, on occasion, produce a creditable and artistically educated piece of work.

I went to say good-by to Miss Hani in her little house and to find out when the new term opened and wish her a merry Christmas.

She and her mother were sitting in their living room and offered me a cup of tea. While I was sipping it, old Mrs. Hani with her half-blind eyes closed said, "It is so good for the girls to be taught English by you. They understand more easily from an Indian."

Feeling something of an impostor, I said, "I wish I understood them a little better. I am afraid I don't teach well."

"That may be true. But how *much* you understand does not matter. It is the wish. . . ." She went on reflectively in her hoarse voice, looking out at the sky darkening for snow, "This experiment which they try now in my country is remarkable in all our history. Is it possible to teach without understanding? My daughter tells me they wish to teach us many things—their culture—that in their books and magazines they write often of the American way of life, American democracy, even the American look. I do not say they wish to *impose* it. Can one, after all, impose a culture? But all this they are eager to teach. . . ."

"I think they are eager to learn, too," I interrupted carefully.

She fluttered her withered old hands indecisively. "It has been many centuries," she said, sounding very tired, "since people have been eager to learn from Asia. It has been a long time since learning is what they came here for." Then she said more briskly, "The term is ended, the year is dying and I am an old woman. I wish you a very happy holiday season. . . ."

Christmas in Tokyo was marked by a slightly more hysterical pace to the parties, new clothes sent out from America, crowds at the P.X. fingering the cheap lacquer and porcelain in the hope of finding presents that all the rest of the Occupation would not already have seen. The embassies gave dances and sent each other dwarf trees, orchids, bunches of flowers, and thanked each other politely three times a day when they met at some entertainment or other. It had snowed a few days before Christmas and the parks

[54]

were still dazzling and white. It was cold enough so that the snow along the gutters of the street had not turned into slush but stayed crisp, with only a black edging of soot. The Japanese with scarlet cheeks scurried about always in their dark winter clothes. Since none of the public buildings, theaters, restaurants or private homes was heated, they remained perpetually in their outdoor things.

Among the foreigners in Tokyo as part of the Occupation and the diplomatic missions, I had many acquaintances and relatively few friends. Among those few were Jean de Selancy, military attaché to the French Embassy, whose sweeping charm and intelligence would have made him very popular even if he hadn't been certainly the best-looking man in Tokyo. Centering on him was Tokyo's "Younger Set," and all that winter we met at parties or went for drives into the beautiful snowy countryside. Faubion moved in and out of this circle in his usual absent way, taking no trouble to hide the scorn he felt for many of the foreigners in Japan, and always returning with relief to his beloved actors and their theater.

Clare Harris, another addition to the Younger Set, I met under slightly different circumstances. I came back to the hotel one evening to find a tall, blonde American wearing that basic black dress that the magazines tell you about, and tapping a pencil on a notebook with every sign of impatience. "I," she said, "was supposed to interview your father but he came in for a moment, said you would be back directly, and has vanished."

Clare, it turned out, was a journalist working in the Public Relations Office of the government. She never did interview my father, but meanwhile she and I became friends. Several things about Clare interested me. First there was her great competence and tough-mindedness about her work which, to somebody like me who is lazy and erratic in her writing, seemed almost miraculous.

Another of her attributes was the extraordinary talent that so many American women seem to have of meticulous grooming. That disinfected, flawlessly exact look is something I have always envied and never managed to achieve. She knew all kinds of little tricks about how to make stockings last longer, or how to dance with a man shorter than yourself, or how to give yourself a face pack when you have only five minutes to spare. She had the American girl's delight in small luxuries—little silk bags of sachet for her clothes, or a massage—combined with considerable money sense.

Clare's reading taste seemed to me perhaps stranger than anything. She read dozens of newspapers and magazines every day; one would often find her in the Ernie Pyle Library wearing horn-rimmed glasses, and flipping through everything from *Harper's* to *Popular Mechanics*. She never read novels, which she considered a waste of time, but worked her way through every new book that came out about politics, by schoolteachers, newspapermen, radio commentators or even politicians, and seemed to retain the facts she got from them. No minute of her day was wasted. Even her fifteen minutes of relaxation before she went out in the evenings were spent under a sun lamp because she knew that her long blonde hair and straight features made her only pretty, but the contrast of the tan made her prettiness arresting.

The Takarazuka Girls' Opera had come to Tokyo for Christmas and Clare and I went to it quite frequently. Their repertoire for the Christmas season ranged from operas like *Manon Lescaut* through *A Midsummer Night's Dream* to original musical comedies complete with tap dancing, swing tunes and chorus lines. They, and the other shows at the Nichigeki, Tokyo's permanent vaudeville theater, provided a curious contrast to the classical theater of Japan in which the ban on actresses is so severe and deeply rooted.

In Christmas week the trial of Hideki Tojo came on at the War Crimes Tribunal. It was almost considered part of the Christmas attractions of Tokyo and for the first time I saw the visitors' galleries crowded by people wanting to hear the cross-examination. Clare and I watched one day of the trial. Tojo was an unimpressive-looking man, small, with a bad posture, his curious egg-shaped head was shaved and he wore heavy glasses and a shabby army uniform.

I could not help thinking that the War Crimes Tribunal was one of the most expensive and futile projects the Occupation had embarked on. As mountains of evidence were produced, as secretaries sorted it, filed it, mimeographed it, as the judges considered it and the lawyers fought over it, only one thing remained clear. No-body—not the Allies nor the Axis, not the democratic leaders nor the Fascist ones—had a clean record.

There was something infinitely frustrating about these trials. Partly, I think, because of the clumsy cross-examination. The long, involved, heavily sarcastic questions were almost incomprehensible in English and after their passage through the wearying machinery of translation and interpretation must have been even more confusing to the Japanese spectators. Partly, too, because one considered the years that this thing had been dragging on, the complete boredom on the faces of the accused sitting day after day in their box. The Japanese people themselves had long since made their judgment on their leaders. These men were failures; that was enough to condemn them.

I was reminded of a conversation I had had with a Japanese some time before about the trials in which I had expressed my surprise at the lack of feeling among the Japanese about their leaders, their easy shift in loyalty from Tojo to MacArthur. I was thinking of the scenes one read about at Nuremberg, the tears, the crowds, the bitterness, the publicity, joy, satisfaction—everything, but anyway *feeling*.

"Do you think," I asked finally, "that they should be shot?"

After a minute's thought the Japanese answered, "I don't think it matters how they die."

Tojo showed more spirit than most of them. He had a good resonant voice and was clearly answering questions for the benefit of the Japanese spectators in the galleries and the reports that would appear in the Japanese papers—not for the sake of the trial records. He knew that he had no chance of surviving, so he was concerned not with defending himself but with defending the system and the Emperor. Most of his answers were acute and impressive. In reply to the accusation that he had treated with the Vichy Government, knowing that it was the instrument of Hitler, he didn't bother with the obvious reply, "So did you." Instead he looked up to the gallery and said, "It was supposed to be the legitimate and recognized government of France, just as the present government of Japan is legitimate and recognized even though it is under the Americans."

One point came up that was clearly beyond the comprehension of the prosecution, but apparently made complete sense to the Japanese. An extract from Kido's diary was quoted in which he said that the Emperor had described Tojo's part in the Indo-China incident as that of "a thief at a fire." With no attempt to defend himself, Tojo very angrily said that it was the lowest possible language and he could not believe that the Emperor ever used a phrase like that.

At intervals throughout the cross-examination the big flood-lights were turned on to illuminate the witness box, the prosecutor, and the judges' bench. Cameras turned, movies were taken, stenographers took down the questions and answers word for word. One day it would all be history, and I did not envy the schoolchildren who would be expected to make sense of it.

Afterward I heard that Tojo's family who had fled to their old home in Kyushu where they lived in obscurity and disgrace, unable to get food and ostracized by the villagers, were suddenly deluged with presents after accounts of Tojo's cross-examination appeared in the papers. Food was piled high on their doorstep and their neighbors came to call.

I tried taking Clare to kabuki plays, but they didn't seem to impress her as they had impressed me. She kept looking for political significance in the plots, which I found most irritating, and on the whole disapproved of kabuki. "Feudalism," she said, "severed heads on the stage, harakiri. It all seems perverted to me."

"Really, Clare," I said, "your standards probably seem perverted to them."

"Well, at least we don't make our defeated generals carve out their entrails—"

"Look, with them it's a point of honor. When your stock market crashed in America, you had millionaires flying through the air of Wall Street to commit suicide. I am not prepared to say which is the more ridiculous point of honor—losing your money or losing a battle."

"Maybe you people understand it, you have *suttee* and things, but where I come from suicide is considered a crime."

[58]

"But Clare, to half the people in the world it's not a crime," I said, rather surprised to find myself arguing as an "Asian" to a "Westerner." "At least they retain *that* dignity. You ought to try to understand them instead of condemning them out of hand."

"Okay, kid," she said tolerantly, "I'm a busy woman. You understand them and tell me about it."

The actors, too, were curiously reserved in front of her. Clare had so strong a worship of the tenet that all men are equal, that she couldn't bring herself to make the marks of deference—in bows or speech—to the old or the great actors. To them such behavior was the ordinary currency of social exchange; to her, the violation of a principle. So she found them arrogant, and they thought her ill-mannered.

14 The New Year came and with it letters from my students of the Jiyu Gakuyen. One of them invited me to a party where we were to cook "unknown soup." Everybody who comes is supposed to bring some ingredients and put them in the soup without letting the others know what they are. When the lid is opened, with what I can only feel is a touching faith in human nature, you drink the unknown soup. Another was both flattering and saddening. "My dear teacher," one of the girls wrote. "Now we are beginning to have great interest to study English than ever before. Because you taught us. . . . I like to study English. If I were supply with many times for my study it will make me very very happy. Because I working at school and at home where need my services every day."

New Year's day brought all the Japanese children out in their fine, bright kimonos playing a kind of battledore and shuttlecock with gaily decorated wooden bats; long processions could be seen going to the temples or visiting the houses along the way. After the New Year, winter set in really hard with deep frost—too cold to snow. When school started I spent my time shivering in the theaters and shivering in the classroom. The girls whose clothing was scarcely heavier than it had been in the autumn sat perfectly still through their classes without a word of complaint. Only once did I hear them refer to the cold and that was when I asked whether the Japanese had become so used to the cold that they no longer felt it. One of my students told me that the only time she really minded was when her fingers became too cold to practice the piano.

A new problem had come up though. The electric power shortage in Tokyo meant that the girls had only one rather weak bulb in their study room by which to do their homework. They got up at dawn to make full use of the daylight hours but even so the long winter evenings did not leave them enough time to finish all their work. When I asked what they did about it I was told that they took it in turns to study under the light and sometimes one girl would read aloud from her homework and the rest sitting in the twilight around the edges of the room would try to take in by ear what they could not read.

My particular excitement at this time was that we had at last been assigned a house, so we could leave the cramped dark rooms of the Imperial Hotel for good. Clare and I went out to look at it and think about furnishings and decoration. Rather to our surprise, when we got there, several little men were dashing about the garden and appeared to be digging up the trees.

"What are they doing?" I asked the driver.

"They remove the trees," he said gently, as though I were a half-wit.

"But half the point of buying this house was the very nice trees."

He said in a tone of sweet reasonableness, "Maybe you did not buy the trees."

"It's hardly the kind of thing that occurs to one," I said. "I thought they would go with the grounds. I never expected these people to come and cut them down."

"They do not cut them down," he pointed out, "they take them to plant them somewhere else."

"Now really!" I said exasperated. "You can't just pick up a full-grown tree and plant it somewhere else."

"Oh yes, they can do." The driver shrugged his shoulders and added, "It must remember to buy the trees."

Clare and I stood by helplessly while one of the trees which was ready was carted away, its roots wrapped carefully in sacking. The men bowed and smiled as they passed us.

The house itself was so large that I was rather unhappy about it, certain that the day-to-day matter of running a place that size would take up my full time and would leave me none for the things I would rather do. I am not really interested in domesticity.

For the first week the house was in utter confusion. We had four maids, two cooks, a housekeeper and a mysterious little band of men who sometimes worked in the garden and sometimes did odd jobs about the house. There seemed to be no way of organizing them into a normal functioning team of servants. One maid attached herself to me and another to my father and all the rest of the servants did whatever jobs happened to come up without any question whether it was their work or somebody else's.

The first day my father's maid turned up in his bedroom at eight o'clock standing around waiting to help him dress. He managed to escape into the bathroom and dressed there in considerable discomfort. The morning after that he got up at seven-thirty and managed to avoid the maid, but the day after that she turned up at seven-thirty rather worried at having missed him the morning before. He said to me plaintively over breakfast that that was the kind of thing I was supposed to organize in a sensible way, otherwise he would have to keep getting up earlier and earlier and finally would not get any sleep at all. "Of course," he said, "if I keep it up for twenty-four days I would again be able to get up at a reasonable hour but I cannot help feeling that that would make the office routine a little unconventional."

I tried to imitate Clare's efficiency and spent an entire morning typing out instructions for the servants: when each one was to get up, all the duties they had and at what time those duties were to be performed. I had each set of instructions translated into Japanese by the housekeeper and pinned up in appropriate spots about the kitchen and servants' quarters. All afternoon the servants came to me one by one congratulating me on the excellence of my typing, thanked me most formally for having taken so much trouble and from the next day continued to operate exactly as they had done before.

I cabled to my mother urging her to hurry to Japan as soon as she could.

15 One Sunday toward the end of January was a beautiful empty day. One of those glistening days you get after frost. The moat around the Imperial palace was frozen, the trees in the park black and brittle, of an improbable delicacy. The Japanese children wore kimonos so heavily padded that they could not put their arms down to their sides and went about all day as if they were engaged in an elaborate balancing act.

I went with Clare for a short walk in the morning and watched the American girls so trim and inappropriate hurrying along in their ridiculous heels and furs to church and to dates. Always walking purposefully as though to the dentist or to meet a train—something specific, something noted in a book, an appointment made several days before—always with brushed and shining hair, careful make-up, an assurance, inevitably brash and inexplicable to us Asians. They called to each other in the ringing air, "Hi there!" or, "Hurry Bernice we're late." Japanese walkers are silent, less full of thrust. Indians, of course, are not silent but it is a different sort of noise.

Japanese parks have no animals, no squirrels run up the trees, no dogs dash across your path leaving misty puffs of breath in the air, no cats promenade insolently along the walls. It was a strange light, that Japanese winter morning light, extraordinary in clarity, yet without the harshness one expects to go with it (as in Switzerland), subtle in coloring but not indistinct. You notice the exact shades, and somehow details seem to be emphasized by it, not exaggerated, just abnormally clear of outline. It explained itself in Japanese painting, which had at first seemed to me a confusion of improbable coloring and fussiness. To a non-Japanese eye it looks unimaginative and too pretty but when you have been there a little while it seems the only possible style.

I felt suddenly very foreign and homesick for India, for our bright colors, and the sun, and said to Clare, "You must come to India someday . . ." meaning that I wanted to go back myself.

"Yes," she said promptly, "I intend to."

"We could go to China in the spring and then on from there to India."

We were to meet Faubion in the afternoon to call on a friend of his, Azuma Harué a very distinguished dancer who was ill and according to Faubion, needed cheering up.

Harué lived in a section of Tokyo which, in the old days was the center for the most exclusive set of restaurants and geisha houses. "There," said Faubion, pointing to a badly damaged house, "that used to be one of the most rarified. It only had about five rooms and orchids dripped from the chandeliers. They only took very special guests, and the geishas were so madly high-class that no bills were ever presented. A collector came around at the end of the month and told you what was appropriate to give."

Harué's mother was a geisha, and Harué herself would have followed the profession but she was so great a dancer that she didn't need to. She could command a thousand yen for a performance. We went up the stairs of her house to a small room overlooking the street. She was reclining near the window, a thin woman, quite plain with that great security that the accomplished artist sometimes acquires.

She gave us orchid tea from Kyoto. You drop a couple of the tiny, salted brown orchids into a cup of very hot water and wait. Part of the pleasure—as in most Japanese food—is in the look of it. You watch the beautiful intricate patterns that the petals of the orchid make as they move about in the water, and when you sip the tea it has a very faint, slightly salty, slightly perfumed taste. With it she gave us the usual little floury Japanese sweets which look charming and taste dreadful.

When we left Azuma Harué, we walked into the winter afternoon to a part of the city which had not been burned. It is still very lovely,

[63]

with old wooden houses and tiny enclosed gardens and the sound of someone playing the *samisen*. "Why," said Faubion, "is the sound of music heard from the street so moving and so sad?"

We walked down to the river where Faubion told us the story of one of the famous courtesans who had lived there and for whom her lover, a rich noble, had built the avenue of cherry trees. Eventually he had distrusted her, certain that she had been unfaithful to him, and sent her down the river in a boat to her death. As she floated down she sang, and the unhappy, unjust lover heard her exquisite singing voice even after the boat was out of sight. This part of the city is rather shabby now, with a lot of its wicked excitement and daring worn off.

16 Clare was writing an article for an American magazine on the women of Japan and asked me if I would like to go with her on some of the interviews. She was after another of those American dreams of hers, a "cross-section of the women in Tokyo." At one end of the poll was the wife of Japan's communist party, herself a leader in it, Mrs. Nozaka, who told us about her work in the women's labor movement before the war, then her sixteen-year exile and her return to women's work in Occupied Japan. At the other end there were interviews with vaudeville dancers who chatted about jazz and clothes. In between were the government workers, journalists and so on, and gradually I began to build up a picture of that new phenomenon of postwar Japan—the career girl. Perhaps the most typical was Kumiko Nomura, a journalist on one of the Tokyo dailies. With her short hair, big glasses and Western clothes, she might easily have been a Greenwich Village intellectual. She had, she explained, given up her kimono and Japanese sandals in favor of dresses and slacks because she found them much more convenient for her chasing about town after stories.

We saw her several times and she seemed quite unembarrassed

at talking about herself. " My mother," she told us once, "used to tell me when I was a child, 'It is a great misfortune to both you and me, Kumiko, that you are a girl. Your days of happiness will be few. Build for yourself another life to which you can retire when the need comes.' "

"Did the need come?" Clare asked.

"Do you not see?" Kumiko said, spreading out her hands. "My mother was right, and now I work on a newspaper."

She took us out to Kawana one afternoon to meet her mother who lived there in seclusion, a bitter, silent woman; she was miserable and disappointed in her marriage, and since her husband's death had scarcely left the house, but spent her time studying the Japanese classics and looking after Kumiko's six-year-old son. Kumiko shared a room in Tokyo with another family and consequently had no place to keep the child. From her earnings she sent her mother money for the child and for food, and the rest of her income went to keep herself alive.

In spite of her mother's protests Kumiko had been married when she was eighteen to a young businessman. Her mother, who had insisted that Kumiko be brought up with the nearest approximation to a Western education available in Japan before the war, had sent her to stay with American missionaries for four months out of every year. "She was certain," Kumiko told us, "that my marriage too would fail, and wanted me to have resources of my own so that I would not have the unhappy old age that she has. You know, Japanese girls were all taught, 'When you are young, obey your father; when you are older, obey your husband; in your old age, obey your son.' So when my father arranged for me to marry this man I could not say no. I had met him, but I did not know him well. His family was afraid that I had 'modern' ideas, so they insisted that the full ceremonies be observed."

Kumiko was dressed in a white kimono for the early part of her wedding day because white is the color of mourning and from that day on she must consider herself dead to her family. Later in the day she wore a red kimono—the color of joy—to symbolize the fact that she was being born into a new family. Finally she was dressed in a ceremonial black kimono for the actual service. Before she left her parents' house she was presented with a small dagger, a remnant of the old custom that a bride should kill herself rather than face the disgrace of returning to her own family if she were unhappy with her husband.

"When I left, my mother's eyes were swollen with weeping, and I wept, too. She said to me, 'Kumiko, this is the most tragic day day of my life,' and I didn't want to leave her. My husband's family were most shocked that we weren't more joyous.

"That night I was so tired—and especially so hungry—that I didn't know what to do. You see, I just didn't know my husband well enough to tell him that I had not eaten all day and I was too embarrassed to ask for a sandwich on my wedding night."

After Kumiko's baby was born, she was left at home to look after him while her husband spent more and more time away. "Everybody—all my friends—knew who his mistresses were and where he kept them. I was so ashamed."

As the war progressed, Kumiko's husband was taken into the army, her small house in Tokyo was burned, and she sent her son to her mother and decided to get a job. "I knew my husband would disapprove so I didn't tell him, and as he was away he didn't find out at first." During the war, with so many of the men away, the newspapers had been prepared to take on women, and Kumiko had found a job writing for the women's section of a paper. At first, all she was allowed to write were sugar-saving recipes and suggestions for austerity menus for housewives. Gradually she worked her way on to a different type of reporting, and finally she wrote feature pieces for the paper.

As a result of the changes in law made by the Occupation government, she was able to get a divorce. Never before had women in Japan been able to divorce their husbands. "My son," she said, "will conduct his marriage in a different manner. . . ."

17 On February 2, we heard of the death of Mahatma Gandhi, and at once began the streams of reporters and people coming to call, to ask questions and to offer condolences. All that day there had been no time to eat, and by the time Kumiko who was writing a piece about the tragedy, came it was quite late in the evening, so she and I sat down to some tea and toast together.

"We Japanese had a great regard for your leader, Mahatma Gandhi. He is a great loss to our country, too," Kumiko said.

The shock of the tragedy, the personal loss which all Indians felt, and the questions and confusion of the day had left me exhausted. I replied more shortly than I normally would have, "I really don't know why that should be true. His first principle, you may remember, was nonviolence."

Kumiko, deeply hurt, smiled in a fixed, tense way. "It is a principle that we, as Buddhists, understand very well. Another of his great principles was freedom for Asia."

"Yes. And was that what brought him close to Japanese hearts?"

With great seriousness she said, "That was what brought him close to our hearts."

"Oh heavens!" I said, in final exasperation. "Wars and murder, conquests and concentration camps, people dead, and people wounded, and everybody poorer and the world unable to right itself for ages afterward—why do we all have to pretend that we have God on our sides when we do these things? Why must we always say it was for freedom or some such thing? Why can't you, Kumiko, be honest and say it was for economic gain, or because you had to, or from fear—"

"Almost all one's actions are from fear, I think. We were afraid of fighting, but other fears, stronger fears, made us fight. But you," she said calmly and furiously, "an Indian, you should understand what we did. You, at last, have your freedom in your country, and you are the first nation in Asia to do that. But the rest of us? Are we not in chains? The Dutch, the French, the British rule Asia. In China the Americans try to build up their idea of a 'good government' with billions of dollars. Siam is so small, and every Western nation has a share in her government. And now we, the last to be subjugated, are a conquered nation, too. Oh," she said painfully and in despair, as though it was an old sore, "if only you had helped us. . . ."

"You should be thankful," I said, sounding like a governess, "that you are occupied by the Americans. They are doing more to set your country on its feet than you could ever have done."

"But," she said, surprised into pleasantness, "that's not what I was talking about. You know I am thankful for some things under the Occupation, just as I hated other things under the old system. But that's not the point at all. I was talking about Asia and its freedom. Look at the movements that have started now, since the war, in Indo-China, Indonesia, in Malaya and Burma, didn't we organize them, arm them, lead them to 'democracy'?" She put the word in verbal quotation marks. "It was only possible for them—weak countries—to fight their conquerors after they had seen the white men beaten. Beaten by Asians, working for Asians—that was when their prestige vanished and the subject peoples had morale enough to revolt. That is why you should have helped us. After the war," she finished quietly, "the 'democracies' returned those nations to their foreign rulers. Like all wars, it ends in mysteries. . . ." She picked up her tea cup. "Come, let us drink to Asia's freedom. It is what Mahatma Gandhi would have wanted, I am sure."

The next day I phoned Clare. "Listen," I said, "on this tour of ours, let's go to Indo-China, Siam, Malaya and Indonesia, too. Shall we?"

"Okay," she said accommodatingly. "What brought this on?"

"Nothing special. I thought it might be interesting. Clare?"

"Now what?"

"Are you serious about coming on this trip?"

"Of course," she said. "What do I have to do? Put it in writing?"

"It'll mean resigning your job—"

"Oh sure, that's already done."

[68]

"What?"

"You have to give the government three month's notice. . . . I thought you said we were leaving in the spring."

"Yes," I said weakly.

That evening I told my father that I thought I should like to make a tour of some Asian countries after my mother arrived in Japan. I said I would like to spend two or three months visiting other parts of Asia on my way home. He nodded and went on with his reading.

"Aren't you going to say anything?" I asked.

He looked up, took off his glasses, and said, "Well, I suppose you will need some money."

"No," I said, "I mean, yes. What I meant was—"

"If I were you," he said, "I should take enough for a year. You always get more involved than you expect."

18 Early in the spring my mother arrived in Tokyo. She worked her usual miracles, and in a few days the house was running smoothly, the servants knew exactly what they were supposed to do, the food improved beyond belief, and the cook learned how to make curry. With those little problems solved, she was ready to tackle something else, and soon I found that whenever I came into the drawing room there would be groups of Japanese women drinking tea and listening to my mother saying, "But if you hope to find answers to any of these questions, you must organize. . . ."

Meanwhile, I made preparations to leave Japan. Jean de Selancy and Faubion had decided to come with us on the trip, which by now we all called The Trip. Jean had managed to get three months' leave from his government, and Faubion, feeling that his work in saving the Japanese theater from excessive censorship and eventual death was about finished, decided to study the theaters of other Asian countries.

The school year at the Jiyu Gakuyen ended in April, and we made our plans accordingly. I took my mother there to listen to some of my classes, and my students, who had lost a good deal of their shyness by then, did a scene from *Watch on the Rhine* for her, asked her to give a speech, and were altogether friendly and easy.

There were many things to do that last month of my stay in Japan, apart from the actual co-ordination of our arrangements for leaving.

Meanwhile, I tried to introduce my mother to the things I had liked best in Tokyo and at the same time said my good-bys to my Japanese friends, the theater (modern and kabuki), the actors and the lovely parts of town. The diplomatic life, of course, was an old story to her, and occasionally there were unusual entertainments —tea with Prince Takamatsu, the Emperor's brother, and a performance of the weird old bugaku dances which came from India one thousand years ago. It is a lost art at home, but here it was preserved by the Imperial family and performed only for them. The masked Hindu gods and dancers of bugaku were until very recently the only stage shows the Emperor ever saw.

The last of my good-bys, to the Jiyu Gakuyen, were all mixed up with the end-of-the-year bustle. Many of my students wept, with the easy emotionality of the Japanese (those inscrutable Orientals), and made me promise to ask my mother to visit them from time to time. Old Mrs. Hani and I bowed low to each other, and she smiled blindly in my direction, "We will not forget what you have taught us."

"I'll try to remember what I have learned," I said, feeling that all the gratitude should be on my side.

"And think of us as people, not as the nationals of a country."

"Yes, of course—as friends," I said.

"Friends or enemies," she said gently, "but at least as *people*. That is more important than anything."

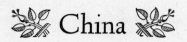 China

19 There is always the thing about a country that people never tell you. In Japan it was the extent of the destruction, in China the fact that everybody wears blue. Clare and I arrived in Shanghai early in the spring to find it exactly like the cheap novels that are written about it, just as improbable, just as extravagantly vulgar and overwritten, just as attractive and full of the jetsam of many nations, ways of life, and above all, of frustration. All the foreigners living there seemed to want to get out, the small talk at parties was often concerned with someone who had just got a visa for the States—that was considered the height of good luck—or somebody else who had finally decided to return to his own country —or the White Russians who were going on the repatriation ships back to the Soviet territory. And one always heard the tragedies of the stateless who had no passport, no papers. Yet they stayed on there doing odd jobs, always thinking of themselves as being in transit, hating China though many of them in ten or fifteen years had never been outside Shanghai—which, as they all say, is not China.

The slightly ordered existence of the International Settlement had gone and the only people who maintained an interest in anything beyond getting out of the place or making enough money to stay there, or anywhere else for that matter, were the Americans who were there for a specific assignment, newspapers or business, and those who owned that perennial bulwark, a British passport.

Sprawling in a confusion of dirty streets, overcrowded with refugees from the interior, neurotic and unstable from inflation, high prices, problems of transportation, housing, getting a job, making friends, using influence, Shanghai and its people had produced a curious, haunted, unreal existence. One felt the people had to keep assuring themselves that they existed because they were certain that should they disappear into one of the many by-lanes nobody would miss them.

Everywhere one heard stories. There was one, concerning in-

[73]

flation, about an American G.I. who bought a case of sardines because he liked to eat sardines. Before that case got to him it had been used in many complicated transactions in barter. Nobody trusted the currency so one dealer who had got the case from UNNRA had exchanged it with another for a bolt of cloth, the second one had exchanged it with another dealer for, say, a fountain pen and so it had been going on. When the G.I. finally got it, he opened it up only to find that the fish had gone bad. In a fury he went back to the dealer and said, "You can't cheat me this way. These damned sardines you sold me are bad."

The dealer said, "If you had only told me you wanted to eat them I could have given you a guaranteed fresh case."

Another sort of story concerned the antiforeign feeling. Apart from tales of people being stopped when they were riding in pedicabs and made to hand over their money and jewelry because they were "damned Americans," there was the often-quoted crack about the Englishman who asked a Chinese why they were suddenly so hostile.

"Because you are foreigners," said the Chinese.

"Foreigners?" said the Britisher. "I'm not a foreigner, I'm British."

All business was accomplished by "squeeze." Graft and corruption were so ordinary that no sensible businessman figured his expenses without them. The stories of government corruption were so usual that people did not even repeat them except to strangers and newcomers. Scarcely anybody knew the official rate of exchange for American dollars or any foreign currency. Automatically they quoted the black-market rate on which all prices were computed.

In Shanghai it was extraordinarily hard to meet the Chinese—any other nationality: the bridge-playing, golf-playing foreigners, or the refugees, but not the people of the country. Every road, of course, was packed with them walking along in their blue gowns or trousers, conducting business from stalls, cooking things in alleys or doorways. Eating seemed to be a national pastime, and the Shanghai streets were always filled with the smell of something frying or roasting, or the strong pervasive smell of soy sauce. One would see the little, fat white dumplings filled with minced meat sizzling in pans, or people leaning against buildings shoveling food from bowl to mouth with great speed before they returned the bowl to the vendor and walked on to complete their errand.

There seemed to be a greater air of release in Shanghai than in Japan. The quiet orderliness of Tokyo streets was replaced by scenes of confusion and a more uninhibited atmosphere altogether. It was impossible to pay a pedicab driver without a brief drama of shouts and recriminations in front of the inevitable audience of interested spectators. On any street there was a mock fight in progress with foreigners or with other Chinese. All this embarrassed Clare dreadfully. She found the open screaming and discussion of money as difficult and uncomfortable as most Westerners do. She never understood the fun of bargaining or the economic necessity that forces you to overcharge a stranger if you can get away with it.

"But Clare," I used to say, feeling that this was much more like India and our way of doing things, "they seem to be a nation of actors, the audience has fun, the kids in the streets enjoy it, and it's not really a waste of time because no one is in that much of a hurry here."

"I don't see why they can't fix their prices," Clare would say indignantly.

"Well, clearly, as long as there are people like you who would rather pay up than be embarrassed in public, it's worth their while not to."

The city was so crowded with refugees from the north that people slept, lived, cooked and played on the streets. Occasionally we saw a body lying at the edge of the sidewalk, either too ill to move or else dead. "How appalling," Clare would say, or, "How callous— they just walk by." The first time she saw it, she was furious. The body lay against a bank building on one of the main streets of Shanghai. Clare rushed into the bank and found a teller who spoke English.

"There's a woman outside your bank," she said, "I think she's dead. Dead on the street, and nobody seems to notice. Can't you do something . . . call someone?"

[75]

The teller looked up with startled eyes. "But if they live on the street, where are they to die except the street?"

In Asia life is not a carefully protected thing, and death is not shocking. It is the one certainty.

Another thing that puzzled Clare was the curious reversal in China of the position of man and his machines. Coming from a country in which human labor is the expensive commodity, and the product of the machine is not—the hand-embroidered hand-kerchief costs more than the machine-made one—she was continually surprised that you could buy a hand-made cigarette case, say, more cheaply than the machine-turned one. Of the three modes of transport in Shanghai, the taxi, the pedicab, and the hand-drawn ricksha, the cheapest was the ricksha although it needed the greatest expenditure of human labor.

"In New York," she said, "you pay the world to go around Central Park in a hansom cab, instead of a taxi, and even that is pulled by a horse, not a man."

Some friends took me to dinner with Mme. Sun Yat-sen one evening. She is a good-looking woman in a neat, plumpish way, and simply dressed. She has a layer of easy conversation over a tremendous reserve. In Shanghai at that time she was virtually a prisoner inside the small house which her husband had left her. She could not leave the city. She was carefully watched by the police and everything she did was under suspicion. Her house which was in the old French settlement was quite nicely decorated in an old-fashioned way. The food was excellent and her kind of hospitality a very appealing one.

While she had been in Shanghai her time had not been spent uselessly. She had occupied herself with social work, dealing mostly with the refugees and the slum children in the city. A few days later I was taken round to see some of her work in actual operation.

In three of Shanghai's most congested manufacturing areas, over a thousand children who could not afford the fees of municipal schools were receiving their basic education free of cost. Their classrooms were sometimes the corner of a Quonset hut, sometimes the steps outside a children's clinic, occasionally a slum shack temporarily vacated by the parents and adults of one of the children's families. Sometimes they even had a genuine classroom which they were permitted to use after class hours. The ages of the students ranged from seven to seventeen and the point that made these classes unique in China and extraordinary anywhere in the world was that the ages of the teachers ranged from ten to seventeen. Conducting classes in reading, writing, mathematics and general knowledge, the children taught each other with all the poise and discipline of experienced lecturers.

The first step in the Little Teacher Movement was to find the most intelligent children from the municipal schools of the slum district. If they needed money to continue their formal education Mme. Sun offered to subsidize them in return for their services. Then three adult assistants gave the children about three months of training in their new responsibilities. One of the teachers told me that the first thing to impress upon the children was that such work must come from the desire to do it rather than from compulsion of any sort. "It should be a voluntary wish to help others."

The techniques that the children were taught were rather different from those that most primary schoolteachers learn. The first principle was that work must continue whatever the conditions or difficulties might be. If there was no space, classes must be held out of doors or in somebody's home. If materials were short the children must write on the ground with sticks. They had begun to write their textbooks, too, partly because they could not afford to buy them and partly because the old reading texts made very little sense to children whose only knowledge of life was a Shanghai slum and the constant fight to eat.

Passages that used to read, "I go to the park with my amah every morning. My amah buys me candy . . ." were changed to, "There are many germs on the feet of the fly. When you eat food on which the fly has rested, you will get sick," or, "It is snowing heavily now. The price of rice and charcoal has gone up. The poor family has no money to buy wood so they burn their benches for warmth." Elementary rules for hygiene, or traffic regulations such as, "The street is a tiger, you must be careful of it," as well as concepts more nearly related to the life and daily work of the children had been substituted for the vague mysteries of parks and amahs.

The children seemed to have accepted the Little Teacher Movement with great ease and the three adult assistants remained only to supervise the work. One of these teachers was a pleasant girl who had been trained as a lawyer but found the slum conditions in Shanghai so frightful that she decided to go into social work rather than start a law practice. She took me to visit a literacy class. It was being held in a small deserted hut next to a barber's shop in one of the most congested manufacturing districts of Shanghai.

The seventeen-year-old teacher was a shoeshine boy in the mornings and evenings, and he taught a class of youngsters during the lunch hour. At night he himself studied in the advanced class. With a schedule heavier than most adult teachers would consider undertaking he found he had no time to himself during the day, and when I saw him he was eating his midday meal while he taught simple arithmetic to his class.

Many of the children were themselves laborers in the factories in the district. Such children grew up young and when I talked to ten-year-old Wu Shaio Mei, the youngest of the Little Teachers, I found it hard to believe that she would have authority enough to keep order in a class of such children, most of whom were older than herself and all of whom were used to the rough undisciplined life of the street. I asked her what she taught.

"I teach Chinese book two but I study book eight myself."

Before she began on a lesson she studied the vocabulary to see if she could understand all the words "because a teacher must not know less than her pupils." Then she tried to make the lesson into a story to hold her pupils' attention.

"Do you have trouble in making them work?" I asked.

"At first they were noisy so I chose two of the cleverest in the class and told them that they were responsible for keeping order. Because they were eager to learn they made sure that there was quiet in the class. Now there is very little trouble. It makes a difference," she said thoughtfully, "if people *want* to learn."

I asked if she ever punished her pupils.

[78]

"No that is the old-fashioned method of teaching. I tell them to stand up and think over what they have done wrong."

"If that does no good?"

"Well I have not so much experience yet. When I have done more teaching I will know."

She had three brothers and one sister. The brothers worked as hawkers and in the fish market and her sister in a factory, though she was out of work at the moment. I asked Wu Shaio Mei what she would do when she grew up.

"When I am fifteen I will go into a factory."

"Would you like to continue your education?"

"Of course, but I must not ask too much. I know we are very poor."

As the movement became more secure and the children more versed in the techniques of teaching, Little Teachers could be drawn from the literacy classes themselves instead of from the regular classes. If any child felt that a literacy class was needed in his district he applied to Mme. Sun's committee and if it was possible an additional class was opened.

To raise money for their own work the children had started a Little Theater group which consisted of the more talented children in dramatics who wrote and performed plays for the children of more well-to-do schools.

While I was watching one of their classes in mime I asked one of the little actors if he could invent a scene for me about Shanghai life. The one he did went a long way to explain the antiforeign prejudice. He acted a drunk American sailor wandering down one of the Shanghai streets. The sailor tries to pick up a Chinese girl, claims that a pedicab driver has overcharged him, gets into a fight with a man and finally when an M.P. comes up, springs to attention and says it was all the pedicab driver's fault. Afterward as a final comment on a mechanical civilization the little boy acted the sailor walking away from the scene of his fight producing a cigarette and a lighter. While the Chinese crowd stands around and stares, the sailor clicks and clicks but the lighter does not work. He walks off in a fury.

A few days later I was introduced to Rewi Alley, a New Zealander, who was the head of a remarkable school in northwest China, called the Bailie School, which trained boys to work in the Chinese industrial co-operatives. The co-operative movement interested me partly because of its application to Indian conditions, and partly because of the publicity it had received during the war. Clare, from her extensive political reading, assured me that it was "the only democratic movement left in China," and that we ought to inquire into it. Accordingly, when Rewi Alley invited us up to the northwest to see his school, we accepted at once, and decided to go there as soon as Faubion and Jean, who were to join us on The Trip, arrived.

During the six weeks before they came, Clare and I did the touristy things, in case we should never get another chance. In Peiping we wandered about the Forbidden City, and squinted up at the golden roofs shivering in the sunlight, sat for hours in the courtyards, improbable and lovely with their white lilacs. We walked along the city walls against that dazzling sky, took picnics to the Summer Palace outside the city, and spent a week end at the University there. Sitting under the fruit blossoms on the campus we listened to the students asking serious intelligent questions about why America was helping Japan—a defeated nation—to rebuild its economy, or what India planned to do with its new freedom. And always there was the sort of underground mutter of the Communists outside the city, and the sympathy for them among the young people inside the city. Every now and again it would break out in student strikes and arrests, barbarous behavior on the part of the Kuomintang police, atrocities, protests and processions, and then another interval of calm with the bitterness intensified, and the Nationalist cause further discredited.

We went to Nanking, too, to see what China's capital was like, and found it—like all governmental centers—dull beyond belief.

We returned to Shanghai in time to meet Jean and Faubion. Jean went first to his consulate and met us for dinner, looking stricken. "What is the worst thing in the world?" he asked.

"A muddle," Clare said, "of any sort."

Faubion said thoughtfully, "Warm gin with a hair in it."

"No. Not getting something you've been looking forward to is the worst," Jean said drearily. His government had recalled him to France for some special assignment, and he couldn't come on The Trip.

Shortly after that, my father asked me to go to America because he had been appointed our ambassador there, and my mother would be unable to join him for three months. So for that summer Faubion went to Peiping to study the theater and to learn Chinese. With his extraordinary facility with languages, it takes him about three months to speak a language, six to speak it well, and a year to read and write. Clare found herself a temporary job on a Shanghai newspaper.

20 The Trip really started when I returned to China in October. Clare, with her usual efficiency, was determined to make preparations, and to organize.... Faubion said vaguely, "The things you prepare for are never what happen, so I don't see that it matters."

We were going to northwest China first, so Clare arranged to have our summer things shipped to Hong Kong to meet us there; we were to take only a small suitcase each with winter things in it. She was always saying things like, "Now, I can lend you a ski suit, have you any gloves? . . . We'd better take plenty of DDT. . . . Faubion, go down to the bazaar and buy some sulfa pills. . . ."

Faubion came back with an enormous bottle of sulfadiazine. "They are only," he said solemnly, "of use in case of gun shot wounds, but they were the only sulfa I could find."

"Soap . . ." Clare was chanting, "toothpaste . . . lanolin cream in case of snowburn . . . cans of soup in case we get dysentery. . . . Have you," she looked at me suddenly, "had your appendix out?"

"Yes," I said firmly. "Really I think this is a lot of fuss about nothing. We're going to be there only two weeks, why can't we eat what they eat and live as they live?"

Faubion only said, "We must get out into the villages. You can never learn about the country from the cities."

Those ten days before we left were busy in other ways, too. Faubion had made friends with Ts'ao Yu, one of China's most distinguished dramatists, and we saw him practically every day because Ts'ao Yu's generosity was almost as prodigious as his literary output and little notes and invitations were always arriving from him. He didn't, he told us, mix with foreigners as a rule but Faubion's great interest in the Chinese theater had in turn interested Ts'ao Yu. He was a delightful man, small and tidy, and spoke very good English.

One afternoon he took us to call on Mei Lan Fang, the greatest classical actor. He was over fifty then, but looked like a youngish man with a rather ugly, pleasing face and beautiful hands. Sitting in his dark, unpretentious drawing room, with its exquisite porcelain and pictures, he talked very softly, guarding his lyric soprano for the stage, and told us about the struggle of Peking opera to survive the popularity of the movies. The old glory of Peking opera will probably die when Mei Lan Fang does. He is the last of the great actors, and although he has a few pupils none of them can match his genius and his scholarship. He did a lot to purify the art, study its history and revive much that was lost, but the tradition continues in an attenuated form only in Peiping, in the provinces, among inexpert village companies.

Afterward we had dinner with Ts'ao Yu—at a restaurant, as usual, because the Chinese seem to delight in eating away from home—and he told us about his tour of America when he was invited by the American Government. He had met many people, but the ones he had most enjoyed were Lillian Hellman and Clifford Odets.

"Didn't you see Eugene O'Neill?" Faubion asked with surprise because Ts'ao Yu's early work had been strongly influenced by O'Neill.

"No," he answered slowly, "I could have seen him because they were very kind about giving me access to people in America, but I felt I had nothing with which to flatter O'Neill."

"Flatter him?"

"I mean my writing is beyond the O'Neill stage—I am not prepared to say that it has *progressed*—" He suddenly embarked on an extraordinary little soliloquy—extraordinary, that is, for anyone of his position and attainment. "You must take everything I say this evening with a grain of salt. I am going through a period of some confusion in my mind and for the past few months I have written nothing. I feel out of touch with the thought and motives of the younger generation, so now I am studying the things that influence them. I am reading economics and sociology to find out how their minds work, and what persuades them to action. Then I must decide whether my way is the correct one or theirs. Already I am beginning to feel that perhaps a writer should concern himself more specifically with the political conditions of his country. So far politics have entered my plays only when they were necessary to the art. Now I am not sure that it should be that way. But," he said, shaking his head and frowning, "I must study more, and see. Forgive me for this self-analysis in public. It is very rude."

I stared at him, amazed at such questioning and humility from someone whose fame and popularity were so great.

Faubion said, "But should you let the students lead you? Shouldn't you lead them? They, of course, are immersed in politics —they are the most politically aware group I have ever run into. But should a writer let the politics come before the art?"

"These days we are all involved, and there is no help for it. For the first time we are *Chinese*, rather than writers, or citizens of— say—Peiping. It is no longer possible to produce art under these conditions."

"Then you will have to flee. To Communist territory? But you are a liberal, not a Communist."

"What *is* a liberal in China these days?" said Ts'ao Yu smiling. "Anyone who is not anti-pro-Communist. I cannot go into these rarified distinctions. All I know is I can't write propaganda, and in Nationalist China I am allowed to write nothing else. So I write nothing. You see, we all go in fear of our living, if not of our life. . . . Perhaps the students are right. We must all help to get rid of the oppression, then perhaps art can flourish . . . perhaps?"

Later he took us to the biggest entertainment center in Shanghai, The Great World, which consists entirely of different forms of theater and vaudeville. For the equivalent of two and a half cents you could spend a long evening moving through the large wooden structure and watch about a dozen plays. In different parts of the building there are continuous performances of modern and old-fashioned plays, comedies, tragedies, Peking opera with all-men or all-women casts, boxing matches, music-hall turns and parodies of famous dramas.

21

Ts'ao Yu's short, casual figure appeared one day to sweep us all off to lunch to meet a friend of his, a woman who had been a labor organizer. "But," he said, looking wisely at Clare, "she has had to give it up because of police pressure."

Clare, as he had guessed, was immediately interested. She found all the theatrical talk rather trying, and was glad that at last we were to meet someone "who really knew the problems." She asked Miss Wang many questions about the women's movement, only to find that the fear of reprisals on their families was great enough to keep women out of public life.

Miss Wang advanced another reason for the absence of a women's movement, comprehensible to an Asian, but horrifying to Clare. "The Chinese woman," she said, "occupies a position of great security and dignity in her family. She can see very little advantage in entering the field of men, and considerable vulgarity in competing with them."

Indignation made Clare sit up straight. "Do you mean that a Chinese woman looks forward to being no more than a wife and mother."

"Oh more than that," said Miss Wang easily. "You might say that the ambition of a Chinese woman is to be a mother-in-law. That is when she reaches the position of most respect in her family, when her sons marry."

Clare said, "Surely there are other things that a woman wants besides the ability to rule her family."

[84]

"But I agree with you. On the other hand," Miss Wang said questioningly, "the daughter of a friend who has been in America tells me that elderly ladies live by themselves in hotels, sometimes when their children have homes and familes in the same city. Is this true? . . . If that is the price of emancipation, the Chinese women do not find it attractive. Here they know they are protected until the day they die. They always have a place in the family, a position in society, and what more does any woman want besides security? You are young," she smiled at Clare, "loneliness becomes more frightening when you start growing old."

"You work with labor unions and things, so you *must* think the same way I do. You *must* see that women should be able to have jobs and independence."

"If they want them. I have only dealt with that small group of the dispossessed Chinese women who have to work in Shanghai factories, and they deserve decent conditions to live and work in. But it would take a braver and more ambitious woman than I to try to change the family system."

Ts'ao Yu said, "I have written much against the family system here, but in a way it is a great institution."

"If you're ready for an institution," Clare muttered.

"Because it is through the family that we have survived, and it is through the family that the Chinese has retained his independence of heart. You *cannot* allow any member of your family to starve while you eat, so to that extent at least wealth has been divided. And when your first and only loyalty is to that small unit—your family—you have no loyalty left for governments, or regimes or ideologies.

"We can't be regimented because governments cannot frighten us, and you can't appeal to us through sentiment—only our family can do those things. This is why in the middle of economic ruin we can still eat, conduct business—and survive; why we can be ruled by fascists or communists—and still be free."

On the way back from lunch Faubion managed to circumvent Ts'ao Yu's generosity for the first and only time. When it came to the moment of paying the pedicab coolies, he said, "Ts'ao Yu, you can't afford to pay these men, you are the greatest writer in China."

This sent Ts'ao Yu into such a spasm of laughter that the coolies were paid before he recovered. The poverty of China's writers, however, was no joke. No writer, not even the greatest, could support himself by writing in China. They all had to turn to other trades in order to survive. Ts'ao Yu was a director in the movies. Sheng Ts'ung Wen, whose two best-selling collections of short stories brought him, over a period of two years, royalties sufficient only to buy three small Chinese cakes, was a professor at the Peking National University. Most of China's great writers had fled to Communist territory, or to Hong Kong to escape Nationalist persecution.

This situation had been brought home to us by a visit to Pa Chin, one of the best-known and most prolific of the Chinese novelists. His masterpiece, *The Clan*, on the evils of the family system, had sold five hundred thousand copies—more than any other novel had ever sold in China. He kept himself alive by working for a publishing firm. He lived in a tiny room in a slummy section of Shanghai. The entrance to the house was through the kitchen, at the top of a rotting, creaking flight of stairs; his room faced onto the little alleyway. Through the window came the shouts of the slum children playing and quarreling in the autumn afternoon, while inside, surrounded by dusty papers and books piled on the floor, Pa Chin talked to us. His voice was halting and sick, and he coughed frequently. He showed us a letter which said that John Day in America, a possible publisher of *The Clan*, had turned down the book because it was too long and too gloomy. However, it added as a compliment, Pearl Buck herself had seen the manuscript.

"Is that hopeful, do you think?" he asked naively in his wasted voice.

"Oh I'm sure it is," I said quickly. "After all, you are so famous in China, there should be translations done of your work."

"Yes. . . . It is not a question of fame"—food perhaps?—"but are Americans interested in Asia? In our stories?"

"I hope so."

"I hope, too."

Pa Chin, from his experience in working with publishers in Shanghai, told us that the situation had reached a point where the long chain of maladjustments led to some strange conditions. Eight American cents would buy almost any book on the Chinese market, but even this was too much for the poor reader. The Commercial Press, China's largest publishers, found that it couldn't pay its authors even the pittance they were accustomed to, couldn't sell the books when it did print them, and had stopped accepting manuscripts at all. Reprints of textbooks brought in some money, and the rest of the paper ration was cut up for stationery. Letter paper was worth more than a best-seller.

Faubion told us a story of two girls, students in a Peiping university. They were watching a particularly lovely sunset and one of the girls admired it. The other said, "No, no. You must not say such things. We must learn to be hard."

"Yes," said Pa Chin, "we are forced either into politics, or—like me—into silence."

Lao Shaw, the only Chinese writer who could make money, did so by his sales in America, although his most brilliant book, *The City of Cats* carried too bitter a message for the foreign reader. A malicious satire, it summed up the situation in China very neatly. *The City of Cats* was the story of a Chinese aviator whose plane was wrecked on the planet Mars. There he found a kingdom of cats, a kingdom of complete social corruption. In schools, degrees were granted on opening day. Money was called "national spirit" and circulated in tremendous abundance. The libraries and museums were empty because the treasures had all been sold to foreigners for vast quantities of "national spirit." A kingdom of dogs, composed of very small, rapacious members, invaded. Even in the face of that disaster the cats continued to wrangle among themselves. Finally the kingdom of cats was reduced to its two surviving leaders, one red cat and one white. The enemy unwittingly put the two in the same cage, and they killed each other. The Chinese aviator, in disgust, made his escape back to "great, glorious and free China."

22 Before we left Shanghai we acquired one more member for The Trip. Michael West was a young English businessman whom we had met at a party. He had taken one look at Clare's blonde head and invited himself along. None of us knew him, and by the time it was established that he was coming with us we had discovered only that he worked for some kind of import-export firm, and that he had a month's vacation which was too short a time to go back to England and too long to stay in Shanghai. He had heard that we were going to the northwest when he was talking to Clare, and after that he spoke to each of us separately, and we all thought that one of the others had invited him. It was settled before we got together.

"Well," said Clare, shrugging and accepting the inevitable, "at least he's good looking—in that stern-jawed way."

He was helpful about money as well. While I had been in America, the Chinese dollar had been "stabilized." After it had dropped to the point where one got several million to the American dollar, a new currency called the gold yuan had been brought in, which was supposed to be fixed at four to the American dollar. Michael said that to be on the safe side we had each better take with us the equivalent of seventy-five dollars (American) with us, and that should be plenty for two or three weeks in the northwest.

Michael had the stately, rather charming manners of the conventional Englishman, and a kind of imperviousness to his surroundings that made him live in China exactly as he would in England, and regard the Chinese as characters out of a comic opera. He had a certain patronizing fondness for them, and often told us stories illustrating their ingenuity or business acumen.

Although he had been in China for more than a year, Michael spoke no Chinese, as he was of the school that feels that if you speak English very slowly and clearly the foreigner is bound to understand. So Faubion was our only interpreter; his Chinese, by then, was fluent and adequate enough for conversations which did not require too specialized a vocabulary.

23 Lanchow, the capital of Kansu Province, is a biggish town. High walls enclose the city which is in the center of a circle of flat-topped hills. One road from the town leads out to northern Kansu, and on to Sinkiang and Central Asia, edged by the Gobi Desert on one side and the rim of the Tibetan plateau on the other. The only way of getting to Lanchow from the China side was by air.

Everything was a desert tan in color. The hills that formed the cup in which Lanchow was placed had no vegetation. The city walls were built of the baked local mud; houses, roofs, roads and alleys all seemed to be carved from an enormous block of caramel. The river outside the city ran like a stream of milky coffee between its eroded banks. Only the main streets were cobbled.

We stayed in the only "Western style" hotel in the northwest. In the Hsi Pei Ta Hsia we were each given a tiny room like a cell, containing a wooden bed, a washstand, and a table and chair. We paid the equivalent of a dollar a day for each room. As we were being shown to our rooms, Clare said, "There are really only two phrases one needs to know in Chinese, one is, 'Where is the ladies' room?' and the other, when you eat in a restaurant, is, 'No sea slugs.' Everything else you can express with your hands." She did learn those two phrases and did manage on just those two all through China.

After dinner we went for a walk in the silence and cold of the northern night. Like all country towns, Lanchow slept early. There were no streetlights, and the only illumination was the faint glow of oil lamps from some of the houses, and a lightening of the outline of things from the starlight. The air in the northwest had a special quality. It smelled slightly of dust, and its dry and penetrating cold reached right into one's head. We walked along the cobbles of the silent bazaars, with the shut wooden faces of the shops turned to the street, through the dead alleys, between the great arches of the city gates, and back through the darkness to the Hsi Pei Ta

Hsia. I remember that we chatted a lot in our nervous foreign voices because it all seemed so remote and closed after Shanghai.

The electricity worked occasionally at the hotel. That evening it had failed, and when I stopped at Clare's room to say good night, I found her sitting up in bed in a frilly nightdress, with her mouth full of bobby pins, carefully putting her hair into those little snails that American girls know how to make. The mirror from her handbag was propped on her knees, and the little oil lamp flickered uncertainly by her bed. There was something wonderfully incongruous about the scene, with Clare so intent on her daily routine. "I like to look my best when I face a new city," she said defensively, as though she were about to be launched as a debutante in Philadelphia.

One was strangely conscious of the sky, in the northwest. At night the enormous, icy stars hung very low, and in the daytime the hurting blue of the immense expanse of sky kept one glancing upward continually. We had been given letters of introduction, by friends in Shanghai, to the governor of Kansu Province, and to Mrs. Han Lo-ran, an English teacher in Lanchow. Mrs. Han lived in part of a house which was built around a courtyard in the usual Chinese way. A bright-red door opened onto the courtyard, and in one corner Mrs. Han and her two small children occupied one room. In most of the Orient, houses present a blank, uncommunicative side to the street or passer-by. The life of the house eddies around the center, and there privacy is not considered important. Rooms open inward, verandas keep you informed of comings and goings, or courtyards that must be crossed to go from bedroom to bathroom, or from meals to leisure, make secrecy impossible. Inside, there may be gardens and trees, the children may play, or a woman may wash her hair in the sun. But the family is shut away from strangers. It is the only privacy in such a crowded continent.

Mrs. Han, the widow of a well-known painter, could not afford a house of her own, so she shared the courtyard with friends. In her padded cotton clothes and knitted gloves she was much more sensibly dressed than we were. The temperature inside the houses and outside was the same. One didn't heat a room, one simply put on

[90]

more clothes. Firewood in that barren country was too rare a commodity.

Mrs. Han, her round pleasant face glowing, looked doubtfully at Clare's beautifully cut slacks and cashmere sweaters and my borrowed ski suit and said, "You had better buy some sheepskins. It gets cold here very suddenly."

We said airily that it did not seem worth it as we would be in Kansu only a couple of weeks. But she insisted, anyway, on our buying warm gloves and the felt shoes which all the people there wear. We hurried behind her through the bazaar to the rows of stalls, with the workrooms immediately behind, surrounded by the chatter of farmers in from the country wearing fur hats and embroidered boots and the citizens of Lanchow in blue quilted clothes.

Michael who was always much struck by contrasts said, "Odd, don't you think? Here men wear gowns and women wear trousers."

"It is the mysterious Orient," Faubion answered gravely.

When Clare and I stopped to try on shoes, a crowd gathered at once, astonished and laughing at the size of our feet, while the women with their tiny feet looked smug. The shopkeeper made faces, muttered and finally gave us men's shoes. Mrs. Han was most ashamed for us at the display of our inelegant and peasant-like feet. Besides the shoes, I bought two of the heavy white sweaters that the shepherds wear and some rough woolen gloves.

Mrs. Han borrowed a spare sheepskin from one of her students for Faubion who had no coat. She assured him the old army uniforms that he was wearing would not be warm enough. Michael had a fleece-lined flying jacket so he was better equipped that any of us.

After our shopping trip we invited Mrs. Han and her two children to lunch. "Oh! that will be a great treat, we so seldom eat out. But," she said with concern, "the hotel is very expensive." The average meal would cost the equivalent of a dollar for four of us. But she insisted anyway on taking us to one of the many restaurants in Lanchow, which are cheaper, a Mohammedan one, it turned out, with the rich cooking and grilled or barbequed meats of Central Asia.

We learned over lunch that Mrs. Han earned three hundred

gold yuan a month from her teaching at the University of Lanchow. That money was only enough to buy the coal that was essential for heating when the winter really set in.

"But what do you do?" Clare asked. Michael who was embarrassed by any discussion of money looked with elaborate unconcern around the dark restaurant room with its earth floor and general air of smoke and dirt.

"What can we do?" Mrs. Han said. "We must just struggle along in whatever way we can and hope that prices do not rise as high as usual this winter. I do extra teaching, of course, and already the children help me with the housework, and then if there is any writing job that I can pick up I try to fit that into my schedule, too." She paused for a moment, looking rather timidly into the future, and said in a voice that was suddenly old, "I suppose we shall survive. The trouble is we are all so tired. The simple business of getting along from day to day requires so much energy and worry and concern that really one only sees China's economic crisis and the strange things that are happening to our country's wealth in terms of one's own exhaustion. What," she asked, "will the really poor people do this winter? How will they eat? What can they expect? Already prices are rising and the faith in this new currency has gone. If only we were not all so tired. . . ."

Something that I had not expected of a small provincial capital was the cosmopolitan air of Lanchow. In the city one saw an astonishing mixture of races and faces: the pale, small-boned Chinese of course; the Mongolians with their scarlet cheeks and distinctive woolen (rather than cotton) clothes; the Tibetans more aquiline in feature, more bronze in coloring, wearing deep furs and silver jewelry; White Russians from Sinkiang dressed sometimes in the dowdy peasant clothes of Europe and sometimes like the Chinese; a large number of Arabic and Mohammedan faces and all the many mixtures of those various races. To us Lanchow may have seemed remote, to them it was the big city, the center of their part of the world.

We found, too, that Faubion's Chinese was comprehensible only to the educated richer businessmen and the bankers. Mrs.

Han introduced us to a good many of her friends in Lanchow—
teachers, businessmen, and a few government officials, sturdy northern types, more direct and more independent than southerners.
The rest of the people spoke their own dialect and would merely
look baffled if one addressed them in the pure Chinese of Peiping.
Fortunately Faubion could read and write Japanese, and since the
written language of both countries is very similar he fell into the
trick that the Chinese have when they travel of writing everything
down when they cannot speak the dialect. One sees customers in
shops rapidly drawing characters in the palm of their left hand with
their right forefinger and being answered in silence by the same
method by the shopkeeper.

24 One day the slogans on the walls of the university of
Lanchow read: THROW AMERICAN ARMIES AND SUPPLIES OUT OF
CHINA. CHINA FOR THE CHINESE. By the next day these had been
erased and the usual Kuomintang slogans were back in place: THE
PEOPLE AND THE ARMY ARE ONE FAMILY and similar sentiments
along with the principles of the New Life Movement.

The university had a spacious campus. Some new dormitories
were being built because the enrollment had been steadily rising
as students from other parts of China had come to the northwest,
the last section to be involved in the civil war.

That day while I was talking to some of the students at the
university I asked them what they thought of the problems China
was facing and what solutions they considered would be most
effective in dealing with them. In contrast with the Peiping students these had no answer, only vague and evasive suggestions and a
change of subject. Finally I asked if there was any political interest
or activity in the university at all.

"No, there is none."

This was particularly surprising because usually the Chinese
students were the most vociferous section of the population of
Kuomintang China. I said, "In Peiping it was very different. It

seems strange that there is no political interest here."

"Here the students do not dare," I was told. "This is a government university and they are afraid to talk about politics."

"But there are government universities in Peiping, too, and those students are concerned with politics."

"Yes there they can afford to. They are so close to the liberated areas and can escape there if they have to. But where can we go?"

"But you do not have to be a Communist to be interested in politics," I said.

"No, but these days the difference between Communists and liberals is not recognized. If you do not support the government, whatever your political sympathies, you still have to prove you are not a camel." The other students laughed.

"What?" I asked.

Then they told me the story that was quite popular in that part of the country. A rabbit was running at enormous speed down the street. Another rabbit saw him, stopped him and said, "Where are you running to so fast?"

"Haven't you heard?" said the first rabbit. "They are putting horseshoes on camels in that town back there."

"But why are you worried? You are not a camel."

"No, but how can I prove I'm not a camel?"

25 With Mrs. Han to interpret for me, I went to present my letter of introduction to Governor Kuo at his office in the old Manchu government building. The governor, a neatly handsome man, came from Anhwei Province and was sent to Kansu during the war, a very strategic area of defense because of its proximity to Russia.

He added quickly, "There is no threat now from the Communists here because the people know the Communists from when they passed through Kansu before. They know the cruelties and terror of the Communists."

Since it was clear from the beginning that this was to be a purely formal interview, I asked him purely formal questions about the problems in his province. The most important, he said, was the betterment of agriculture. They have on paper extensive schemes for irrigation and reforestation, to check the enormous erosion of land and the dearth of water of the northwest. If the land can be irrigated Kansu can be an enormously fertile province, entirely self-supporting in food. Already, Governor Kuo assured me, the days of famine from drought were over. This point did not quite fit in with what we had heard from one of the officials in the Forestry Department who had told us that the few irrigation schemes that had been carried out had benefited only the rich, the big landowners who had the best lands nearest the rivers. The poor farmers still had no water. As for reforestation, a couple of attempts were made, but without machinery to protect the trees, so as soon as the trees were old enough to be used for firewood they were cut down by the fuel-hungry people of Kansu.

The interview was very short because it was quite obvious that he was going to tell me only what the government wanted the foreigners to believe.

26 After a few days in Lanchow, we thought it was about time to move on to Sandan, where we were going to stay with Rewi Alley in his school for training workers in co-operatives. The only means of transportation in that part of China is by road. Only trucks and jeeps can negotiate the road which would shake any other car to pieces. Hitchhiking on the mail trucks, and occasional trucks of the China Petroleum Company which go up to the oil fields of northern Kansu, is the elegant way of getting about. Otherwise one can buy a pony, or walk. The system has the complicated logic of most Chinese systems. The trucks, which are mostly American army surplus, have signs on them saying how many tons they can carry. The company wants to get the most service out of their trucks so they load them to capacity. In China, unlike more technology-conscious countries, the machine is the servant of man, so by bribing the driver of the truck you can get a ride on top of the load. Since as many as twenty-five poeple can do this at a time, the government disapproves of the system because it is dangerous, and further overloads an overloaded truck. However, the government officials themselves have no other way of traveling about the province. So a sort of two-way blackmail keeps this method of transportation running. The officials don't report the drivers, and, in return, are allowed to ride free and in the cab beside the driver—out of the cold. The officials are called "white fish"; the paying passengers are "yellow fish"; and the occasional soldiers who stop the truck and under the threat of their guns demand free rides, and their meals along the way, are called "black fish."

Mrs. Han explained all this to us, and on a morning late in October we waited outside the city gates with our suitcases for a truck.

We found the place where the yellow fish usually wait, and in the chill, slanting sunlight walked about and speculated excitedly about our fellow passengers. There were a few soldiers, without guns, some town dwellers in long, padded gowns, a few peasants in sheepskins (worn with the fur inside). None of them carried much luggage, and each one had a bedding roll on which he sat, with his hands inside his sleeves, apparently impervious to the cold.

When one of the oil trucks came along, it stopped at once near our little group on the roadside, and the negotiations began. Clare and I were very lucky, managing to get seats inside the cab next to the driver by paying him a little more. Sandan is on the road to Sinkiang, so the truck would certainly pass it. It would be a two-day journey, and the cost for us would be the equivalent of seven dollars each. The others climbed on top of the truck with all the luggage, and the machine jolted off.

The road was unsurfaced, but we traveled along in considerable comfort between the barren, eroded mountains. Here and there were rocky outcroppings, but on the whole the same desert-colored countryside continued making one—since there was no contrast in the coloring—very conscious of shapes, of the flat-roofed, cubistic look of the little walled villages, of the strangely old look of the mountain masses. Occasionally the light powdering of green in a small patch of cultivation struck the eye with a feeling of unfamiliarity. We passed many pony trains, a few rows of camels, and often the peasants walking behind their herds of sheep.

By midday it was comfortably warm, and we stopped for food. I don't think there is any Chinese village that doesn't have a restaurant that can produce a decent meal. The driver turned to us and said "*Che-fan!*" and made motions of shoveling food into his mouth.

The restaurant was small and dirty. Faubion, very sensibly, pointed to the most prosperous looking of the yellow fish, and said, "We want the same as them." The restaurant keeper seemed to understand and brought us rice, chicken cooked with green peppers, a dish of mixed vegetables, an unidentifiable meat with a thick, sticky, sweetish sauce, and a small bowl of bright red, very sharp chilies crushed together to make a seasoning. He wrote down the name of each dish. In this way we soon collected quite a repertoire of meals we could order in a restaurant. The whole thing cost less than fifty cents.

After lunch, we stood and watched the driver fiddling with the engine of the truck, while the children in the village collected to watch us. It was pleasant standing in the sun, with only a row of huts and a wall between us and the hills. We were in no hurry, which was just as well because we learned the first lesson of truck travel in China. The truck, naturally enough, is sure to break down.

"Is something wrong?" Faubion asked.

"Yes. Can you drive?"

"Yes, I can drive. Why?"

"Well then," said the driver, "see if you can mend this."

"I can *drive*," Faubion explained, "but I don't know about the inside of trucks."

The driver straightened up and stared at Faubion in amazement, then repeated to one of the yellow fish, "He can drive but he can't mend the engine." They all smiled and looked puzzled.

Here, we learned, you are an apprentice driver first. You travel on the truck with a veteran driver and your job is to fix it when it goes wrong. You get a cut of the money the yellow fish pay, and

[97]

only appeal to the driver for help when the breakdown is beyond your mending capacity. By the time you graduate to the position of driver, you are naturally an experienecd mechanic as well.

Eventually, whatever was wrong was mended with a piece of wire, and we drove on, climbing steadily onto the Central Asian Plateau, until evening. The truck stopped for the night at a small town called Wu-wei, on the edge of the Gobi Desert. We asked the driver where we should spend the night. He looked at our clothes and our luggage doubtfully and suggested that we should find Dr. Shu because he was a very kind man, and we had no bedding of our own, so he might put us up in his hospital.

We had no trouble finding him because apparently in every Chinese village everyone knows exactly where everyone else is at any moment of the day. Small, painfully thin and with a smooth, saintly face, he was, as promised, exceedingly kind, and rather to our surprise spoke English. He immediately took charge of us because Rewi Alley was a friend of his and he was pleased to find people on their way to see him. Over dinner he told us about his work, the problems of keeping his tiny hospital functioning and supplied. "Sometimes I can cure a disease or perform an operation —and there is plenty of such work because I am the only doctor within a hundred miles of this town—but what can I do for people whose real disease is too little food, insufficient clothing? And what of the diseases of the mind? The eternal worry of staying alive, and the fear—always the fear?"

"Surely," Michael said, "one could teach them to keep clean" (the dirt of China bothered him a great deal). "That should cut out at least some of the sources of infection."

"If I tell them to wash their clothes, which they wear all winter long, what will they do even for the time it takes for their clothes to dry? No, they have to wear them until they rot off their backs. Which of them can afford the fuel to heat water for washing? No, the coal must be kept for essential things like cooking food. And I can deal only with the effects, not with the sources." He leaned across the table, his tightly stretched skin glistening in the wavering light of the oil lamp. "The most usual disease here is tuberculosis, and what am I to say to my patients? This is a condition of poverty? You need isolation, good food, a healthy climate, plenty of rest?" There was a look of pain round his eyes. "Oh there are so many people in my country, it is scarcely noticed if some die. But what about the living? . . ."

He gave Clare and me the room of one of the nurses who was away, and Faubion and Michael accommodated themselves in the dispensary.

The next day's journey took us up through the high pass between Wu-wei and Sandan. The wind across the plateau was icy, and there was a light sprinkling of snow on the ground. The driver seemed very pleased that the truck had managed to negotiate the pass, and began singing excerpts from a Peking opera, and produced a flask of *pai-gar*, the strong liquor distilled from *kaoliang*, a kind of millet. He offered it to Clare and me in a hospitable way, so we all took swigs from it and managed to keep warm until we reached Sandan.

27 Rewi Alley is a stocky, red-faced man with tremendous drive and great charm of manner. He had come to China first in 1926 as a factory inspector in Shanghai. He got into the habit of taking his summer holidays in the interior of the country, learned Chinese and studied village life. Gradually he became interested in a village co-operative movement for China, and for over twelve years—since the Japanese invaded China—had devoted his full time to organizing co-operatives. The Bailie School was a more recent project intended to train young Chinese in the techniques of organizing such co-operatives. The boys received a high school education as well as technical training in the use of simple machines and in new forms of agricultural implements.

Remote, difficult to reach, Sandan had been chosen as the best place for such a school largely because it was in a very poor part of the country where the Bailie School experiments in farming and mining would be of great immediate use to the surrounding countryside. The school was supported largely with funds from relief organizations in America and New Zealand.

Rewi Alley had taken over several Chinese houses and a few

[99]

deserted temples, and these were made into classrooms, dormitories, tool shops, and houses for the machinery. The school tried as far as possible to be self-supporting. Inside the town walls of Sandan, the school functioned as part of the community. The pottery, cloth, buttons or farm produce were sold to the citizens after the school's own needs had been filled. Outside were the experimental farm and the school's coal mine.

Our first day in Sandan was spent learning about the school and seeing some of the classes at work. In some of the temples, lathes or looms had been set up in front of the huge painted Chinese images with their staring eyes and savage expressions. In others, students sat on benches and took notes while their lecturer stood against a contemplative Buddha or a huge, peeling mural.

We walked through the town and watched the Sandan women on their minute bound feet, like the hoofs of little animals, totter to the market with baskets of vegetables; the village school with its huge Kuomintang slogan painted up: A SENSE OF DUTY, A SENSE OF SHAME . . . the principles of the New Life Movement. From the walls we looked across the curved roofs of the temples, with the colors of peacocks and gold, to the dry expanse of the country and the hills.

In the evening we went to dinner with Rewi Alley and his three adopted sons—little boys whose parents had been killed during the war—they flashed their chopsticks between bowl and mouth, finished their meal in a few minutes and ran off. We, too, left immediately after dinner to go to bed, already falling into step with the country life which starts at daybreak and ends with the fading light.

28

"I call them Peter Pans," Rewi Alley said the next day, "these children who work in the coal mines here. They never seem to grow at all, from the time that they start work, at the age of eight or nine, to the time when they have to retire as old, broken men of thirty." He had taken us out to the pits in the hills some miles outside Sandan. All around us were the mine workers—tiny, shriveled, dark-skinned gnomes, known to the local population as "ants" or "blackfaces"—and the scattered encampments where they lived. They see nothing except their bleak hills, and the pits until they die of scurvy, starvation or mine accidents.

One of the projects of the Sandan Bailie School was to prove by demonstration in the coal pit they had acquired that better conditions of work for the miners were in the long run conducive to a higher yield and more efficient production.

Until the previous few months when the school began to work its mine the usual custom there had been to allow the children to start work as soon as they were of an age to earn for the support of the family. Often if the family could not afford to buy their food during the winter months the children were sold to the mine owners and from then on there was no further control—governmental or parental—on the conditions under which the children worked. The number of hours a day as well as their wages were determined by the mine owners without reference to either humanity or to law.

To all of us it seemed incredible that children could survive under such conditions. Usually they were without shoes, socks or trousers even through the bitter northwestern winter. In Sandan the temperature drops to twenty-five degrees below zero.

The children started work when they were between six and nine years old. Most of them were diseased and stunted, but they hoped that they wouldn't grow much because a shrunken frame was an advantage in that job. The shafts were so narrow that only a child or a wizened man could fit through them. They earned the equivalent of fifty American cents a month.

As we walked over the dry, sand-colored hills, those mining villages presented an extraordinary sight—no shops, no restaurants, no amusements, just the black holes of doorways in the mud huts, the silent, half-naked miners and their old little children sitting on the ground, grimy and expressionless. Only the scavenging dogs barked at the strangers and sometimes the babies giggled and clung to their mothers as the cold of the evening intensified.

Rewi Alley brought us at last to the pit that the schoolboys were working. At first the other miners hadn't trusted them because they said that "white faces" could never work a real mine, but gradually as the Bailie School experiments continued the miners were acquiring a little more confidence in the new methods. With the introduction of simple and cheap machinery, safety measures and better living conditions, the lives of the impoverished miners might slowly be benefited.

It was nearly dark when we walked back across the hills and only little sparks of glowing light told us that one or two of the encampments could afford a fire.

In the following days we went outside the town to see the school's agricultural experiments: special plots where new crops were being attempted, irrigation trenches were being dug, a new variety of sheep grazed and new machinery was being put into operation. In the school itself we sat and watched the boys at work studying and doing manual labor. After one of Rewi Alley's English classes he gave us some of the diaries which his students kept as part of their English curriculum. They showed more clearly than talking to the boys how the peasant minds had reacted to some of the skills they were taught in school.

Chen Ing Kwei who was a refugee and an orphan from the war area of China had been studying automobile mechanics. He wrote in his diary:

I think of bygone days. How lucky I was to be able to run away from a famine district and from the war. Also to get to the Bailie School after all.

I have learned much. The first truck I saw in the country, I saw turning a corner. The driver sat at the steering wheel. I looked through the window, and was very happy when I saw how the truck worked. I decided I would make a simple one with a wheel. I said proudly to my friends, "A man sits in a small room. He turns a wheel and the wheel turns the truck." Then I saw another kind of truck on the road. The exhaust was blowing a lot of smoke out and there was dust and smell. I was very, very happy to see it all and ran home fast and told my friends, "I have seen another kind of truck which works different. A man sits in a room and lights a fire and the fire makes smoke which drives the truck."

Then one night there came a truck and the lights were on. The lights were very bright. I wondered for a while, "Oh wonderful! How can they make the oil lamps so bright? How can they set them? Doesn't the oil come out when the truck goes? Oh I wonder how they work!"

Now the years have gone on and I understand these things. I have driven trucks. I have made light.

Altogether we spent about two weeks in Sandan learning a little more about the various projects that the school had started, including the free clinic where there were always piles of eggs or chickens or baskets of vegetables left on the doorstep by grateful peasants for the treatment they received.

29 When we were leaving Sandan, instead of returning at once to Lanchow we thought we would follow the old silk route further north to Kanchow to see a city which was a flourishing trading center in the old days and one of the richest towns in the northwest. The road is flat all the way and is flanked on one side by the Great Wall of China. Kanchow immediately shows its prosperity by its huge, beautifully kept city walls, elaborate gates, busy markets and even a few stone houses.

Here, too, it was with a feeling of surprise that we saw a flourishing commercial center in what we had always thought of as a remote desert area. Horse caravans, strings of camels and yak trains marched solemnly into the city through its four enormous gates; from Ninghsia, Central Asia, from distant parts of China and from Russia traders came to do their business in Kanchow.

After only a day there we decided to return to Lanchow and on that return journey two of the strangest days of my life were spent. We had not been able to find places together on a truck going south so we divided up and I found myself alone on one of the most unreliable machines that I had seen in China. We had been stopping for repairs almost every time the truck had to negotiate an upgrade and by the time we reached the high pass between Sandan and Wu-wei the truck collapsed entirely with an awful clatter of machinery which made me think that the engine must have fallen out.

[103]

It was about five-thirty in the evening when I got out and stared at the desert. It had become bitterly cold and there was a blizzard blowing up from the mountains. The driver made signs to me that we were to spend the night on the pass and I thought only of Rewi's stories about the history of Kansu and how invading armies had frozen to death on that pass and wondered what sort of idiocy had persuaded me to let the others go off with the luggage and whatever coverings we had.

One of the yellow fish came and stood beside me. He was a Tibetan, I gathered from his enormous fur hat and high embroidered boots. He asked me the standard opening question, where did I come from? Was I "Inguo?" I said "No, Indu." He said "Ah?" very interested and immediately rattled off a lot that I could not follow.

The soldiers from the top of the truck had already started stretching blankets between the wheels and putting their bedding underneath the truck. Presumably they would be settled there for the night. The Tibetan tapped me on the shoulder and motioned to me to follow him and by then I was too desperate to do anything but obey.

We must have walked about two miles into the darkening desert to a tiny village—really just a row of mud huts surrounded by rather dilapidated walls. By then it was that curious half-luminous time of the evening that one gets in that mountainous part of China. The stray dogs of the village started their lonely, hysterical barking as we approached. I noticed in the twilight two skulls stuck up on poles on top of the wall—the usual warning to bandits.

We walked down the only road of the village, no more than a clearing in front of the huts, and noticed the dim lights from one or two of the houses where the evening meal was being cooked. The biggest hut was the last one and we went in. The Tibetan talked to the old woman who came to the door. She was very surprised and asked a lot of questions and eventually let us in. There was only one room with a k'ang running across one side, and very faintly in the gloom in the other side of the room I could see vegetables piled, and a small heap of wheat. Garlic and chilies hung on strings from the ceiling. Across the back of the room was a half-wall and behind it were the stables for the donkeys.

The entire family were sitting on the k'ang—an earthen platform built right across one side of the room—two boys, a girl and a small baby. The old woman surprised me by taking up the baby and starting to nurse it. I had thought from her looks that she was much too old to have a child so young. The old man was lying across the wall and one of the boys was massaging his legs. Every few minutes he would stop and prepare something over the tiny charcoal burner and put it in his father's pipe. From the sweet, sickly waves of smell that came from it I gathered it was opium, which was pretty cheap in that district and really the only luxury that the peasants could get. The old man hospitably offered the pipe first to the Tibetan and then to me but I was too frightened to accept and the Tibetan apparently did not smoke opium.

The Tibetan indicated that I should sit near the burner and get warm and told the old woman to give us some food. She picked up the single lamp, which was a bowl of oil with a wick in it, and held it up to my face and asked a whole lot of questions which I could not understand. Eventually she gave us a meal of half a bowl of noodles, a couple of limp green leaves and a bowl of hot water. These people were too poor to afford even tea.

I was gradually losing all touch with reality. It seemed impossible that I was in some obscure Chinese village of which I did not even know the name, with no means of getting anywhere else and without even the ability to communicate with the people.

After the meal the family gathered around me, still talking excitedly, and began to feel the material of my clothes and examine my watch and the contents of my handbag. They made me stand up to see how tall I was and pulled my hair out to watch it snap back. Curls, to the Chinese, were the strangest thing about my appearance. The old woman said, "Mao fan tse," and led me out to a small space enclosed by low mud walls, with the stables on one side and the village wall and the desert on the other. When I returned, the Tibetan indicated that I should go to sleep at once because I might have to walk to Wu-wei the next day. I was not sure that I understood him correctly because I had gathered that Wu-wei was more than thirty miles away. However, I was uncertain enough to do anything he suggested.

The charcoal burner had dimmed and it had become very cold. The Tibetan unrolled his bedding on the k'ang and told me to get in. I asked where he would sleep and he pointed to his sheepskin and said he would be warm enough. The entire family stared spellbound while I took off my coat and shoes, made a pillow of them, and climbed into his sleeping bag with all my clothes on. I was thankful for the dim lamp because it made it impossible to see how dirty the bedding was. By then I was not even slightly concerned about the animals that must live inside because the sleeping bag was made of two sheepskins sewed together with the fur inside. Soon after that the rest of the family spread out their poor coverings on the k'ang and went to sleep, too.

I remember waking in the middle of the night feeling lonely and sick from the pervasive smell of the opium. And because things like that always seem so much worse in the middle of the night I felt myself on the edge of tears. "If only I can get out of this. . . ." I thought I had made no noise but a hand came out from the Tibetan's bedding next to mine and very gently traced a line along my face from chin to eye and then vanished still in silence. It was curiously dramatic at the time.

In the morning the Tibetan made the woman bring me water to wash in and everyone stood around and stared while I stood with dripping face and hands waiting to dry. I had no towel of course. The woman had called in her friends from the neighboring huts to see the foreigner and they all came in to examine my clothes and belongings even more carefully now that it was daylight. While they stood there the door from the stable opened and three donkeys marched casually through the room out of the front door and onto the fields.

Breakfast was another bowl of hot water and a lump of potato bread. After that the Tibetan indicated that we should go. I felt by then that I had spent most of my life with him and thought vaguely of the years stretching ahead when we would live in word-less but scrupulous courtesy in obscure mountain villages without ever knowing each other's names. I produced a card which said in useless simplicity and a flowing script *Miss Santha Rama Rau* and that is all. He smiled and put it away without looking at it and I realized that, separated from one's possessions and without a lan-guage, one had no identity at all.

I asked him by producing my wallet whether I should pay for the food and lodging, but he became very embarrassed and waved the money away. All the way back to the road I composed long and elegant phrases of thanks and recited them to him in the most complicated and archaic sentence structure I could think of. He smiled and nodded and smiled some more.

When we reached the truck we found the soldiers still gray with cold trying to light a fire by the side of the road. I found a place where I was sheltered from the wind but still in the sun and sat down to see what would happen. My Tibetan wrapped himself up in his sheepskin, put his bedding roll under his head and promptly went to sleep by the side of the road. I sat and wondered whether it was worth trying to walk to Wu-wei and what I should do now that the Tibetan was tired of looking after me.

It must have been about an hour and a half later that a green truck came down the road. The Tibetan woke up at once, sprang into the middle of the road, stopped the truck, and began to explain something long and complicated to the driver. Everyone gathered round and they all laughed and asked questions and made com-ments. Clearly it was the funniest thing that had happened to any of them for some time. The driver of the truck pointed up to the roof but the Tibetan said no very firmly and showed him how thin and silly my clothes were. There were two men in green uniforms sitting next to the driver in the cab. He made one of them get out and sit on top of the truck and insisted that I be placed between the other two for warmth. This was apparently a mail truck that went to Sandan once a week.

I tried to thank the Tibetan and asked if he weren't coming too, but he shook his head, waved off his amazing kindness and went back to the side of the road to settle down for another nap. The man in green said, "Inguo?"

I said, "No, Indu."

He said, "Ah," as though that explained everything.

From then on I traveled in the greatest comfort. The driver and the other men insisted on buying my meals and wine whenever we stopped and the official would scatter the change to the beggars outside in a most magnificent manner. In Wu-wei they arranged for me to stay in a Chinese inn and explained that I must remain outside the city gates because the truck would start at five in the morning and the city gates did not open until daybreak—about 6 A.M.

30 Lanchow, on our return, seemed like such a large and busy metropolis that we were surprised at how our perspective had changed.

The winter had come with the suddenness of which Mrs. Han had warned us, but we still didn't buy sensible winter clothes because, now that we had been to Sandan, we thought we might as well fly down to south China. We spent a few more days in Lanchow.

During that time Clare dragged Mrs. Han firmly around the schools and hospitals because she "wanted to get the picture," she said. The only nursery school there was a charitable enterprise, we were told, run by the Women's Work Committee—a Kuomintang project over which Mme. Chiang presided. It turned out to be anything but charitable and seemed to benefit only the children of the rich government officials.

This made Clare angry. "But why don't the Chinese help themselves," she said, her fair-mindedness making her speak vehemently. "Why are all the things like the Bailie School run by foreigners? You know the abuses of the Women's Work Committee, why don't you start your own charities?"

"Charity," said Mrs. Han, "is a Western idea. We can't afford it."

"You people seem to think only in terms of your family—"

"Because we must," Mrs. Han put in almost under her breath.

"—and you blame your government for your economic mess, but everywhere in China there is black-marketing and corruption—on any level. We pour money and supplies into your country, and what happens? Are we supposed to fight your war, too?"

"I hope not," said Mrs. Han.

"Then why don't you people help yourselves? Most of the people we meet think as you do, but you all complain and nobody does anything. Why should we do all the work?"

"Indeed," Mrs. Han was forceful for the first time, "many Chinese ask the same thing."

Clare turned abruptly, "Do you mean that you want the Communists to win?"

Mrs. Han said wearily, "You are the ones who are afraid of communism. What can communism bring us that is worse than what we have? Can you talk to the Chinese peasant about civil liberties and free enterprise?" She said to me, "You, of course, understand all this. Your country, too, is poor. First you must eat. If you have not life, where is the use of anything else?"

"People," said Clare uncertainly, "must be prepared to die for freedom," and feeling that "freedom" sounded silly, amended it to, "I mean, for a better way of life."

"Oh yes," Mrs. Han said, "we will die in any case."

31 Faubion, as usual, had discovered all the theaters in Lanchow, and insisted on our going several times to see the northwestern version of Peking opera. Michael, who was heartily bored at the Chinese theater, commented only on the comedy scenes. "The Chinese have no sense of humor," he announced to Clare. "Really, it's all on the banana-skin level." It was a remark that interested me because most Asians feel that the Westerner has no sense of fun, and lives in a terrible gloom of financial ambition.

This and his other curious, rather formal ideas about Asia must have been instilled into Michael, as into most Westerners, during his infancy and schooldays—long enough before, anyway, so that he didn't remember acquiring them—for he was constantly surprised by the Chinese bewilderment at his opinions. One day when we were going for a walk with Mrs. Han, we passed a man beating his overloaded pony quite fiercely. Michael, filled with his usual indignation at the poor treatment of animals, shouted to the man (in English) to stop beating his pony. The man stared at the foreigner for a moment, but naturally enough took no notice.

"Really," Michael said furiously, "the cruelty of the Chinese is incredible."

Mrs. Han turned her alert little face to the man, blinked her eyes rapidly against the cold, and said, "For beating his animal?"

Faubion said, "But if a Chinese *man* isn't treated as well as an English horse, a Chinese *horse* must be treated worse than the man. It's a descending scale, and it simply depends at what point on the scale you begin. You wouldn't for instance, feed your horse caviar and champagne."

"Of course not," said Michael overcome by this outlandish statement, "it would be very bad for the horse. Make him sick, I dare say."

"But look at the man himself. He's carrying proportionately as much as his horse. He's not being cruel, because he treats *himself* the same way."

"That's no excuse," Michael said. "The thing I shall remember longest about a Chinese village is the screaming of a dog being tortured. Do you remember how often we heard—"

"Those," Mrs. Han said, much puzzled by this conversation, "are children that tease the dogs. The older people haven't time."

"They should be trained not to be cruel to animals," Michael said grimly.

Faubion, with a gleam of malice, said, "But wouldn't that be cruel to the children?"

Mrs. Han pounced on this as the first sensible remark spoken so far. "I have often thought," she said eagerly, "that the foreign friends I have are cruel to their children. It is a Western idea, is it not, to make the children go to bed when they are not sleepy, eat when they are not hungry, forbid them to play when they want to, and perhaps make them go and play when they would rather stay at home? It must lead to much trouble in their minds later on. We find it very cruel to the children."

"Which," said Faubion gravely, "is far worse than being cruel to animals."

Mrs. Han nodded in agreement, and Michael, feeling somehow betrayed, blushed hotly.

32 The variety of the food in Lanchow was one of the minor delights of the town; we would pause at the many stalls to taste what they were cooking on the street and for every meal we would try out a new restaurant. We used to buy great disks of Sinkiang bread, made by a few stalls in the bazaar to meet the demands of the travelers and traders from the Russian frontier who came to Lanchow from time to time with their caravans loaded with sheepskins, wool and carpets. The bread was about eighteen inches in diameter, very thin and crisp, and shaped like a soup plate. It took about half an hour to bake, and just before it was ready, tiny shreds of onion and peppers were sprinkled across it so that the flavor was drawn into the bread without making it soggy. While it was still hot we used to spread it with yak butter—a curious taste something between butter and cheese—and walk about the town eating it and spitting our the yak hairs. We never worked out how to clean the butter.

Michael still had a week of his leave left, which he thought he could extend to ten days, so we decided to go to Chinghai, on the Tibetan border, rather than spend the time in Lanchow.

We each still had about fifty dollars of our original seventy-five, and since we had been told that in Chinghai nobody trusts paper money, we changed the equivalent of five American dollars into Chinese silver dollars. The rate for those worked out at two to the American dollar and was about the only stable currency in China. For this reason Chinese silver dollars were very hard to find, and we could get only ten each.

The night before we left, we had a "feast" with Faubion's friends,

[111]

the actors and the manager of the theater. Afterward they accompanied us back to the Hsi Pei Ta Hsia, chattering and laughing in the icy night. "It will be a full moon the night you get to Sining," the manager shouted back to us, as they walked away, "it will be beautiful."

33 We took the mail truck to Sining, the capital of Chinghai, and again it was a two-day journey. The cold had a new penetrating quality, and Clare and I huddled together next to the driver, and Michael and Faubion rode at the back with the other yellow fish. Dust billowed away from us in clouds, and the ponies on the side of the road gave way to yaks as we approached the edge of the Tibetan range of mountains.

When we stopped for lunch Clare and I hopped out of the truck and walked to the back to wait for the others. Michael appeared to have become an old man in a few hours. His hair was white with dust, and his clothes looked like firmly set cement. Michael presented this extraordinary picture, Faubion told us, because with foolhardy gallantry he had insisted on taking the worst place in the truck—on the edge, at the back, and consequently caught all the dust. He was helping the women off. We began to laugh hysterically because there was something irresistibly comic about an Englishman in the middle of Asia saying very solicitously, "Now, watch your step there . . . here, I'll help you . . . *that's* right." The women gave him frightened smiles and darted into a restaurant.

"What are you laughing at?"

"Michael, dear," said Clare, "we're impressed at how your training holds good."

"I see no reason for not being polite simply because I'm in another country," Michael said huffily.

"Of course," Clare said with unaccustomed gentleness, "you're perfectly right."

That night we had our first experience of a poor Chinese inn in which there was only one room for everyone to sleep in. You could hire quilts—though the other yellow fish would think you were mad not to carry bedding—wrap yourself up in them, and range yourself with all the other bodies like a row of shrouded corpses on the k'ang. The k'ang is sometimes heated from underneath but that particular one was not, because the innkeeper didn't feel the winter had really started yet. The next evening we arrived in Sining.

You can tell when you cross the border into Chinghai because there the trees start. The change comes as the biggest surprise because the rest of the northwest has such a shaved look that a bush seems like a landmark even from miles away. The roads smooth out suddenly when you reach Chinghai, and the trees make them into long avenues reaching to Sining. The city itself is obviously prosperous. It is, besides, astonishingly clean, well cared for, and there are no beggars.

At the post office, where we stopped, an official came out and stared at us. "Foreigners?" he said. "You should go to the government hotel. All foreigners are the guests of the government here." He directed the coolies to carry our luggage, and sent a note off to someone in the visitors' bureau to meet us at the hotel. For the first time in China, the coolies didn't argue or throw scenes about the money we gave them.

The guesthouse was partly Chinese in style, and partly Western. Men in dark-blue uniforms bustled about and delivered us and our luggage to our rooms and ushered us in to dinner at once.

In the middle of the table was a large silver bowl on a stand. From the center of the bowl rose a perforated silver chimney. The chimney contained glowing charcoals, and the bowl around it was half filled with water which was bubbling quietly when we sat down to dinner. The servant then brought on small dishes of spices and salt and some yak butter. These were added one by one to the water until, after a few minutes, a thin soup was simmering in the bowl. More dishes were brought on, this time containing slices of raw lamb, onions, spinach, coriander, white cabbage, chilies, and slices of raw liver. The servant picked up some chopsticks and threw a few slices of each ingredient into the thin soup, left the

[113]

rest on the table and retired. Within about five minutes the mixture was ready and we helped ourselves and immediately put more of the raw ingredients into the bowl.

After dinner Mr. Mao, another government official, came to see us. He was a short, strong man, with a rather large, white, circular face. His features seemed to have been crowded into the middle of his face. He was very friendly and jolly, and told us that he was to be our guide and interpreter.

Faubion's friend in Lanchow had been right. That night from my window I watched the full moon over the battlements of the city wall. Enormous and very close, it drained the color out of everything leaving the silent city looking like a strangely luminous photograph. It was incredibly cold, and even the stove in my room couldn't take the bite out of the air.

The next day Mr. Mao, with great pride and a flow of explanation, showed us around Sining. The shops and bazaars were richer more ordered versions of other Chinese cities, but the state institutions of that extraordinary province were surprising beyond anything we had expected. Surrounded by mountains, connected by only one road with the outside world, with its boundary on the Tibetan side as yet undecided and further muddled by warring mountain tribes, Chinghai had schools, colleges, hospitals, state works—all functioning smoothly, all provided by "Our governor," Ma Bu-fang.

"Our governor" had also brought in some excellent doctors who had opened a hospital and free clinics. They had managed to make the enterprise almost self-supporting by an elegant separate wing for ailing Tibetan princes or landowners from Sinkiang who would make the long cross-mountain trek to Sining for modern medical treatment. A great deal of the doctors' time was occupied with the wounded soldiers. Ma Bu-fang's army, with a reputation of having the only troops which had inflicted a conclusive defeat on the Communists, had a discipline and a drive far above the general standard of the Chinese army. He insisted, too, on their receiving free and prompt medical service. The common wards were filled with disabled soldiers returned from the fighting in east Kansu when the Communists had attacked there some months earlier.

One soldier lay propped in bed, chatting to the casualty in the next bed. We found, on questioning him, that he was twenty-five years old, and had been in the army eight years. "My mother," he said, "does not like it. I am an only son and that makes it difficult for her."

"Can you send money to her?"

"No. My pay is one gold yuan a month" (about twenty-five American cents), "and I spend all that."

Clare said in a shocked voice, "Why on earth don't they all desert?"

Mr. Mao solemnly translated the question, and the soldier replied, "The food is better in the army than I could get at home. We get clothes and a place to live. Besides," he said, indicating his wounded arm, "how can I work in the field now?"

We were shown nurseries and maternity homes, state-supported mosques and religious colleges. Everywhere Mr. Mao repeated, "Our governor, Ma Bu-fang," has done this, or arranged that or given his people something else. Finally we asked whether it would be possible to see the fabulous Ma Bu-fang. Mr. Mao was rattled for the first time. "I will find out," he said. "The governor has not seen foreigners for some years. He spends much of his time in the villages . . . I will see."

Left to wander about the town by ourselves in the afternoon, we came upon a couple of things that interested us. The streets of Sining, crowded with people from many different parts of Central Asia, are a lesson in geography by themselves. We walked into a sweet shop. Inside, a Mongol and his wife were buying cakes. They were wearing finely cured, white sheepskin robes, heavy silver ornaments and embroidered boots. We stared at them, fascinated by their clothing, and they stared at us fascinated by ours. After a moment, Faubion apologized in Chinese, stated our nationalities, and explained that we were interested in the foreign clothes. The Mongol smiled without surprise, and in halting Chinese, said, "We

[115]

are foreigners, too. We are Mongols. We, too, are interested." All of us, tourists together, bought our candy and stared at the foreign Chinese shopkeeper.

Chinghai is a country of minorities. It has the atmosphere of a large friendly camp of displaced persons. Tibetan traders, with their faces and bodies smeared with yak butter, come in to trade their mutton and skins. Mongolians visit Sining to replenish their yearly needs and then return to their nomadic life in the mountains. Uigurs and White Russians have their own settlements in the city. The Moslems, who make up 40 per cent of Chinghai's population hold the major positions in the governing and running of the province. Although they are Chinese in everything but their religion, still Ma Bu-fang and his government look to the Near East for much of their inspiration. The Han Chinese are uneasily conscious of their "foreign" (Moslem) government. And, finally, the lamas in their wine-colored robes are religious refugees from the political authority of the Dalai Lama in Tibet.

On our walk back to the hotel we passed an alley where scenes of great confusion were going on. Yak trains, and horse carts were jammed into the narrow passage, and peasants with sacks of grain were crowding into an arched gateway. There two uniformed officials with long whips beat back the peasants, checked the loads and whipped them again if there was anything wrong. This was the quarterly government tax collection.

"I bet we weren't supposed to see *that*," Clare said.

At the hotel one of the boys brought us tea. He was evidently full of curiosity about the foreigners, so Faubion answered questions and began the inevitable little chat about who we were and where we came from. When the boy was more at his ease, Faubion asked, "Ma Bu-fang is a good ruler, isn't he?"

"Yes, very good."

"He is a Moslem?"

"Yes, of course. Most of the government officials are."

"And the police?"

"Some are Moslem, some Han Chinese."

"What are you? A Moslem?"

"No," said the boy fiercely, "I am Han, and we all hate the Moslems."

"Why? Do they treat you badly?"

Suddenly he looked wary. "No, no," he said, "we are all friends."

"But you just said—"

"Our governor is very good." He escaped out of the door.

The next morning, Mr. Mao came to breakfast and we all ate bread and yak butter and sweet malt together. He was even jollier and more full of laughter. "Our governor will see you this morning. It is very unusual." He bowed to me, "He wishes to meet the Indian. Never before has an Indian girl come to Chinghai. He is most happy that an Indian comes."

Ma Bu-fang did, indeed, seem most amused at the idea of my coming to Chinghai, and laughed and made jokes about it. He had sent his car for us, a magnificent conveyance. It was a rather old Buick covered on the outside with leopard skin. His own appearance was even more impressive. Very tall, very handsome with a thin spidery beard and shrewd eyes, he was much younger than I had expected and was dressed in a long, black padded gown. He came striding into the small sitting room in one of the courtyards of his elaborate maze of office buildings. It was a charming room. The red-lacquered window frames showed a view of a neat courtyard with a couple of leafless trees, their trunks wrapped in straw coverings against the winter. Opposite the windows were cases of porcelain and bronzes. On the floor, thick, bright-colored carpets from Ninghsia were spread, and the furniture was low and comfortable, made of lacquered wood. Ma Bu-fang radiates a sort of good-humored energy that makes it impossible to notice anyone else in a room.

"I am always glad," he said, "when foreigners come to Chinghai. Are you comfortable? Are you seeing whatever you want? Mr. Mao, when friends come from so far, no hospitality can be enough." He twinkled at us at though he were engaged in performing a parody of a successful war lord.

We assured him that we were not only comfortable, but that we neither expected nor deserved such hospitality.

"Now," he said laughing in an out-doors kind of way, "you look embarrassed, and that makes me an even worse host!" He settled us all in chairs, and when he sat down it was something of a relief as he seemed to fill up so much of the room. "You look as if you want to ask questions," he said. "I am delighted to answer them. Chinghai is my life, and no detail is too small for my interest. But first let me tell you what Chinghai was like when I first became governor. My father handed me a province torn with war. Racial antagonism," he smiled at Clare and Faubion, "and religious fervor," he nodded slightly in my direction, "as in other countries, had produced rebellion, slaughter and inevitably poverty. These problems I am sure you understand from your own countries." His point was perfectly clear. "However, I don't think I am making extravagant claims when I say that now, after twenty years, they are settled."

"Yes, but how?" Clare muttered.

Although he couldn't have caught the words, he caught Clare's tone for he replied, "Our army, naturally, had to be strong. It has turned out to be useful to other parts of China, too. We—ah—lend our army to the Generalissimo to help him sometimes." He managed to include us on his side in a vast contempt for the central government. We had heard before that the sort of hereditary dictatorship by which Chinghai was governed received its strength from the army. It had been built up originally by Ma's father, and had as its nucleus the fanatically disciplined and obedient Chinese Moslems. Ma Bu-fang had put it to the use of uniting and consolidating his state and his own position, and had recently turned over the command of the army to his son, while he devoted himself to civil administration. Although technically it was integrated with the Nationalist army, its strength and bargaining power (because the Moslems' first loyalty was to their own governor) was so great that they could refuse to fight for the Nationalist cause except when the boundaries of their own northwest were attacked.

Michael asked how his armies had been so successful against the Communists, even though they had been outnumbered.

Ma Bu-fang answered, "If you are sure you are right and have a job to do, then don't play with the enemy. Chop him up into bits, and take no prisoners."

Once he had established the strength he needed to ensure respect, Ma Bu-fang set about rehabilitating his province. "The salvation of our desert was in the tree." The importance of trees in preventing soil erosion was explained to every element of the population. Education teams were sent out to remote villages, and even contacted the nomadic tribes. "Sometimes the co-operation was not enough, and then I went to my people myself and explained to them." As much revenue as possible was diverted to the purchase and importation of the hardiest tree—the poplar—which grows fast enough to produce quick results, and yet is resistant to the intense cold. Literally thousands of trees were brought into Chinghai and soldiers, civilians, men and women were conscripted into tree-planting gangs. "Within ten years the desert of Chinghai began to look again like the garden to which my ancestors first migrated from Arabia."

Faubion, who is entirely at home in the oblique style of Oriental conversations, said that in Japan, too, trees were important. In fact, in one of his favorite kabuki plays there is a beautiful cherry tree which bears the notice, "For every branch broken from this tree the perpetrator will forfeit a finger."

Ma Bu-fang roared with laughter. "No, no," he said, "how can there be a punishment for damaging the trees? The people are poor. It would be only natural. No. I have taught my people to *love* the trees. *That* is why they are not chopped down for wood as in other parts of the northwest."

"Yeah," said Clare.

He turned to her rather seriously, "The people respect the trees because they see their importance. You cannot beat people to gain respect." With a sudden twinkle he said, "In the paper I read that Chiang Kai-shek beats the Communists. Do they respect him?"

To meet the expense of all this Ma Bu-fang perfected the system of tax collecting. Unlike the other provinces of China, his collectors were paid well enough so that they did not need to make their own percentage on the taxes. The standard of honesty all over Chinghai was very high. The taxes themselves were simple: half the grain and half the number of animals belonged to the government. Anything that the individual wanted to sell had to be traded through government channels and exchanges. The advantages were that there was no starvation and the minimum needs of all the people were met.

We had noticed that the Moslem women of Chinghai wore no veils. They covered their hair with hoods—white for the old women, black for married women, and brighter colors for the girls. I asked how Ma Bu-fang had persuaded them to give up their veils.

"Wherever there was opposition, I called the women together and explained that the progressing world was dispensing with such backward signs. All over Islam the women were discarding symbols of repression and were joining side by side with the men. As a father instructs his child, I taught them—directly and personally."

Clare brought up the classic argument against a paternalistic despotism. "This is all very well while you are in power, but how can you guarantee that the next governor will not abuse his strength and exploit his people?"

Ma Bu-fang nodded with complete understanding. "Ah yes, Miss Harris. You are an American; you believe in your democratic principles, and you distrust anything that seems to you like a dictatorship. This does not always lead to wisdom in action. The Americans," he said with a glint of malice, "who I am told are good businessmen, are willing to throw away many millions of dollars in proving that Chiang Kai-shek's 'democratic' government is better than the Communists'. But when you crusade for your form of government, does it never occur to any of you that what is suited to Americans may not be suited to others? Perhaps it meets your needs. Do you never wonder whether it meets ours?" He leaned forward and spoke earnestly. "We are a people old in government as in civilization. The centuries have impoverished our land, but they have not obliterated our wisdom. We are both too simple and too complicated to be betrayed by the ideas that every man is equal or that the majority is always right. History has shown us often enough

[120]

that a mass of people can bring about their own destruction even as an individual can fling himself from the city battlements. And we are all—are we not?—concerned with survival."

"But a dictatorship," said Clare a little more uncertainly, "can lead to the worst sort of oppression of its people. There are no checks to the power at the top."

"I agree, I agree," Ma Bu-fang said at once. "The step between my position and the position of a tyrant is a very short one. But you must recognize, too, that only the rich can afford a democracy."

34 The next day the governor's car came to the hotel. Mr. Mao bounced in and told us that Ma Bu-fang had thought that we might want to go to Kumbum, so he had lent us his car. Much excited by this unexpected opportunity, we drove the fifty miles to the fantastic desert lamasery. Along the way the land with its carefully tended plantations of trees stretched away, and beyond, glittering in the morning sun, were the eternal snows of Central Asia. Peasants carrying loads of hot, scarlet chilies stared at the car. A bride dressed in blue, riding on a donkey, her groom who was leading the animal, and the whole wedding procession stopped to gaze.

Kumbum is extravagantly beautiful. Its lavishness and theatricality didn't appeal to Michael who felt it was "ostentatious," but there is something most attractive about such decorative abandon. Monasteries of whitewashed plaster are tiered against the hills in asymmetrical rectangles. The golden roofs of temples and immense meeting halls flash their own light across the land. Ornamented stupas, painted and lacquered pavilions, courtyards and gardens where two thousand lamas live and pray make up the rest of the lamasery. The monks in their red and purple robes walk in thought between the scarlet pillars and painted peacock walls, or throw themselves full length on the dull gleam of the lacquer floors as many times as their bodies can bear.

At festival times an extra two thousand lamas come down from the hills to turn each of the thousands of prayer wheels and sit

[121]

in meditation in the gloom of the inner temples with the images and offerings. Everywhere there is the gentle hum of the spinning prayers and the chanting of the monks. In every temple there is the smell of burning yak butter from the huge bowls of offerings before the images.

At the center of the religious fervor of Kumbum is the Panchan Lama. Traditionally he is the religious head of Tibet, but a few years ago after a quarrel and religious schism with his political superior, the Dalai Lama in Lhasa, he fled to Chinghai. Rumor, greatly embellished and passed on by the anti-Chinese Tibetans, says that the Panchan Lama is a political prisoner of the Chinese. The Kumbum lamas themselves say, "The Panchan Lama has only to set one foot in Tibet and the Dalai Lama would kill him." To him, and to his following of Tibetan lamas loyal to the Red Sect of Lamaism, Ma Bu-fang had given sanctuary in Chinghai, and had allowed the Panchan Lama to build up his own fantastic Vatican in Kumbum, and to rule it as he saw fit.

On the drive back to Sining, Mr. Mao explained the spiritual freedom protected by Chinghai's government like this: "Everyone except the Han Chinese is in a religious minority here. And the Han Chinese have no religion anyway."

35 We got back to Lanchow in the third week of November to be faced at once with rather unsettling news. Mrs. Han came up to the hotel to see us. She looked sad and said quickly as though she wanted to get it over with, "You know, of course, that the new currency has broken?"

We were all in Clare's room where Clare was sitting cross-legged on her bed painting her nails. She put the brush back carefully, and asked, "What do you mean 'broken'?"

"The new currency, the gold yuan, it was all a trick of some sort. It had to happen of course, prices were rising so fast, and the winter here. There was no doubt that it would come, people were hoarding food and cloth and supplies. All our savings are gone. When this currency came in we were told to trust it—it was backed with gold. I had then fifty American dollars which I had collected to keep toward my son's education. . . .I gave it to the bank—trusting them—and now—" She sat down suddenly beside Clare, looking very small and shabby, and smoothed her woolen gloves in her lap. "What will become of us this winter?" I could scarcely hear her voice.

Faubion went out and bought a newspaper. Translating slowly for us he said, "The crash has come in Shanghai apparently. Inflation has started all over again. You remember Chiang Kai-shek's son was put in charge of the economic controls there? Well, he has resigned because his disciplinary methods have proved useless. It used to be a capital offense to black-market in currency—a couple of people were shot while I was there—now that has been withdrawn. People will start hoarding gold bars, and the spiral will rise again. The gold yuan is fluctuating wildly between forty and eighty to the American dollar."

Rumors that the government would fall within a matter of weeks were all over the place. Every boat, plane or other means of transport from Shanghai to Hong Kong were booked for three months to come, and the queues before the booking offices extended around several blocks. A small system of profiteering had been started by Shanghai kids who would get up very early in the morning and take their place in front of the booking offices before the crowd got there. Then they would sell their places to later-comers. The price went up as the day wore on. Meanwhile, one could not buy food or commodities of any sort because everyone was hoarding. You can always eat rice, but what can you do with money?

In Lanchow people didn't seem to care too much what happened to the government. They had never had any faith in "those southerners" or their currency. Except for the city of Lanchow, most of the transactions in the northwest were conducted in silver, gold or by barter. They felt no loyalty or identification with any part of China except their own.

For us the break of the currency meant a drastic change of plans. We had, by now, thirty Chinese silver dollars between us, and a handful of almost worthless paper. I should have had the equivalent of forty-five American dollars left, but now it was worth less than five dollars at the best price. Clearly, flying back to Shanghai was out of the question, particularly since we would not be able to leave Shanghai once we did get there. We hadn't between us even enough for one air passage to Chungking.

Faubion said, "Well, we'll just have to yellow-fish it to Chungking. We can probably get some money there." Whatever trains there were had been cut by the Communists, but the road to Chungking was still open.

"Can we even afford to do that?" I asked.

"Well, we've got to do something, unless you'd rather walk."

"We can't," said Michael fiercely, "ask the girls to *walk*. I'll wire my firm to send us some money."

"Don't be stupid," said Faubion. "If they wire you money it'll have to be through official channels, and your air fare will cost you about five hundred dollars that way."

"*I* certainly can't afford that," Clare said.

"Well, no. . . . In that case. I mean." Michael said vaguely.

I went to see the governor to ask him if he could help us. He seemed rather amused at our predicament and said he could give me a letter authorizing us to travel free on any army trucks going to Chungking, but it would be up to us to find the trucks, persuade the drivers to let us get on as white fish, and make our arrangements along the way. He could guarantee us nothing more.

"How long does it take to get to Chungking?" Mrs. Han translated for me.

"Four or five days, I think—if you are lucky in finding the trucks, and if the weather is good."

I returned to the hotel triumphantly waving the letter. "At least we can travel free, and the rest is up to us. It only takes four or five days. I think we should leave while we can still pay our hotel bills in paper money."

We went at once to the army transport depot to find out if there were any trucks going to Chungking. The officer looked at our letter, read it, showed it to his friends, discussed it, asked us all how we liked China, and finally said, no there weren't any.

"Have you any going part of the way?" Faubion asked.

"Tomorrow one is going to Hwang-hsi-pu."

"Is that on the road to Chungking?"

The man nodded.

"Fine. We'll take it."

The gold yuan just covered the bills and left enough to tip the coolies in the morning. We spent the evening walking about Lanchow saying good-by to our friends at the university, to Mrs. Han, the actors, the officials. We ate Sinkiang bread with onions for dinner because it was the cheapest thing, and returned to the hotel to pack.

36

We left Lanchow on the twenty-sixth of November, a clear, sunny day, cold, but with little wind. We hadn't even discussed the purchase of furs or bedding, partly because we couldn't afford it, and partly because we naively believed it would be only a four-day trip. There was one free place beside the driver, and Clare and I took it in turns. We started in the morning, cheerful and rather excited by our little adventure.

Faubion and Michael were by now used to the technique of traveling on the tops of trucks. They showed me that the best place is near the front so that you don't get the dust, and with one row of yellow fish between you and the edge so that you are sheltered by them from the wind. If it is possible to persuade someone to sit on your feet, then you are really fortunate because the slow freezing of your hands and feet is the hardest to bear. The truck was carrying large barrels of oil south from Sinkiang. We climbed on top of the barrels, and realized for the first time the intelligence of carrying a bedding roll. The other yellow fish sat on theirs, and it didn't take me long to learn that, once the truck is moving, the cold and draught can attack you from the most extraordinary angles. A

Mongolian climbed on at the village where we stopped for lunch, and Faubion immediately christened him the Mongolian idiot, partly for his looks, and partly because he had placed a large dead goat in Faubion's place while we had been eating. The ethics of yellow-fishing dictate that you cannot take someone else's place if you are a late-comer but nothing prevents you from putting your luggage there, as the other yellow fish can always sit on it.

"It isn't that it is uncomfortable," Faubion said, "It is simply that I have become Chinese enough to feel that one should respect the dead." However, the other yellow fish patted the goat and congratulated Faubion on having such a warm, resilient seat.

A pleasant camaraderie springs up among the yellow fish on such a journey. Since they suffer from no inhibitions about asking what they want to know their questions are direct and to the point. Only Michael was embarrassed by what he called "personal questions." Faubion, of course, was delighted because, being of a very inquisitive turn of mind, it gave him the perfect excuse to ask dozens of questions back. The opening questions are always, "Where do you come from? Where are you going? What are you doing in China?"

When Faubion answered, "Just traveling about and seeing your country," they were entirely satisfied. They had an easy conviction that China was certainly the greatest country in the world. The character for the word "China," which also means center, or the Middle Kingdom, seemed to them a literal statement of the truth. Of course China was the center of the universe, so of course foreigners would come there if they could.

The Mongolian idiot turned out to be a most engaging young man. Huddled in his furs, jolting along a road which was growing progressively worse, he asked more questions than anyone. "Which of the two men is she married to?" he asked nodding at me.

"Neither."

"Then where is her husband? In India? Why does he let her travel with foreigners?"

"She is not married."

The Mongolian and several of the other yellow fish turned at once and comforted me, "There is still a little time. But do not waste it. You must marry as soon as you return to your country. Certainly you cannot marry a foreigner." The women smiled cozily at me.

"The American sitting with the driver," pursued the Mongolian, "she is married to the Engishman?"

When Faubion translated this, Michael turned scarlet and stared with passionate interest at the receding hills. "No," he said.

"Ah? Not yet? But she will later on?"

"I shouldn't think so for a moment," Michael said in a strangled voice.

Most of the yellow fish were soldiers and their families. One of the soldiers, whose padded khaki uniform made him look like a Teddy bear, lifted the ear flaps from his cap to hear the conversation better. When he heard Faubion was an American he was very excited, and his round peasant face puckered into a smile. His skin was taut and shining from the cold, and his teeth were green and badly rotted. "Roose-velt," he said with delight, "Tru-man!"

"Wonderful. Where did you learn that?"

"In our army we are taught those names because your country helps us. *Mei-guo ren ding hao!*" he said, laughing and turning his thumb up. He introduced us to his wife, a shy little girl who was carrying a baby. He asked why we didn't fly to Chungking, "Foreigners are rich."

"We aren't," Faubion said, "we can't afford it."

The soldier was at once full of sympathy. "Then you must come with me when we reach Ting-hsi. I will arrange for you to stay in the soldiers' inn. It is cheaper."

Ting-hsi, which was scarcely even a village, looked in the light of the setting sun as though it were quite deserted. As soon as the truck stopped there, however, children, dogs, and adults dashed into the street and surrounded the truck. Heated conversations and questionings began at once. We waited patiently while our soldier friend explained who we were and what we were doing, and then were conducted to the soldier inn. It was built around a square courtyard, clean and bare, and groups of soldiers squatted on the

[127]

ground chatting and singing. We ate dinner with the Mongolian and some of the other yellow fish, and returned to the inn to find that the soldier had hired quilts for us, arranged two rooms, and was haggling with a man about the price of a small basket of charcoal so that we could have a fire.

I woke very early the next morning feeling stiff from the board bed, and with all kinds of unsuspected aches from the truck ride. I hobbled to the door of our room and found the courtyard a sheet of white. It had snowed heavily during the night, and the moon paling behind the last of the snow clouds gave the snow a weird luminous look, as though it were lit from underneath.

At first when we got up and drank our tea we were still warm from sleep and didn't realize that the winter had arrived, and from now on would grip the northwest until the spring loosened the ground, brought the rain, and allowed the lives of the people to thaw into an easier pattern that was not built entirely around escaping the cold.

It was my turn to ride inside the truck, but after we felt the wind and the dense cold outside, Clare and I decided to divide the days rather than take alternate days in the cab. "Only another three days," we kept telling each other, "and Chungking should be much warmer."

At the lunch stop, Clare climbed painfully off the truck, scarcely able to straighten her frozen joints. Tears were streaming down her face and for the first few minutes inside the restaurant she couldn't hold a tea cup. I had wondered how Faubion would survive, because he had returned the sheepskin he had borrowed from the university student in Lanchow, and had only a raincoat over his army uniform. The Mongolian, appalled at his stupidity, had lent him his own sheepskin, and had pulled out the covers from his bedding roll for himself.

In the afternoon I began to understand Clare's state. I was wearing three sweaters and a pair of flannel slacks underneath Clare's ski suit. The suit itself was wool, with a windproofed jacket, but the blizzard across those deserted hills swept through as though I had been wearing muslin. Clare and I rubbed cream all over our faces, but nothing seemed to prevent our skin from cracking and flaking. The only thing that redeemed the situation was that under snow the country looked beautiful. The flat surfaces of the villages—roofs, the tops of walls, window ledges—caught the snow and gave an architectural effect to scenes that were normally monotone and two-dimensional.

That night at Chingan, where there was no soldier inn, we followed the other yellow fish, and learned the importance of the k'ang method of sleeping. The slight warmth of the other people does reach you through furs and quilts and bedding, and keeps you alive through a night that you couldn't otherwise survive.

Overnight the cold had intensified so greatly that further snow was unlikely, but the remains of the blizzard on the roads had frozen solid, leaving a wildly slippery surface to the narrow uncertain road with a sheer rise of mountain on one side and a precipice on the other. The truck, of course, had no chains. I shut my eyes and buried my face in the Mongolian's dead goat. Faubion with all the curiosity frozen out of him didn't say a word until we were nearly in Tienshui, our next stop.

I was wondering, in a lightheaded and rather detached way, whether I would live through this trip. It was hard to explain why, since my whole body was numb, it should ache so violently. I had never realized that cold could be painful. Faubion said in a strange cracked voice, "Look."

I brought my face out of the goat's flank and saw a row of men in a sort of uniform, straggling along in the snow and ice of the road outside the town walls of Tienshui. They were roped together, wrist to wrist, guarded at both ends of the column by armed Nationalist soldiers. The men were barefoot.

"Those must be the first prisoners of war we have seen," Faubion said. He asked our soldier friend what battle the Communists might have been captured in. The soldier laughed with all his rotten teeth showing, and said, "Those are not Communist prisoners, those are new recruits to the army."

Faubion turned to me and said very bitterly, "It's the usual thing apparently. To recruit new soldiers they send a few men with guns

[129]

into the villages; they pick the men off the streets, rope them together, and march them into a military camp."

"Their shoes—" I said, horrified.

"The shoes are taken away. It makes desertion harder. As soon as possible they are sent away from their home provinces. That makes it harder still."

37 Tienshui turned out to be a fair-sized town. Our soldier and his wife, who were immediately involved in conversation when we arrived, told us that the town was full of troops at that time and that all the inn space had been requisitioned. We went with them to an inn entirely filled by soldiers, where after much argument and gesticulating the innkeeper said he could give us one room (normally his own room) for the four of us. We walked through the very dark and dirty restaurant to the room at the back. It was tiny, dark and extremely cold. It had one narrow plank bed in it and a table. The soldier smiled, waved his hand and vanished. We all sat in a row on the bed too depressed to speak.

"Well," Michael said at last, "it's only for one night. Faubion and I don't mind sleeping on the floor." We stared at the earth floor which showed clearly the places where people had spat and thrown tea dregs, as they do in all Chinese restaurants. The smell of mildew was strong from the sweating walls. Somehow the room managed to combine stuffiness with bitter cold. There was no window.

"We could always," said Clare with an unsuccessful attempt at lightness, "phone the Waldorf." A large rat strolled casually across the floor. Clare suddenly started to cry, "Oh damn it!" she said. "It would have been worth every penny of five hundred dollars!"

Two small children came and stood in the doorway. The soldier had sent them to us with a couple of handfuls of nuts as a present. Their parents were sharing a room with our soldier and his wife and all three children. They stayed and talked to us for a while. The little girl, about six years old, was the older and by far the more intelligent of the two, but when they were showing us how many characters they could write and what big figures they could add, she always deferred to him. Already she knew the place of a girl in the family.

Faubion asked her the price of the little felt shoes she was wearing.

"Fifteen gold yuan," she said.

"Isn't that very expensive?"

"No," she was most emphatic, and recited off the prices in other villages she had been through on the journey south.

"But we bought some like that for only eight."

"Then you must have bought them more than a month ago, because since then money is not worth so much."

"Yes, that's true."

Our soldier came in to tell us that he had been talking to the truck driver and had heard that we wouldn't be leaving Tienshui for two or three days. The roads were impassable.

Michael stood up with sudden decision, "We'll have to do something. We can't stay in this room for three days. Ask the man if there are any foreigners in this town."

"Yes," said the soldier, rather surprised that after a whole hour in Tienshui we shouldn't know all about the town. "There are some Christians."

The Catholic fathers in the Tienshui Mission, when we eventually found it, were most cordial and seemed delighted to see new faces. Most of them were German, a couple of Spaniards and one American, Father Rudolf. They gave us a couple of rooms in their little hospital, which are normally kept free for the Fathers themselves, served us mission-made wine and biscuits in front of the old-fashioned stove in their refectory, and then sent us off to collect our luggage.

At the inn our soldier was waiting for us. Rather shame-facedly we told him that we would stay at the Mission while we were in Tienshui. He seemed to think it a good idea, "You like to be with your own people sometimes," and suggested that we tell the inn-

[131]

keeper that one of us was ill, and that was why we were moving. It would save his face, and in any case he would find out where we were staying.

Meals at the Mission were extraordinary. Fifteen bearded old men sat around the refectory table eating solidly German food—sausages, meatballs, sauerkraut—made by the nuns who helped in the hospital. The cabbages had to be specially grown in their own garden—Chinese cabbage somehow isn't quite right for sauerkraut.

Tienshui, which means Heavenly Water, was at one time a well-known cultural center of China; since then, the increasing poverty of the soil has scattered some of the population. It still has many schools and some beautiful old buildings and temples which the Chinese rather casually use to keep their cattle in. Gazing at one of the temples, Faubion remarked, "The Chinese must be the only people in the world who have evolved a code of ethics—or manners if you want to call it that—without a 'fear of God.' They can lead a good life, when they do, without the need for a religion in the accepted sense." Then feeling that this was not precisely the remark to make to a missionary, he went on by asking whether the Mission would be disbanded since the Communists were so near to Tienshui.

"No, no. This is our home. Some of us have been here for thirty and forty years. Why should we leave now? One of our fathers went back to his village in Europe for the first time in thirty-eight years. He saw his first movie and heard the radio for the first time on the ship going over. Most of us don't even take our home leave."

We were shown around the hospital, a series of cottages built in the Chinese way, but dazzlingly clean, whitewashed and well cared for compared with most Chinese interiors. The haggard men rotting away with syphilis, the children with brilliant cheeks and tuberculosis, the wasted mothers waiting for children to be born who would live no longer than their previous ones. It was easy to understand why movies and radios were unimportant.

38 Three days later the truck left Tienshui. The days were still overcast and rigidly cold. We were all grimly depressed at the thought of facing more of those agonized days of truck travel, particularly since we had learned that only the most ignorant amateur at travel in China could have hoped to reach Chungking from Lanchow in four days. It takes at least ten in the very best weather.

The roads were still frozen and we skidded recklessly along over the treacherous passes south of Tienshui. We got to the top of one long hill which was entirely iced over. At the top of it there were three trucks and several ox carts and horse carts waiting to go on and afraid to try the downgrade. The animals were too precious to lose by broken legs, and the truck drivers didn't feel up to risking their necks.

Our driver decided to be brave and told us all to get off the truck while he took it down the hill. He started off with a crowd of enthralled yellow fish watching him. We all stood well out of the way on top of the hill. The engine roared, a cloud of smoke from the exhaust hung in the frozen air, and a few yards down the truck skidded so violently on a road that was too narrow even for overtaking that it whirled around in its tracks and teetered madly on the edge of the precipice. Horrified gasps from us, and gales of laughter from the yellow fish and the other drivers. Our man got it back under control when the truck was facing up the hill again. We looked down the cliff to see another truck caught halfway down where it had fallen the evening before after rashly attempting the same descent.

Slowly the driver got the truck back up the hill, and then all the drivers got together and had a conference. Faubion, naturally, was listening avidly, but I didn't even bother to try to understand what was going on because I was feeling immensely happy and exhilarated. The sun had come out for the first time since we had left Lanchow. During the previous few days we had all developed

[133]

large, painful chilblains, and a passionate worship of the sun. Every few minutes we had gazed at the sky, looking for a break in the clouds. I hadn't thought it possible that one's life could come to revolve with such fervor around the appearance of the sun.

We were on the wrong side of the hill so the sunlight, pale and without much warmth, reached us only for about an hour, but during that time I couldn't seem to take seriously the fact that we would probably have to spend the rest of the day and all night on that hill without food or bedding. Michael, in his matter-of-fact way, said, "Look, we've only got about three hours of daylight left. I think we should abandon the truck and walk to the next village and get accommodations for the night. We're bound to freeze to death if we stay here."

"What about the luggage?" Clare asked.

"We'll just have to leave it."

Clare checked through the things in her handbag—bobby-pins—lipstick—toothbrush—comb—and finally said, "Okay. Let's go."

Faubion explained our plans to our soldier friend and told him that in case the truck had to go back or cracked up completely, he could have whatever he wanted of our luggage.

The next village was about seven kilometers away, but when we got there we could find no restaurant. There were about twenty huts in the village, and we asked at each one, but they all said that food was too scarce, and that there was no room to sleep. We walked on until after dark to another similar village to receive the same replies.

We were sitting dejectedly at the edge of the road, too tired and cold to talk. Two brilliant beams of light came swinging around the corner, and our friend shouted to us from the top of the truck. They had managed to get it down the hill, the soldier said, by digging into the hillside and getting out cans of earth. They all sprinkled this on the road and finally made a surface that the truck could manage to grip. I had never ridden on top of a truck after dark before, and I found that the cold of the first days of the trip was like a pleasant summer breeze compared to the icy winds of the night.

[134]

Several hours later, when we did get to a small town (of which I never discovered the name), my limbs were entirely dead. I tried to climb off the truck but I couldn't grip with my hands, and slipped and fell rather heavily on my right wrist. In the panic of the moment I was certain I had broken it. People from the village and the yellow fish from the truck stood around laughing as though they had never seen anything so amusing.

Clare, in a fury of worry, yelled, "For Christ's sake get a doctor! Don't just stand there grinning!" They laughed again at her anger, and stood where they were. She turned on Faubion, "Aren't you going to do something? Or do you think it's funny too?"

Faubion said to someone in the crowd, "Is there a doctor in this town?" They smiled and chatted with him while Clare and Michael led me off to the inn. We walked through the usual sort of restaurant with people sitting about playing the finger game and gobbling their food. Little cups of oil, each with a wick in it, flickered on the tables. The room at the back opened onto a small, filthy courtyard with two enormous pigs in one corner, and chickens walking disdainfully around in the refuse. A pervasive stink came from the latrine in the courtyard—both doors had gone from it, and there were just the two little mud-walled cubicles. Across the walls the frozen fields stretched in the starlight. At least tomorrow would be a clear day.

I lay on the k'ang in the back room and listened to the rats, feeling too sick to eat. I could just hear Clare and Michael in the restaurant, just outside the door, whispering. After some time Faubion came back with a man in a blue gown. The doctor was obviously terrified at the idea of dealing with foreigners. He looked at the wrist. It was beginning to swell. Faubion wrote out the characters of "Is it broken?"

The doctor asked me to clench my fist, which I could do, but it was painful. He wouldn't touch it except to paint it with some dark-brown liquid on a dirty bit of cotton.

Michael said, "He's scared that if it gets worse he'll have to take the responsibility. In Shanghai foreign doctors get a written guarantee from a patient before an operation that they won't be

[135]

taken to court by the family if the patient doesn't recover. Under Chinese law they can be sued for manslaughter."

"Isn't there someone that knows about American medicine?" Clare asked.

The doctor caught the word "American," apparently, for he produced a box of pills which he said were American medicine.

"Sulfa?" Clare asked. The doctor nodded agreement.

"Aspirin?" Michael said. The doctor nodded again, smiling.

"Oh, hell," said Clare, "better let it go. It probably isn't broken if you can move it. Does one put hot things on a sprain or cold things?"

None of us knew, so we did nothing. The doctor left a name of a Chinese ointment with us, and said, expecting an argument, that his fee was five gold yuan (about thirteen cents at the time). Clare said, "And cheap at the price—the education, not the treatment." We found out much later that the ointment he had suggested was something like Iodex, and perfectly good for a sprain.

All night, since I couldn't sleep, I lay and listened to the sounds of a Chinese village. I tried to keep still so that I wouldn't disturb the others, but nothing seems to disturb a Chinese when he is sleeping. He may wake at a particularly loud noise, but he sleeps at once right afterward. Equally, he has no hesitation in making a noise himself when others are sleeping. In the early part of the night a few people talked and laughed in loud voices, heavy steps trudged across the courtyard to the latrine. There was the clatter of bowls and chopsticks being put away, or tea cups still clinking against the pot—none of it subdued at all. A child cried, somebody shouted to somebody across the street, then there was the sudden dead silence as the day ended for good.

In the night a rat ran across Clare's leg, and she sat up and screamed. Only Michael woke up and said, "What's the matter?" Somebody else on the k'ang grunted and muttered something. Then there was silence again until the animals started waking up in the courtyard and the sound of donkeys being led down the road began.

39 Hwang-hsi-pu was a crossroad for military transport from Kansu and Shansi. There we had to leave our first truck because it wasn't going any further. We asked in town whether there were any foreigners in Hwang-hsi-pu who could tell us what to do about a sprained wrist. A Chinese boy conducted us to a place where he said foreigners had lived. We found a deserted mission house—the foreigners had evacuated leaving a couple of uninterested Chinese to continue the work of the Lord. We asked why they had left. The boy didn't seem to know, but suggested, "Perhaps because of the fighting?"

"Has there been fighting here?"

"No, not recently, but there is fighting in China. . . ."

We had a last festive dinner with our soldier and his wife. He told us that things were often difficult for soldiers in cities; everybody was against them. He said, frankly, that he could understand it because they were on the whole irresponsible and aggressive— but what could they do when they were paid so little? They often commandeered theater tickets, refused to pay in restaurants, or demanded free transport in public buses. But how else were they to get about? If, for instance, they had a furlough, the army simply let them go without money enough to pay for transport of any kind— even yellow-fishing—how were they to get home?

He told us, too, about the system of conscription which we had heard described as "semivoluntary" whatever that might mean. Except when things were critical and men had to be picked up off the streets as we had seen outside Tienshui, the system had a sort of lunatic logic which fascinated me. One month of the year was chosen as conscription month. If you could prove that you were a college graduate or still a student you were exempted from military service—or if you had enough money to buy such exemption. If not you could be conscripted. Each province in China was divided into shens or counties, which in turn were divided into pau, groups of one hundred families. Suppose each pau chief were asked to produce one soldier from his group. He would go to each family suggesting that they contribute a son, but one family might have only one son on whom several relatives depend for their support, another might have several sons, but might need them all for working in the fields. So each family would contribute two Chinese silver dollars and the *pau* chief would buy a soldier with that money—keeping, of course, a cut for himself. The soldier who finally goes off to the army may be one of those rare Chinese men without family responsibilities or he may simply need the money very badly. The prices for a soldier vary, being highest in Chinghai—about five hundred dollars—because there the army discipline is stricter and very difficult.

Our soldier took us to see the officer in command of the troops in Hswang-hsi-pu, and we were told that there was a truck leaving the following day on which we could ride. It would be going part of the way to Chungking, picking up loads on the way.

This time there were no seats in the cab so we all rode on top, but by then it was beginning to matter less. We were further south, the weather had finally broken, and while the sun still had little heat, at least the cold was easier to stand. We had come into the part of the country where American troops had been stationed during the war. The wayside restaurants were still decorated with the strings of flags representing the Big Four of the Allies. The little paper flags hung in rows: the Chinese sun, the Stars and Stripes, the Union Jack, and then a gap where the hammer and sickle had been. Only frayed paper edges on the string still showed.

Our new yellow-fish companions looked a little more prosperous, and there was even one fat old lady who traveled with a servant. Just before the truck left Hswang-hsi-pu a small boy leaped on and hid himself among the luggage and the bedding. Clearly, he hadn't paid. At every stop the driver looked over the yellow fish to see that there were no such stowaways, but between us we managed to keep the boy hidden for most of the day. Everyone contributed bits of their food to him, and he grabbed them without a sign of gratitude, but clearly all the yellow fish were on his side. Tiny and petrified, he crouched under cover, until the driver stopped unexpectedly

[138]

for some minor repair. Then he was seen, hauled out of the truck, beaten with a piece of rope, and left on the roadside. Nobody had asked him where he was trying to go, or why.

In Paochi we saw oranges on sale for the first time. We were so starved for fresh fruit—or fresh food of any kind—that we bought a basket each, and made ourselves very sick eating about thirty oranges straight off. We had, by then, become used to the sight of the new recruits to the Nationalist army being bullied by armed guards and made to do the kind of work one normally associates with convicts. In Paochi they loaded our truck with steel cabinets which made for the most uncomfortable riding we had had so far.

40 On December 3 we reached Kwang-yuan, an extraordinary town where we stayed three days because we couldn't get another truck at once. Kwang-yuan was built on the bank of a beautiful river, the color of celadon. There was no bridge across the river, so all trucks or other vehicles had to be ferried across on several flat boats lashed together. Since this was the main road south to Chungking the traffic was fairly heavy, and the fact that there was no bridge had made Kwang-yuan a wealthy town instead of a small wayside village. The boatmen, of course, made money from their ferrying, and were in a strong position because people couldn't quarrel about their prices. On the riverbank, refreshment stalls and little food counters made money from the travelers who were waiting to cross. Whenever the river was in flood all traffic was held up, sometimes for weeks, and then the entire town made money; the inns and restaurants would be crowded, the shops and markets filled with people stuck for a week in a place where they had expected to spend a couple of hours. Ricksha coolies, beggars, everyone got their cut. Naturally, the town had refused to let a bridge be built.

A flood was just subsiding when we got there, so our wait was relatively short, and we were lucky enough to find an inn that would take us for that time even though the population of the town had doubled during the previous week with troops and travelers. We had time enough to see something of the town, to visit some Ming tombs and pavilions a couple of miles outside, and to pass a little colony of cave dwellers in a hill behind the town. Clare, of course, was horrified, and insisted on our going into the dank little homes blackened with smoke and smelling frightful. The bundles of rags on the floor turned out to be babies. The bent old mothers blinked painfully as they came to the mouths of the caves. They stood about without comment or question while we peered into their homes, and turned back with indifference when we left.

In town there were dozens of restaurants with excellent food, and we tried a new one every meal. Clare longed for sweets—the one thing that seems to be absent from the Chinese diet—and in one restaurant we asked whether they could produce anything for her. A bowl of water was put on the table, and next to it some strange white cubes covered with thick caramel sauce. The waiter showed us how to pick up one of the cubes, wind the caramel around it, dip it quickly into the water so that the outside of the caramel sets hard while the inside is still soft, and hold it just long enough so that it won't burn your tongue. Clare was delighted and wanted to know the name and how it was made so that we could order it again.

Faubion said it was called *pa-tse*, which meant "pull-string," because as you pull out the white cubes the sauce stretches into long strings of candy. The cubes which we had guessed were sweet potato or perhaps apple, turned out to be, in fact, lumps of pork fat. Clare put down her chopsticks and swallowed a couple of times. She pushed away her bowl, unable to finish the meal.

Eventually, when we did manage to get on a truck to continue our journey, it broke down as soon as we had crossed the river. By then we had all lost the sense of time or urgency with which we had started our journey. We didn't bother to count the days, and even Michael never referred to his firm or the necessity of communicating with his employers. The yellow fish on the truck, in their usual way, had immediately made a little encampment by the side of the road. We decided to walk on to the next village, and two of them offered to help with our luggage. As we marched off up the hill we saw the wisps of smoke from their cooking fires beginning

[140]

to curl upward. The weather was much pleasanter, and the country had lost the drama and the beauty of the northwest. The hills were gentle, the soil fertile and well cultivated, and there were trees.

We reached a village just before nightfall, and an inn where several soldiers were drinking and gambling. We sat in the courtyard of the inn, in the tepid evening, eating our first out-of-doors meal and talking calmly of the distant time before we had started on this journey, when our lives did not revolve around trucks and yellow fish, the sun and a place to sleep at night.

41 The roads, hills, villages, inns, and the days slipped away behind us until, eventually, on the evening of December 12, seventeen days after we left Lanchow, we reached Chungking and a life of newspapers, obligations, decent clothes, foreigners, and the day-to-day trivialities of their way of life. "I suppose," Faubion said dismally, "we will have to take baths." It would be the first time in over two months.

We had expected almost anything of Chungking except that it would have no hotel. The enormous, untidy city sprawled about along the Yangtze. Its famous fogs obscured the surrounding hills and the river, and dimmed the neon lights and advertisements in the wide, unfamiliar city streets. Already the easy life of village restaurants and inns, the comfort of k'angs and chatty country people seemed part of a sadly lost past. We stood in the middle of an unfriendly road and said, "Well, what do we do now?" and, "We can't very well just march into someone's house and ask for accommodation for the night . . ." and, "No, we're in a city now . . ." and, "We can't just stand here the rest of the night."

Michael said, "The British Consul?" and we all began to laugh because that familiar recourse of the tourist seemed fantastic after the previous weeks.

"In any case we couldn't reach him at this time of night."

"We could phone."

"Oh a *telephone*—" Clare said as though she had never heard of the instrument.

We went into the Sing Sing Café—Western food, electricity, beer, and a radio relaying dance music from Hong Kong—and the well-dressed Szechuanese stared at us while we asked the proprietor about phoning one of the consulates. None of them seemed to have private phones. We moved indecisively further down the street and saw a sign: CANADIAN MISSION HOSPITAL. Clare looked thoughtfully at me and said, "Your wrist ought to be x-rayed, you know."

The Canadians were exceedingly nice to us, and also very surprised that we were still in China. Didn't we know that all foreigners who hadn't necessary work in the country had been told by their consulates to leave a month before? "Most of our people have left."

"Well, we haven't been anywhere where we could hear news like that."

"You'd better get in touch with your consulates tomorrow."

Michael and I went to the British Consulate the next day, and were told by the pleasant young man who had been left to run the place alone that we should rush out of China as soon as possible. They could take no responsibility for us as all foreigners were supposed to be out weeks before. Michael said, "But I must go back to my firm in Shanghai. I'm already three weeks late."

"Well you'll just have to be later. We can't possibly allow you to go back to Shanghai, the city's surrounded and, in any case, how do you expect to get there?" He promised to wire the firm and ask them for instructions for Michael.

While we waited in Chungking for an answer to the wire, we made arrangements to continue our journey to Hong Kong. The river boats to Ichang and Hankow were the only way open to us, and all of them were commandeered by the army. Tremendous troop movements were underway, and everywhere one heard the angry gossiping of the Szechwanese who were afraid that the government might move for the second time to Chungking. We gathered that they found that a most unattractive possibility because their innate sense of independence was great, and if they allied themselves

[142]

with any part of China it was the northwest. They had no use for the "foreign" government.

The day that Michael got his reply telling him to go on to Hong Kong and await instructions, we managed to get places on a troop ship going down the river, and Clare developed a temperature of 104 degrees, and chills. The doctor at the hospital called it Chungking fever and gave her atabrin. He asked me whether we had been drinking bad water.

"No, that's the one thing you can't do in the interior. They always give you tea—we even used to brush our teeth in it. So at least I know we only drank boiled water."

We decided to take her on the boat in any case because we didn't know when we could get another, and the journey was only three days downstream. It was with no surprise that we found the journey actually stretched out, with delays, confusions, and changes of boat, to ten days. The soldiers were packed on the boat in every cabin and on all the available deck space. When they saw that Clare was ill, they cleared a tiny cabin for her. It had two wooden bunks and a tin basin on a shelf. While they helped us move in, they said brightly that thousands of troops were being sent "to the last stand of Nanking." They laughed and jostled and said, "Of course Nanking will fall."

Clare and I stayed inside the cabin nearly all the time; she because she was too sick to move, and I because the effort of fighting my way to the rail was just too much. I gave the famous Yangtze gorges scarcely a passing glance. Faubion and Michael had to sleep on deck and got lice.

We never did discover what Clare's ailment had been because by the time we arrived in Hankow, on Christmas day, she was better. We went directly to the British Consulate where suddenly we realized that the journey was over and we were practically out of China already. In the drawing room was a Christmas tree, Murray McLehose, the consul, was opening presents, and colored paper and ribbon were all over the floor. He gave our extraordinary clothes and generally battered appearance a look of only mild surprise, produced Scotch and soda, arranged for us to stay with friends of his, rushed us through baths, changes of clothing and dinner, and swept us off to a Christmas dance given by the foreign community.

The journey by train to Canton was three days of reasonable comfort following the southern coast of China through the lush fields and rich countryside. We stayed in Canton only long enough to find out that the Cantonese, even more than the Szechuanese, dreaded the rumors that the government would move to their city. As hardheaded businessmen they realized that it would be more of a liability than an honor.

On New Year's Day we arrived in Hong Kong where Michael had to leave The Trip.

Indo-China

42 Coming up the Saïgon River—forty miles to the city itself —Clare appeared on the deck in shorts as the final proof that we were at last in the tropics. The river banks were green with palm trees. The Annamese boats, more Western in design than the Chinese junks, skimmed about the water. The people were much darker than the Chinese and vaguely Malayan in feature. The city itself was unimpressive from the river.

Saïgon looks like a complete French provincial town. In the morning the French housewives appear in their cotton dresses and flat-heeled shoes, with a string bag for groceries to do their shopping. At twelve o'clock everything closes except the restaurants where one eats (as opposed to the cafés and bars) and stays closed until 3 P.M. This is true of most of the offices as well. About 4 or 5 P.M. the girls appear again. This time in silk dresses and high heels to sit in the cafés and eventually to dine. With the particular genius of the French for making their streets sociable places where one chats or has a drink, the Saïgon streets are friendly, but the houses which the French keep for their family life have that closed interior look.

There was very little entertainment in the evenings because there had been several cases of hand-grenade explosions in cinemas, and the theater to which touring companies used to come before the war had been bombed. There was a midnight curfew.

Just outside Saïgon is the Chinese city Cholon, whose enormous Chinese population the Annamese hate even more than they hate the French because, as in so many Southeast Asian towns, they have monopolized trade. The French do most of their business with the Chinese. Thousands of Annamese are in debt to the Chinese so all the commercial activity does not profit the country at all. The proceeds are sent back to China. It is a strange sort of creeping imperialism.

At first we met mostly members of the foreign community in Saïgon, the consular and the business groups. It was very like the curious colonial life we used to know in India, seen this time from the other side of the fence. It is a society of foreign clubs, lavish entertainment, foreign food, a standard of living which most of the people could never afford in Europe, servants, and apart from amahs and coolies no contact with the life of the country itself. The foreigners spoke adequate French but not the language of the people even after many years in Indo-China.

One morning wandering about the city I went into a bookshop to ask for something on the history of Indo-China. There were quantities of books there in French and English, novels, biographies, poetry and that sort of thing, but when I asked my carefully framed question, the girl looked very surprised, "We have no such books."

"That is very strange. Have you no stories, no travel books even?"

"I am sorry, madame, nothing at all."

"Why is that? Is no one interested. . . ?"

"But it is a regulation. We cannot sell such books."

This was hard to believe and to make sure I went into the biggest bookshop in Saïgon, but the answer was the same, "It is useless, madame, you will not find such a book in all Saïgon."

A friend had given me a note of introduction to the first Annamese I met socially, Madame Francine. She lived in a shabby section of Saïgon in a small house with two bedrooms and one living-dining-everything-else room which she shared with her mother and various other relations. Her husband was a Resistance leader in the Viet Minh area. She was not quite certain where he was. A small, thin woman with the kind of soft, mobile face that photographs badly, she looked very lovely in real life. Her voice was surprisingly authoritative and she spoke perfect French and a little English, so we conversed in a combination of the two. As soon as she heard I was Indian she was cordial. "Ah we are so interested in India and all your news!"

"As we, in yours. . . ."

"Yes, the story is the same. The fight here is another chapter in the same struggle. Now that your time of trouble is over, I hope you will not forget us."

Rather embarrassed, I said, "Of course not," knowing that already we are beginning to forget. "Tell me what is happening in Saïgon."

She answered, "What is there to tell you about Saïgon? The history of a few foreigners? The news is in the free area and we so seldom hear."

"Your husband is there?"

"Yes, and my children." She watched my face, "It is important for them that they be brought up in a free atmosphere."

I told her that my mother was particularly interested in the Women's Movement and had made me promise to find out something about what women worked at in Saïgon.

"But that is very hard. How can we work here? The Women's Movement is in Viet Minh area. We are so carefully watched that we must confine our activities. We know from experience that reprisals for activity can be very terrible."

"Would you tell me something about yourself? Your name, for instance, is French. Are you partly French?"

She looked at me amused as though I had committed a social error. "No, naturally that is not my real name. I have no French blood. I went to scool here in Saïgon. At school all the Annamese girls are compelled to take French names. My own was Francine. Since the time when my husband has been in the free area I have reverted to this name because it is not safe to carry his name in Saïgon. But," she continued, covering up my ineptness, "it is not surprising that you think I am partly French. I had to go to France to complete my studies, my husband and I are both lawyers. We were practicing together here before the war."

"Do you continue your practice now?"

"How is it possible now to practice law? One must have the possibility of justice, don't you think?" She shrugged her shoulders.

"Did you like France while you were studying there?"

"Certainly. Paris was wonderful and beautiful and the French in France are the most tolerant people in the world. The difficulties come when we return. What do we know of our own country? Can we read our own literature? I can tell you the number of kisses

[149]

Napoleon gave Josephine, but what do I know of my own history?"

"And you and your husband joined the Resistance Movement during the war?"

"Yes, like so many of us. It was not, you see, merely that the French had been defeated by the Japanese. We had seen them collaborate and work with them here. Then after *that* when the old tyranny came back, it was too much."

"One is told here that this is a Communist movement—or anyway Communist-inspired. Your leader for instance—"

She broke in passionately, "How tired I am of that word! Certainly Ho Chih Minh is a Communist. I am a Catholic and so is my husband. *Could* we find common cause with the Communists except on the fundamental issues such as our liberties? Of course there are Communists in the movement—that is no secret—but if you see us fighting side by side with them, is it not because the movement is primarily *Nationalist* and therefore concerns *all* the people of Indo-China whatever their individual coloring? The French will tell you we are all Communists. Stupid people on the Viet Minh side will tell you that none of us are. I will not insult your intelligence by telling you that both are wrong. All parties are represented but believe me this is a Nationalist not a Communist movement." She paused for a moment and the bitterness had left her voice when she continued. "Come upstairs. I want you to see some photographs."

The pictures she showed me were among the most remarkable I had ever seen. Her original point was quickly made. There were pictures of Catholic priests ("This one was the priest of our parish here in this city, a scholar as well as a good man. He is now in jail") being unfrocked in the Viet Nam area by French soldiers. Pictures of priests taken before their robes had been taken from them. Then there were pictures of the constructive work done in the Viet Minh territory. She showed me adult literacy classes usually taught by wounded soldiers unfit for active combat, new methods of agriculture. Children in class learning their own language and history for the first time, who would not have to study such things after their formal schooling was over as Madame Francine had done.

[150]

There was one photograph of children with guns, and I asked if it was a youth corps and whether they trained with guns so early.

"No, no. Those are children rehearsing for a play. Children do much propaganda for us in their theatricals, their dances and by singing the Viet Minh songs. Here in Saïgon it is a criminal offense and if you will come with me one day I will show you the children in the jails here—ten and twelve years old—who have been arrested for singing one of our songs in the street. The children help in other ways, too," she added. "They carry messages across the lines to keep families in touch with their members."

She showed me atrocity pictures. "These stories you will not find in the newspapers," she said. "These are the villages burned by the French, those are the bodies of those who died under torture. Here is a girl who was raped and killed, and if you need further proof, here is a picture of a French soldier—you recognize the uniform?— with a Viet girl he has just stripped. Afterward she was raped—one of many in that village. The man who took this picture was shot. I do not show you these things to shock and horrify you. Atrocities there are in every war but we must realize that they happen on both sides. Perhaps one is not responsible for one's actions in war—one is only responsible for the purpose—the morality if you wish. In this case and in this fight the morality is with us."

43 Clare spent most of her time in Saïgon wandering ecstatically through the shops and trying on French clothes.

Faubion, to the horror of the various consulates, announced that he wanted to go to the Annamese theater. People shifted uncomfortably in their chairs and said grenades had been thrown, they could take no responsibility, it was bound to be dull and the theater would be dirty, it was in Cholon where one could not get a taxi to bring one back at night, and so on.

"Where, after all, was one safe these days?" said Faubion.

The theater turned out to be most elegant; proper seats, microphones, good lighting made it both more comfortable and cleaner than those in China. The play, which was a combination of low comedy and then a sort of court drama, was strongly influenced by the Chinese in technique, stage design and plot. The costumes and the language were Annamese and the music modified to suit the softer Southeast Asian taste.

An Annamese girl who came with us to interpret told us that she was never allowed out in the evening unchaperoned, never went out alone with a man and that all Annamese girls of better families were brought up very strictly. The foreigners were considered fast. The final disgrace was to marry a Frenchman or be seen out with him. The French, on the other hand, were extremely tolerant in their social relations, more so than most colonizers. For them there seemed to be no stigma attached to marrying an Annamese.

This question of colonialism kept coming up in the conversation and gradually we began to understand the curious combination of characteristics that made the French the worst colonizers in the world and at the same time the most appealing and the most liberal. So deep is their delight in their own culture and so firmly convinced are they that it is the greatest and has the most to offer to other people that many of them seemed genuinely to consider a demand for independence from the people of Indo-China as ridiculous. They felt that the subject peoples were amply rewarded by their access to French culture, by the fact that when they go to France they have the full privileges of the French citizens and French passports and on the whole a fairly easy interchange on a social level.

We were introduced to one extremely sensible businessman, M. Ricard, who put the matter to us, on the whole, very fairly. He had no illusions about the French Government in Indo-China. Certainly they had treated the natives badly. No, the rebels were not all Communists—about fifty-fifty he would say. On the other hand, the Cambodians and the people of Laos dislike the Annamese and Tonkinese. They have reason, from their history, to fear imperialism, and consequently fear also the imperialism that spreads from the east coast into the inland provinces. They wanted to keep their kings and their rather lackadaisical provincial governors under modified French control.

[152]

"When you go to Cambodia you will see why. It is an astonishingly rich country. The people there have everything they can ask for right at hand: a tropical climate, sufficient water for agriculture, fruit at all times of the year, kapok and cotton for their clothes, and rivers so full of fish that I have seen the natives merely put baskets into the river to bring them up full. It has, however, a history of subjugation and of forced labor. Now that that period is over, they do not breed ambition. In them you have a contented but not very energetic race. If a Cambodian has enough to feed his family for the day or the week nothing will persuade him to work until that is expended. They are not very clever. I remember going up to Cambodia on business which involved an interview with their minister of finance. Well," M. Ricard said, turning down the corners of his mouth and making a slight face, "as a businessman I assure you I would not hire him as an office boy in my company—and that is the minister of finance!"

I wondered whether such a minister was chosen by the French or rose from ability. However, he continued, "Such people, you can see, are very susceptible to conquest and oppression, particularly from the Tonkinese who come from a state with the densest population in the world—denser in parts than Belgium—who need to expand, and have the Viet Minh forces with them. Naturally our propaganda will emphasize this fact. Can one wonder that the Cambodians do not feel a part of the 'Nationalist Movement'?"

Since the beginning of the fighting in Indo-China, travel had been nearly impossible. Business in Saïgon, M. Ricard told us, was almost at a standstill. Rubber, kapok and rice, the main exports of Indo-China before the war, could no longer be transported to the coast from the interior. The dollar and sterling situation was so hard for the French that import and export from Saïgon had fallen off fantastically. "We close our offices at one o'clock every day and never go back to work in the afternoons."

"Then why is the city so surprisingly crowded?"

"Ah that, too, is the same cause. There are the French refugees coming in from the plantations, the inland towns and even the suburbs. In the old days this town used to be a very pleasant place to live in—for a Frenchman to live in—now it is no more than a large internment camp. We cannot even go to the beach for a week end."

We decided to leave Saïgon within a week of our arrival because it was simply too hard to meet the people of the country with conditions in the city as difficult and unsettled as they were. All foreigners were suspected, and in any case none of us were much amused by the nationality-less atmosphere of port towns. We decided to take M. Ricard's advice and go to Cambodia. There, perhaps, we could get into the villages, and besides there would be the enormous compensations of seeing the Angkor ruins.

44 Pnom-Penh, where we spent a few days, is the capital of Cambodia. It is a small friendly town in which one passes the same people on the streets several times a day. There the king's fantastic palace glitters in the strong sunlight, mirrored and painted inside and out. The enormous royal barge floats at the jetty opposite the palace at the point where the Mekong and its tributary meet. From it the king watches the extraordinary semiannual phenomenon of the Mekong, when the water stops flowing south and starts flowing north. Afterward he leads the celebration in the Festival of the Waters and watches the sports competitions, the parades and the pageants on the other barges.

M. Ricard had given us a letter of introduction to Guy Porée, the cultural advisor to the king. His wife, Eveline Maspero, an ethnologist of considerable distinction, and M. Porée himself were among the most charming and informative people we met in Indo-China. Talking to Mme. Porée turned out to be a series of delightful surprises and her knowledge of Cambodia and Cambodians, enthralling.

One night, over dinner, Faubion said with only slight curiosity, "The women here blacken their teeth. Is that a mark of beauty or what?"

Mme. Porée, with sudden animation in her face, turned to him. "Oh I have just been working on that. There are a number of legends I have found about it. This one pleases me most: The first king of Cambodia married the daughter of a demon. He was a very powerful demon, and to make the kingdom of Cambodia for his daughter, he ordered his servants—the waters—to withdraw from this land and leave the country for his daughter. The young king did not know that his bride was a snake. [The snake turns up often in Cambodian mythology and, like the fox in Japan, means magic and the ability to transform itself into the shape of a beautiful girl.] She bore the king a very beautiful daughter. But while her magic was great enough to keep the king from discovering that she was a snake, she couldn't conceal it in her daughter, so she blackened the child's teeth and then the king was not able to see the fangs of the snake and was kept in ignorance." She paused for a moment still filled with her enthusiasm. "There is another version which is almost as nice. In that legend the king discovered that his wife was a snake because every seven years she had to return to her father. The king, who was devoted to his young daughter, was very worried by his wife's first disappearance and was afraid that someday she might take the child with her. Finally he thought of a scheme to keep the mother from recognizing the child so that when she returned she would not be able to maintain her influence over her daughter. He blackened her teeth, and his scheme was successful. Since then, at all important times—such as marriages, when the girl is most desirable to the demons—and even all the time, a girl's teeth are blackened, for in that way the snakes cannot recognize her and take her away to their kingdom."

Clare, who felt this was all a little frivolous, asked Mme. Porée about marriage and divorce laws.

"Divorce?" said Mme. Porée smiling. "Here it is too simple. In fact I can never keep the stories of my servants straight. Let me see, the old woman who has been with us for many years has been married three times, the younger amah is in her second marriage now. And in choosing their husbands there is a great deal of freedom—it is not a matter necessarily arranged by the family."

"Is there any stigma attached to a divorced woman?"

"No, no, it is the most casually accepted thing."

"Who gets the children? Is there any system of compensation for the wife?"

"The mother usually keeps the children, and if she doesn't get married again, works to support them—the husband has no responsibility in that direction. There is no great fuss made about such things, you understand," she said, twinkling a little at Clare.

Faubion had any number of questions to ask M. Porée about the dancing and theatrical activity of Cambodia. His notes on the Chinese theater were to be extended into a survey of theatrical matters all through the Orient. We learned that the old and lovely classical dancing of Cambodia was rapidly dying out. The troupe of palace dancers continued only because of the great interest of the old Queen Mother, but even they—the only troupe of dancers left—performed very seldom.

M. Porée had organized a modern theater group which was sponsored by the palace. He had collected some boys from the villages to train them as actors, and they in turn told friends, and the news got about until quite a number applied to join the new group. They lived in a converted garage in the Porées' compound, and had built a small temporary stage in the back garden. Before the fighting in Indo-China began they functioned as a repertory company and toured the villages with their plays to raise money for a dramatic school in Pnom-penh. During their recent enforced inactivity they only rehearsed, wrote new plays and built up their stock of costumes.

The Cambodians have a very easy, outgoing sense of theater. The boys put on a show for us in the garden, and they seemed happiest in their comedy parts. They had made a strange and most amusing adaptation of The Merchant of Venice. Because the play concerns a moneylender, and indebtedness is a great problem of the Cambodian villagers, they had set the play in Kashgar—the most distant place they could think of. Of course no Cambodian moneylender could be so wicked. They performed some village dances and a short farce for us as well.

[156]

45 With our arrival in Siemreap, the village near the Angkor ruins where tourists stay, we moved into a curious world of several layers ranged one on top of the other like a Neapolitan ice. The life of the Cambodian villagers overlapped scarcely at all with the life of the French soldiers stationed in Siemreap. Their circle and activities hardly ever crossed that of the Cambodian and French government officials. The archeologists and students were a tight group by themselves. The tourists, living all together in the one hotel, came for a few days, saw Angkor Vat, ate in the hotel dining room, drank on the terrace, read guidebooks, and left on the next plane. They were simply the whipped cream on top of the ice.

We stayed in Cambodia about a month and consequently fitted into no particular layer, and saw a certain amount of each. The first couple of days we spent in exploring the tiny town itself. Siemreap, built on the banks of a narrow but important river, is for the most part a cluster of Cambodian houses built of woven palm leaves, bamboo and thatch, and placed on stilts to provide room for the animals underneath. The section of the town around the tourist hotel is more Western in style. There are a couple of restaurants, a few shops, an open market place and the barracks and offices of the soldiers. To Faubion's delight he discovered that there was also a tiny Cambodian theater.

Eagerly, we began our first tour of Angkor Vat, a few miles outside of Siemreap, the best known of what is probably the most important group of buildings in the world. I had expected it to be impressive, of course, but was not prepared for the tremendous emotional impact of Angkor Vat. Uncompromisingly beautiful, gray, much bigger than I had imagined, and terribly dead, it made even Faubion chatter nervously about styles and centuries and history— as if it mattered. When we were a little more accustomed to it, and had returned to it several times, we were in more of a position to notice detail. All around the outer walls of the main building are carved in bas-relief stories from the *Ramayana* and the *Mahab-*

harata, the old Hindu epics, with a fantastic display of precision and design.

"Now," Faubion said, "I hope you'll realize that it isn't only the West that's imperialistic. Do you know that the whole of this area, as well as most of Southeast Asia was colonized by Indians? They conquered the Khmers, a magnificent-looking people. If one can believe these sculptures," he said, pointing to one of the huge bas-reliefs which showed most graphically how the subject peoples were empressed into slave labor, "here is the proof."

At the time I could think of nothing to say, and kept a rather irritated silence. Conversation with Faubion is like a perpetual birthday party. Some of the presents are very nice and exactly what you wanted, some you can keep to give away to someone else later, and some are simply horrid. Later on, after some analysis, I thought that there are really three kinds of imperialism. The first began with a cultural expansion and ended by the southern Indians actually taking over the governments of the countries which they entered. But the important point about that kind was that, having conquered, the invaders then relinquished all temporal allegiance to the country of their origin. The second kind—still continuing—is best illustrated by the Chinese in Asia. Large communities of them are settled in every major city of the Orient where they proceed to take over the commerce and business of the towns, and eventually of the entire country. Never do they attempt to take the responsibility for the government, and always their allegiance (and much of their profits) goes to their homeland.

The third, and I think the most dangerous of the types of imperialism, is the Western sort that combines the characteristics of the other two. Not only have the French, Dutch, and British in Asia taken over the governments of their colonies, but they have also exploited them economically. Both these aspects become dangerous when the colonizers retain their allegiance to their home countries, for then the colonies are drained economically as well as weakened in their social structure.

A Cambodian friend, who had worked on the reconstruction of some of the temples with French archeologists, introduced us to the Conservateur des Ruines d'Angkor, M. Henri Marchal. He is a

[158]

small, bearded, entirely delightful old man, with the look of a highly intelligent goat, and is affectionately called by the local population *la plus belle ruine des ruines*. He is also the kind of expert I worship, for whom no question is too stupid, no comment too banal, and no statement—however ignorant—not worth listening to. "You never know," he once told us, "if the passer-by in the street may not give you the clue to complete a theory."

M. Marchal had a great feeling for the drama and the magic of Angkor. One night over dinner he lectured us gently about it and about the interest and the work of his life. Gesturing with his forefinger near his face like an old-fashioned schoolteacher, he said in his diffident voice, "The Angkorean period which extended from about eight hundred to thirteen hundred was at once the height and the finish of the Khmer people. During this period, with an unimaginable concentration of energy they accomplished the greatest architectural feats in the history of the world. In *thirty* years," he leaned across the table shaking with excitement, "the magnificence of Angkor Vat was completed—that is one-third of the time it took us to construct one of our Gothic cathedrals. Thousands of artisans, artists and laborers gave their lives in frantic carving and chiseling. It was a great outburst of Brahmanic, and later of Buddhistic fervor that made the kings of Cambodia deify themselves in these buildings. The people thought of their kings as gods, and their gods as kings. And now," he leaned back smiling sadly, "now our most eminent archeologists cannot tell you whether these buildings are temples or tombs. It is a comment—a well-worn one—on the passing of glory, is it not? And what is left? A people drained of their energy and their wealth, men who are entirely content with a handful of rice and a thatched roof over their heads. . . ."

With Henri Marchal we went to several more of the six hundred constructions which form the Angkor group of ruins, to Ta Prom, a sort of nunnery, smothered by the dark-green jungle, to the weird, magnificient Bayon with its fifty towers each composed of four, huge, half-smiling faces set back to back, so that everywhere you walk in the terraces and grounds surrounding it hundreds of tired, wise smiles, and hundreds of enormous eyes follow you.

"In the old days," said the scholarly voice of M. Marchal, "each tower and shrine was a storehouse of gold and jewels . . . it has all been looted, of course."

To all the ruins in the Cambodian forests, with the exception of Angkor Vat itself, we had to be escorted by a truckload of French soldiers. The authorities were afraid of ambushes. One day, at one of the temples still half-submerged in jungle, Faubion and I got lost in the trackless and confusing twilight of trees and bushes. For an hour we wandered about, and were at last found by a worried soldier carrying his gun ready in his hands. As soon as he saw us he slapped Faubion on the back and said, "Vous vous amusez?" and chatted to us all the way back to the truck about the army and the life in Cambodia.

"How lucky you are," Faubion said, "to be able to spend so much time near the ruins."

"Well," the soldier said, "you get used to them and after a while you don't mind them."

"But these patrols," Faubion insisted, "must give you a wonderful chance to see all the buildings in the Angkor area."

"The patrols wouldn't be so bad," the soldier explained carefully, "if we weren't so badly equipped. Some of us aren't even armed, and most of us have only about twelve rounds of ammunition. And after that, c'est tout; c'est fini." This phrase which we heard so often in Cambodia became for us afterward the standard description of any hopeless situation. "Even our medical supplies are so short that there is no good fortune in being merely wounded rather than killed."

We invited him to the hotel for a drink with us that evening, and when he got up to return to his barracks for dinner, he suggested that we meet him and his friends at the local bistro for a cognac afterward.

46 The little bistro which the soldiers frequented was the dividing line between the Cambodian houses and the Western part of town. It was one narrow, bare room, with a bar at the end, and a few tables. Travel posters decorated the walls with French cathedrals and castles on the Loire. It is hard to describe the atmosphere of the place: it had a loneliness and yet a feeling of rather desperate camaraderie. It was small and dirty, of course, but the liquor was good and cheap. The soldiers came there for a change of scene—certainly, unless there were tourists or foreigners like us there, they couldn't expect a change of company. They sat around and drank and played the wind-up gramophone, old records, and preferred the sentimental or the Spanish ones. They asked any girls at all to dance—girls were too rare to miss an opportunity like that. If the place was not crowded you danced between the tables, if it was you danced on the pavement of the street outside.

And of course every soldier had his story. After a few drinks they would tell you about the wife who had gone off with another man, the Cambodian mistress, the possibilities of return to France, the boredom and isolation of Siemreap, guarding, patrols, the muddle of jungle warfare. Always there was the refrain of homesickness. "Mine is a small village in the south. But there I am king. I am the only one who has traveled. . . . There I could give you wine compared with which this is vinegar. . . ." Eventually, late in the evening, they always started singing songs. "*Mon village au clair de lune*", "*J'ai deux amours, mon pays et Paris*," or their favorite song which they told us was forbidden in the army, *Les Africains*, "Although you are only seventeen and have no woman except your mother to say good-by to you, still, all you can expect is a bullet in your head or a bayonet in your side. . . ." It was the song of the lost battalion in North Africa.

That evening our soldier was already there with his friends when we arrived. He was in a very jovial mood at the idea of being able to introduce new people to the other *sous-officiers*. He ordered

[161]

drinks, yelled to the patron to play the gramophone, and when we asked if the Cambodian *sous-officiers* ever came there, he said "Of course not—how would we discipline them?"

He then sat back in his chair and said, "It's not bad, is it? When you are drunk enough you can almost imagine it is a little bit of France."

"I suppose," I said, "you are longing to get back home."

"Of course, but who can earn a living there these days? Many of the men talk of emigrating—Canada, Australia perhaps?—our days are past."

"Past in Indo-China, too?"

"But without question! This business here is merely a matter of waiting. What can we expect? Greater losses, and in the end, withdrawal. Then *c'est tout, c'est fini*."

Clare said, "Ask them, what they are all doing up here. In Saïgon they told us that Cambodia was quiet."

"In Saïgon?" said Justin (our soldier) scornfully. "What do they know, the businessmen? Already the countryside belongs to the Izaracks—we hold only a few towns. I am a man of the land. I know that if you have not the land, you have nothing." (Izarack is a Cambodian word literally meaning Free Men, used by the French to mean 'rebels')

People in Saïgon had told us that the reason for continuing the war in Indo-China was to stop communism. China was lost, so that left the Viet Minh as the best-organized pro-Communist front, and the most continually erupting little volcano.

To this Justin said, "But who are we, mademoiselle, to talk of fighting communism? Our own country is half-Communist. Let us begin there if we are serious in this aim."

Justin suddenly smiled, "An end to this gloomy talk. Some more drinks! I know what—I'll order you crêpes suzettes such as you will never taste outside of France!"

The patron, also a soldier, was a charming southerner. He was already half-drunk, and came to join the table. He was married to a very pretty Cambodian girl whom he had bought from her father for five hundred piasters—a high price because she was seventeen

[162]

and a virgin. He ordered her around in a friendly way and she didn't seem to mind at all. She laughed and served drinks as though it were a game. She and Clare and I danced with all of them until late at night.

The soldiers said they would take us back to the hotel in their army truck. The patron wanted to come with us, but the Cambodian girl, far from being the subservient little wife one expected of a village girl, shouted, "If you don't come back tonight I will not be here in the morning! I assure you!" She flounced back into the bistro. The patron turned quietly around and followed her.

All the way back through the silent little town the soldiers sang the songs of their country.

47 Within a very short time of our arrival in Siemreap, Faubion insisted that we go the theater. We took with us an Annamese from the hotel to translate. He was a curious, rather sulky person, who told us that he was not very popular in the town partly because he was Annamese, and next to the Chinese they are the most disliked, and partly because he worked for the French. "I know," he said, "that people dislike me for working for the French, but I work for money and that is all I am concerned with just now. I hate the French, too. I know that I am considered a valuable link in their dealings with Cambodians because I have no loyalty to the Cambodian side—but then I have no loyalty to the French either. I earn good money and soon I shall be independent."

The theater, where traditional Cambodian plays and sometimes vaudeville were performed, was a small barn with a platform at one end. The audience sat on the floor or on benches, or in our case, as foreigners, on little folding chairs. The children crowded round the edge of the platform and stared with their eyes just over the level of the footlights.

Our second introduction to Cambodian entertainment came at the time of the Annamese and Chinese New Year. That evening classical dancers were to perform their ancient art on the stone terrace before Angkor Vat. The setting was most dramatic as the whole stone avenue to the central building and the terrace were lit with torches of dry rice stalks. Everywhere there was incense burning.

The dancers were four local girls, not especially good except for the lead dancer who seemed more familiar with the dances and still had the remnants of tradition and grace about her. The orchestra, on the other hand, was wonderful, and played the way one feels an orchestra should play, with enormous enjoyment in the music, clearly having fun. We sat with the orchestra because Faubion, who before he had been drafted into the American army had been a concert pianist, wanted to see the musicians close to. One of the boys spoke to us in very hesitating French and told us that the first of the dances was a ceremonial dance of welcome and good fortune. He told us to watch only the lead dancer. Although she was now over fifty and had five children she had been very accomplished as a girl. Now that she was old she had lost her spring and grace, but we should look at her hands because they were still beautiful.

Casually, she threw her elbows out of joint as she danced, giving a strange, rather lovely angle to her arms. Her hands were very like the sculptures on the walls of the Angkor ruins, those extraordinary, flexible, curling hands which you think must be impossible in real life.

The second dance was part of a *Ramayana* story which ended in a very beautiful *pas de deux*, a love dance between Rama and Sita. The last concerned one of the first kings of Cambodia beset by hostile tribes. He has no army left and is wandering in the forest alone. At last he grows hungry and puts a handful of rice to his mouth, but he is too unhappy to eat so he throws the rice to the ground. In the places where the grains scatter, armies rise up to support him.

After the dances Faubion asked the leader of the orchestra whether it would be possible to have the dancers and the musicians perform for us again the next night. The lead dancer, Mme. Ott, was consulted. There was much talk and questioning. It was very sur-

[164]

prising. No one had ever asked for it before. Yes, they could arrange it. The price was fixed at the equivalent of six American dollars for a two-hour performance.

The soldiers who had come to Angkor Vat, partly to see the dances, and partly as protection "in case the Izaracks became energetic," joined us after the performance and took us back to the bistro.

48 The next morning we were invited for a drink by the local French Conseiller, M. Challier, to the government and were expecting the usual colonial product. He received us in his cool, pleasant house, and turned out to be a great deal better than that. Realistic in his views about this province and charming and amusing to talk to, he had that quality that makes French officials—at least those that I had met—so much pleasanter than their counterpart elsewhere, the quality of being a minor authority on local history, actual and mythological. A Britisher in his position, for instance, would be apt to fill in his spare time with club life and sports rather than by taking an interest in the country he is working in.

M. Challier first explained to us the difficulties in the government of the province now and before the war. In the old days Cambodia was a flourishing protectorate, but after the Japanese had taken Indo-China, naturally the French could not return to the old form of government as the Japanese had made even the easygoing Cambodians conscious of their Nationalist Movement. So after the British occupied Indo-China and returned it to the French, Cambodia received a high degree of provincial autonomy, a government modeled on the French plan but with the king still in place as a constitutional monarch without political power. M. Challier himself had only an advisory capacity.

I asked whether there was any sentimental attachment among the people to their king that might destroy the authority of the elected representatives.

"There is still an attachment, yes. Many people even now will write a letter directly to the king explaining a grievance or asking for justice, but on the whole they will accept the government of the elected ministers."

"How is the government chosen now?" Clare asked.

"By adult suffrage for everyone except the women, priests and soldiers."

"Do you find that the Cambodians are able to govern themselves?" Clare's voice took on a studied casualness.

M. Challier smiled, "What nation is able to govern itself, mademoiselle? There are good governors and bad, honest ministers and dishonest—this you will find anywhere in the world." His Cambodian servant brought in drinks and handed them round. "For myself I find I am much more at ease here now. I was in Siemreap fifteen years ago and in those days one had the responsibility of the police, courts, the government—everything. I learned the language and became very fond of this country, but now, for the first time, I can have friends here—that is why I asked to come back to Siemreap after the war."

Clare leaned across and said, "Is there a Nationalist Movement here? In Saïgon they said that the Cambodians are a pleasant, friendly people who do not wish to shake off the French rule. Yet here we find we must go everywhere with a military escort, that trucks and soldiers must convoy tourists from place to place."

M. Challier said calmly, "Certainly there is a Nationalist Movement here. It is small, perhaps inspired by the Annamese. As far as I know there are no Communists involved in it. This small group wants complete provincial independence—from the Viets as well as the French."

"You do not sound as if you take it very seriously."

"The situation is not grave. You see, here you do not have intellectuals leading the Nationalist Movement as you have in the Viet Minh. Cambodia has produced few intellectuals."

Faubion asked whether Cambodians, seeing their extraordinary legacy of Angkor Vat, Angkor Thom, and the many hundreds of buildings and temples scattered about in the area, had any feeling

[166]

of their past glory and sense of their own history, and consequently a resentment against the conquerors.

"They see the buildings," M. Challier said, "but they do not connect them with their history. If you ask one of the natives here who built these incredible ruins they will tell you, 'They were built by the Gods.' They feel no personal glory in them. Then you must remember that the building of these things has quite exhausted this country. No state can stand such an expense of life, in the many thousands of slave laborers who died in transporting the stone; of art, in the concentrated production of these buildings, sculptures, paintings; and of wealth, in the cost of the food, the support of thousands of people who were unproductive while they were empressed into this construction, and the cost of thousands of jewels, the gold and the ornaments which decorated the images and were kept in the temples." He thought for a moment. "We who come as transients here can say it was worth it. To the Cambodians, whether they have a sense of history or not, Angkor represents their greatest tragedy. They have been conquered many times because they are not a fighting people but never were they drained by a ruler as they were by Jayavarman VII."

Jayavarman VII, the last of the great "constructor-kings," and an extraordinary ruler, was responsible for a large part of the building in the Angkor area. A megalomaniac and, according to legend, a leper, he built, besides temples and palaces, over a hundred hospitals in his efforts for temporal relief from leprosy as well as hope for an eternal reward in his afterlife. Over each hospital was the inscription, "The ills of the people are the ills of their ruler. As the people suffer, so does their king. . . ." However, his mania for building ended his kingdom and ruined his people, the Khmers.

49 That evening, after the dances which were performed for us at the little theater, we took Mme. Ott to the bistro for a drink. Our Annamese friend came along to interpret because Mme. Ott spoke no French. We found, on questioning her, that the dancers

got about fifty cents of the six dollars we gave them, and the rest went to the Chinese owner of the theater. She told us that she had studied dancing since she was a child. Her parents hadn't liked it at all, but she had insisted and had given it up only when she got married. Now that her husband was dead and her children had left her she would have liked to return to dancing professionally, but she was too old, and in any case people no longer wanted to see the old dances. They preferred the new, rather jazzy ones that came in from Siam.

Mme. Ott was a short, sensible-looking woman, with a square, strong face, her teeth black and rotted with betelnut, and her hair cropped short like most Cambodian women. She came to offer a return invitation one afternoon a few days later, when we were sitting on the hotel terrace gazing rather dreamily at where the central tower of Angkor Vat was visible above the jungle.

She came into the hotel by the backway looking very elegant in a new purple-silk sarong and invited us and our Annamese friend out to her house. We went wheeling away in cyclos past the town and a couple of miles into the country and there in a small coconut grove were a few huts. Mme. Ott ceremoniously escorted us to hers. Like all the native huts it was built on stilts and had bamboo struts with palm-matting walls which were removable from any side to allow the breeze to come through. The floor was slatted bamboo with a sheet of palm matting spread over it when people wanted to sit down or sleep.

We took off our shoes, climbed the short ladder and sat down on the mat around a low wooden crate which was used as a table. On the table were bananas, small, sour, wild mangoes and two glasses. The hut was very clean and Mme. Ott's belongings—a comb, mirror, pencil and that sort of thing—were stuck neatly into the palm-matting walls to leave all the floor space clear. A flimsy screen divided the hut into two small rooms.

As soon as we arrived the entire village gathered outside. More glasses were supplied from neighboring huts, green coconuts were cut and we were each handed one to drink the milk. Mme. Ott carefully gave us some salt to put in the milk because otherwise, she said, it was bad for the digestion.

Once we were all settled and eating, various members of the village came in to stare and to ask questions. Mme. Ott explained in the curious rattling Cambodian language who we all were and where we came from. One of them asked, "Is it not strange that an Indian should be traveling with Americans?" We explained how we had met in Tokyo.

Then Mme. Ott turned to Faubion and said, "You are very old not to be married."

Clare and I listened, delighted that for once he had to make the explanation. He said he traveled around the world too much to marry.

The Annamese said that he had translated that as, "He goes from Siemreap to Bangkok and to America all the time. He would need a wife in each place."

Mme. Ott said, "Naturally, I understand that would be very expensive." She added that she would like to go to America but was afraid of airplanes.

We discovered that it was a fairly poor community. They were rice cultivators and had, besides, their own banana and coconut palms. They ate twice a day, at seven-thirty or so in the morning before work and at six in the evening, with perhaps some coconut milk in between sometime. Their normal meals were two bowls of rice and the dry fermented fish that one saw spread on every roof. This was supplemented sometimes with vegetables grown in the open space around the huts. They had four rice harvests in that special area and felt very lucky because of it. Apparently the water supply and the climate around Seimreap are just right for such intensive rice cultivation.

The women worked in the fields and did the extra chores of washing clothes, marketing and so on. Mme. Ott asked whether this was the same in America.

Faubion said, "God no! In America men do all the work and women do nothing."

She said, "Yes, I can believe that. Here women are afraid of the men but with the Americans it seems that the men are afraid of their women." The young women apparently worked quite as hard as their menfolk, so hard, in fact, that the classical dances were

[169]

dying out. Nobody could afford to send their children to be trained from the early age that Cambodian dancing requires, and even if they had that early training, as young women, they would not have time to keep in practice. However, Mme. Ott told us that the old people in the village still loved the old dances and sometimes she danced in her ordinary clothes for her friends.

As we left we said thank you and good-by to the entire village. They all escorted us to the main road and then Mme. Ott and a friend of hers insisted on seeing us back to the hotel.

50 M. Challier had given us a note of introduction to the Cambodian governor of the Siemreap districts. He provided us with a different point of view on conditions in Cambodia, some more information, and a new and delightful friend. The governor was a very gentle, rather retiring man, with several brilliant gold teeth and a graceful, stooping walk. His house was decorated with copies of the bas-reliefs from the temples, tooled in leather by local workmen—the same workmen that make the huge leather puppets for the shadow plays which are Cambodia's most popular form of entertainment. Several statues and isolated decorations from entirely ruined temples were placed in his house and garden.

We had heard that he had the reputation of being very honest although his assistants had not. We asked him about the trouble in Cambodia and especially around Siemreap. He said, "This is not a political movement at all. They call themselves Nationalists yet we are the Nationalist Government elected by the people, and we can be legally deposed by the people. If they were Nationalists, they would not need to resort to methods outside the law."

"Communists perhaps?" Clare asked.

"No, no, they are bandits who take advantage of the unsettled conditions and smuggle American arms in from Siam. You will notice that although convoys are attacked it is seldom that people are killed, and even then very few people—everybody is robbed."

After we left him Clare said, "The questions one cannot ask are whether or not he owes his position to the French. If he does he is in a nasty situation because he owes the security and normal functioning of his state to the foreigners, yet at the same time he has to persuade his own people that it is their government, and I should think that it would make it just that much harder when he has to tell them, too, that the taxes are imposed on them by their own people."

"On the other hand," I suggested, "it would account for his theory about the bandits. He cannot admit that they are Nationalists but they are certainly not Communists. I imagine he has to face the difficult decisions that all well-intentioned men do. He probably is a sincere Nationalist with the good of his state at heart, looking for a solution that will not involve extensive bloodshed through armed revolution."

Besides that he had a minority problem to deal with in the Chinese and the Annamese communities. The law tribunals for Cambodians are composed of Cambodians, but for the others they are French and there is a good deal of difficulty between the groups and, consequently, bitterness where the authority overlaps. The governor had said, "You must remember that our king is not a king of Cambodia. He is a king of the Cambodians."

"Another thing," Clare said, "that rather bothers me is the way that always, for one reason or another, America is to blame. It was the same in China, and now here. We're wrong if we do send arms and wrong if we don't. Why does everyone expect handouts from America?"

Faubion said in a puzzled voice, "Isn't it strange, I was just thinking that we are the ones who expect handouts. We want Asia on our side and expect it to conform to our way of thinking."

51 One day Henri Marchal said that he was going to a distant temple in the jungle, Banteay Srei, one of the most beautiful of the buildings. He had some special work to do there, and would we like to come along. Very excited at this unexpected opportunity we set off with M. Marchal, fifty soldiers and a truck of arms and ammunition. Banteay Srei was about thirty kilometers from Siem-

reap and, under the prevalent conditions of fighting and ambushes in the jungle, was usually inaccessible to tourists.

It was a trip that took all day, but by some muddle food had not been brought for the soldiers, so on our way there we stopped at a village and the soldiers went in to negotiate for food. It turned out that a short while before the entire village had been made to evacuate and the place had been burned down because the villagers had harbored some rebels.

As we went into the village which was about one hundred yards off the road in a small clearing carved out of the solid jungle, the children sat huddled under the couple of remaining huts, silent and frightened. The villagers, the few that were left, could only give the soldiers a little dry rice out of their store because they had not been able to get their fields working again yet. One of the soldiers turned to us after they had taken the rice and said casually, "Now presumably they can expect reprisals from the Izaracks for helping the French."

When we reached Banteay Srei our soldier escort asked us, as usual, how long we planned to stay in the temple because if one stayed longer than an hour or, in remote places, an hour and a half, that gave the Cambodians time to send word to the nearest guerrillas who could return to attack the party at the temple. M. Marchal's wrinkled, charming face shone with delight as he led us into the temple. He said, "In this temple I can tell you the history of each stone. Banteay Srei was scattered all over the jungle and we reconstructed it block by block. Here," he said, flinging his hand out, "is the result, a miniature, a perfect temple, small and infinitely fine in workmanship. It is a carved jewel."

He gave us time to admire it. "It is," he said, "a *Citadelle des Femmes* of the tenth century, dedicated to the worship of Shiva and his wife Parvati." He bowed slightly to me, "Do I pronounce your Hindu names correctly?"

The temple is rose-colored, and glows with its own light against the dark-green night of the jungle that entirely surrounds it. It was, as M. Marchal said, entirely perfect.

On the way back we took a different route winding dustily

through the forest to Banteay Samré, another of M. Marchal's favorite buildings, but he did not have for this the same sentimental attachment as for Banteay Srei. It was a larger, more curious structure with cloisters, and looked as if it might have been a monastery at some point. It had not the detail or the polish of the smaller temple, but it had considerable graciousness and a generosity of design.

Banteay Samré was constructed to the glory of the "king who loved cucumbers." The story is that there was a Cambodian king who was very fond of cucumbers and so he had given his gardener permission to kill anyone he found trying to steal his cucumbers because they were of a very special variety, sweet and tender and the seeds had come from the gods. One night the king woke up and, overcome with a hunger for cucumbers, went out to get one from the garden. His gardener, following instructions, killed the king in the dark. He could not see that this was not an intruder. After that the ministers brought the gardener up for trial in front of the people to decide whether he was guilty of assassinating the king or whether he had merely followed instructions and was therefore not guilty of regicide. At this assembly an elephant came up to the gardener and bowed down before him. The people took this as a sign that he should be appointed the next king. But after some years of trying to govern the country as carefully as he had tended his garden, he was so disgusted by the dishonesty and self-interest of his ministers that he resigned the throne and went back to his vegetables.

52

Toward the end of our stay in Siemreap we heard that the palace dancers were to perform in Angkor. The government had some idea that photographs of this occasion would encourage tourist traffic in Cambodia. Naturally, we were delighted at our good fortune and for a few days our lives revolved entirely around the dancers. The night of their arrival they gave a performance on the inner terrace of Angkor Vat. With glistening skins and brilliant

[173]

eyes the Cambodian crowd stood about in the darkness watching the dancers, uncertain whether they were gods or fairies, dancing girls or demons. It was most exciting to see the old dances performed by professionals—the only professionals left for this kind of dancing. The slow, magnificent characters from the *Ramayana*, heavily jeweled and dressed in brocades and velvets, moved through the great old stories. The sacred dances, commemorated in every bas-relief of the temples, had a magical degree of technical and artistic development.

On one side the orchestra of xylophones, gongs, drums and horns made of elephant tusks kept up the liquid Cambodian music from the beginning to the end of the performance without pause.

The next day Faubion insisted that we call on the teacher and chaperone of the dancing girls, the Kru. She was a tough old woman with a suspicious eye, who had herself been a dancer. She thawed out, however, when Faubion began asking questions about her beloved dances.

The palace dancer has a strange life. It begins at about eight years of age when her family voluntarily presents her to the king. For this gift they not only receive a spiritual reward after life, but a monetary grant which depends for its size on the beauty of the girl. Her training at the hands of the Kru begins with her entry into the palace.

Practice hours are from eight to eleven, and from three to five every day except Sundays. At first the pupils learn the exercises. Because the hand is the soul of the dance, the first exercise is to press the fingers backward until they touch the wrist. Sometimes, if the pupil is too diligent, this exercise may leave the fingers knotty where the tendons break. But the majority master the exercise without incident, and their hands develop a flexibility which enables them to curve gracefully backward with no effort. The sweeping curve which the dancers produce at will makes one seriously question the Westerner's concept of the graceful, a limp, straight-fingered hand.

Further exercises follow, such as pressing the elbow backward until it seems to fold with equal ease either way. Legs, shoulders,

[174]

and especially feet all have special exercises to develop that easy and complete articulation necessary for Cambodian dancing.

When all these are mastered, the girl is ready to start learning the actual dances. To teach her, the Kru grips her shoulders tightly from behind and maneuvers her through the routines. In this way the movements become engraved on the dancers' mind and body for life. Once the dances are learned there is a strict order of precedence about the roles she may play. No matter how talented she is, the young dancer must play youth's roles and minor attendant's roles until she is fully grown. Then, according to her height, she is placed in masculine or feminine leads.

By thirty her career as a dancer is over. She then either becomes a teacher herself, a singer, a time-beater or a servant in the palace household. Nowadays it has become possible for her to marry and live outside the glamour of the palace.

Faubion asked the Kru what she considered were the most important qualities for a dancer. She answered with no hesitation, "First, grace and precision of movement; second, physical beauty; and third, personal conduct, because what you are inside and how you live is bound to show in your art."

Later she took us to see the fabulous costumes and jewelry of the dancers. They are heavily guarded by men from the palace whenever the dancers travel, because all the jewelry is real. The high, spire-shaped headdresses are elaborately worked and made of gold. The crowns of the leading dancers have enormous diamonds in them. The clips they wear at their shoulders and waists are rubies and diamonds, and their bracelets and anklets are gold. The clothes which had flashed and glittered in the torchlight the night before turned out to be embroidered with gold paillettes and brilliants on the velvets and lamés.

The dancers gave several more performances—at Angkor Thom, and in the market place of Siemreap for the local people who had not been able to walk as far as the ruins—and of course we went to all of them, each time more enchanted with the dances.

53

Going to the bistro most evenings had become such a habit with us that Faubion and I were rather surprised one evening to find it closed because of some holiday. A man told us to go over to the theater, we could get a drink there.

We walked across the seedy little village-green to the theater, and found a number of stands on the street outside, each with a bench in front of it. This was where the soldiers (not the *sous-officers*) took their Cambodian girls after the theater and drank. We sat down at an empty wine-stand and ordered cognac sodas and listened to the noisy music and laughter from inside the theater. The stands were on the village-green side of the narrow dust road, and Cambodian girls stood behind them to wait on you. I don't know whether they or their menfolk owned the stands.

Three girls were standing behind ours, one was feeding a child at her breast. I smiled at the mother, and she smiled back, unwrapped the baby to show me that it was a boy, giggled shyly and moved away.

Several very drunk soldiers came up. One sat down next to me and said, "Excuse me, I see you have French cigarettes, may I have one?"

"Of course, take the package."

"No, no, just one to remind me of home. They send us these— English or American—take one in exchange."

"No, really, I have plenty."

"Please, madame, or is it mademoiselle? Take the package."

"No, seriously, I have another package here, look."

"But I entreat you, I will be very hurt if you refuse." He was extremely drunk. He put the package of something called Sheffields on the white cloth of the stand. Behind us his friends were singing.

Two soldiers, pale and wavering in the light of the oil lamp, leaned across us to the Cambodian girl's array of bottles and helped themselves to cognac which they drank directly from the bottle.

[176]

They did not pay. Both were very young, one had a soft, pathetic down on his upper lip where he was trying to grow a mustache. A third soldier reached over and picked up an entire bottle of rum which he put in his pocket.

The boy next to me put both his elbows on the table, "I have suffered," he said.

I watched the Cambodian girls behind the stand. Except for a slight weariness, their expressions did not alter and they did not look at each other. This must have been a fairly ordinary occurrence. Slowly and regularly they started putting the bottles away under the stand. Systematically, first the most expensive drinks and the bottles with the most in them, working down to the bottles of soda.

The boy was saying, "If you knew how I have suffered. I killed a woman." He stared at Faubion, "You know how? I cut off her ears. I slit her throat. I killed a woman, a Cambodian woman."

His friends, still singing, were forgetting the words in an effort to make more noise. They grabbed another bottle. The girl said nothing. So far they had not noticed her actions.

"Yesterday," the boy repeated, "I killed a woman. . . ."

"Why? What had she done?" Faubion asked.

"Why? Why? She was sleeping with a damned Viet Minh."

"Is that the punishment?"

"I was ordered to. My commandant told me to kill her in front of our men. Like this, with a knife, across the throat." He suddenly gripped my arm, "Don't you believe me? I'll bet you a million piasters. Come with me to the barracks now, come along, I still have her ears in my pack."

I turned to Faubion, "Quickly let's go home."

As we stood up, the boy reached for a bottle of white crème de menthe just as the Cambodian girl had her hand on it. "Let go," he shouted. "Give it to me or I'll hit you." He grabbed the bottle by its slender neck, the round bulb ready to strike. "I've killed one of you bitches, I can kill you, too."

I held my breath. The girl said nothing. She put a bottle of soda under the counter. His friends had stopped singing and were staring at the girl. One of them raised his arm and slapped her. I felt sick and I did not know what to do. I said to the tall boy with the mustache, "Sing me that song—the one about the colonials."

"Ah, *Les Coloniaux!*" They all began singing.

At the end of the first verse we started to walk away.

"You are going then?" The tall one called. "If you would stay . . ." he said, "you're the first European woman we've talked to for months."

"I am not European—"

"Oh, American. Stay with us."

The boy from the stall took Faubion's arm. "How I have suffered—" he began.

The tall one leaned toward me, "Tomorrow we leave for Tonkin, for action, to fight the rebels. The damned, dirty Viet Minh."

The short one who had stolen the rum hiccoughed, "We shall die."

They looked at each other, laughing. The short one patted the bottle he had pocketed.

54 Near the end of February 1949, we decided to leave Cambodia and go on to Siam. We did, after some discussion, take the military convoy to the Siamese frontier in spite of the possibilities of attack, because otherwise we would have had to return to Saïgon and go from there. For the previous few days we had been hearing the disturbing sound of gunfire in the forest around Siemreap, but Clare said, "Think what a wonderful story it would be if we were attacked."

We spent our last day in good-by calls on M. Marchal, Mme. Ott, the governor, M. Challier and our friends the soldiers.

The military convoy took us from Siemreap to Sisophon which was about fifty kilometers from the Siamese frontier. The ride was entirely without incident, though every bridge had to be examined for mines and the roads along the wooded sections were patrolled by foreign-legion troops. As there was no way of getting from Sisophon to Poipet on the Siamese frontier except in a private car, the head of the Sureté there offered to drive us in his jeep. Poipet had the friendly seedy look of all frontier towns, and from there we again hitched a ride with the Sureté man across the frontier to Aram Pradet, in Siam.

As we drove through Poipet we saw that one section of the town had been burned down. "The work of the Izaracks," the Sureté man said. Later he said, "Forgive me for going slowly, this road is usually mined." He pointed to an overturned car on the side of the road, "One sees that quite often." We passed acres of burned rice fields, "Again the Izaracks. This used to be rich rice country, now the peasants have had to leave."

As we came to Aram Pradet he said, "I prefer the Cambodians to the Siamese, they are more docile, not very clever, but they do what they are told and are respectful."

Faubion said coldly, "Beastly independent for natives, the Siamese."

The man said thoughtfully, "Yes, that's true."

It's very hard to be sarcastic in a foreign language.

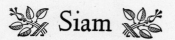 Siam

55

Clare pointed out the first interesting thing about Siam. All the signs at street corners, on the railway station, the police department, or the customs were in Siamese, with no translation into any European language. It felt strange to be in a country where the people speak only their own language and expect the foreigner to learn Siamese if he wants to be understood. We started on our nine-hour train trip from the frontier to Bangkok with a surprising feeling of gaiety and relief at being for the first time in the only country in Asia that has not been dominated by a foreign power.

The miniature Siamese train moved southward through the rich plantations and rice fields. It stopped at tiny stations where we bought cotton candy on sticks and watched the children eat the local form of ice cream—chopped ice crushed into lumps with a little syrup poured over it. The food in the train itself was delicious as it simply didn't occur to the dining-car people to serve anything but Siamese dishes, so one didn't have to put up with the shocking attempts at Western food that one gets in other parts of Asia. Here there had not been generations of ruling foreigners who insisted on eating the same meals as they ate in their home countries.

This is a point worth emphasizing because it is a matter of great bewilderment to people in Asia that Westerners should, with such determination, carry their manners with them. Perhaps it is a by-product of imperialism that in any town or village in Asia a Westerner in a restaurant is served with plates and knives and forks because nothing will induce him to eat as the local inhabitants do—except, perhaps, once or twice out of curiosity. Were a Chinese to ask for chopsticks in a Paris restaurant, or were I to insist on eating with my fingers at El Morocco, we would be considered either affected or insane. Equally, one would think that the logical thing for a traveler, or for someone living in a foreign nation, would be to eat the food of the country he is in. However, homesickness (to be charitable) takes strange forms.

A Siamese businessman who was sitting next to us in the train,

[183]

had been watching us with interest and amusement, so we introduced ourselves. He spoke a little English and, of course, asked us our impressions of Siam.

Clare said, "The only things I know about Siam are from the movie, *Anna and the King of Siam*. Did you see it?"

He said coldly, "It ran in Bankgkok for a while, but we didn't like it much. It wasn't true, you see, and then it was rather insulting." He turned to me and said, "I was glad to hear it was banned in India."

"We have had a good deal of experience with such movies—about India, that is," I said. We smiled at each other with complete understanding.

56 In Bangkok we had two introductions, both of which turned out to be so enthralling that we never moved out of Bangkok until we finally left Siam altogether. The first was to Prince Kukrit Pramoj who was an aristocrat by birth, a liberal politician by ideology, and an artist by nature. A completely fascinating man in any role, he came to our hotel to have a drink with us one afternoon soon after our arrival. As he walked in, Clare whispered, "Ooh Daddy, buy me *that*!" because Kukrit's good looks, like most of his characteristics, went in extremes. He was a little suspicious of Clare and Faubion to begin with because, he told us later, they were foreigners, and "I know them too well. I was educated in England." His voice always sounded a little tired, a little drawling, so that it was hard to believe that his reputation as a public speaker was so great that he was the only man in Siam who could draw a crowd to a political meeting.

"But aren't the Siamese *interested* in politics?" Clare asked, rather appalled at the laissez-faire atmosphere of the country.

"But my dear Miss Harris," Kukrit said, looking amused, "why *should* they be? There's nothing *in*—tr'sting about politics. They are rich and wellfed, their government is not oppressive, why should they worry?" He added a little more seriously, "We haven't the problems that the rest of Asia has *because* we are rich. You can't

[184]

make Communists of us any more than you can make imperialists of us. You can't even get us particularly interested in trade and economic development. All that is handled by the Chinese and the Indians here."

"Well," said Clare hotly, "why are you so concerned with politics, then?"

Kukrit shifted his long elegant figure in his chair and said with infinite vagueness, "Oh *I?*" as if he had never heard of himself before. "Well, I suppose it's because I have an insatiable appetite for gossip. I am a political dilettante, you see."

Clare looked shocked. Politics should be *serious.*

Kukrit continued more briskly, "It has its advantages, the threat of being turned out of office means nothing to me. That is why the other politicians fear me, and also why I am secure." With considerable irony he said, "Don't you find me very Western at heart? —I have to have that extraordinary thing, a hobby."

Three times in the previous year he had been a cabinet minister, and three times he had resigned after sensational speeches in the Assembly. He had no hesitation in accusing various members of the government of corruption. He was extravagantly feared by the officials, partly because he had access to, and used, accurate information about their practices, and partly because nobody had yet been able to question his own honesty. However, he was always the center of a bath of gossip about both his private and public life—none of which he bothered to deny because, he said, he liked to give people so much to talk about.

Until 1932 the government of Siam was an absolute monarchy of a fairly progressive sort. With the rise of Pridhi Panomyong politics became "a sort of game played by the intellectuals and the army. At no time were the people much involved. Our politics," said Kukrit, trying deliberately, I think, to startle Clare, "are arranged on a very high level."

Pridhi was a man of poor parentage who had managed to get himself educated and decided to break into public life. He talked a number of high army officers into backing him in the first of Siam's famous *coups d'état.* He persuaded them that they could

[185]

have more power through him—as indeed they did. Without the army to support him, the king was helpless and had to submit meekly to the proposals that a new constitution be formed limiting his power. It established a lower house whose representatives were to be elected by adult suffrage and an upper house whose members were to be appointed, technically, by the king, actually, by the people involved in the coup d' état—who, of course, appointed themselves. Thus Pridhi and his group had half the government and the king under their control.

"I hope," said Kukrit, "you are not naïve enough to think that this was motivated by any high democratic ideals. Like nearly all politics it was merely the wish to change the source of power to somebody's advantage."

However, certain social measures did go along with the new constitution, compulsory education, adult literacy classes and that sort of thing. There was a five-year intermediary period set for people to get used to the new form of government before general elections would be held, but this period was extended for a further ten years. Before it had expired, war broke out in Asia, and eventually Siam allied itself with Japan and put up with certain Japanese-inspired changes in their government. During the war three different constitutions were brought in. "And now," Kukrit said, as though it were the most ordinary thing, "we are working on our sixth. Perhaps it will be final."

Clare said, with a return to her former belligerence, "Why did Siam collaborate with the Japanese during the war?"

For the first and only time that we knew him, Kukrit looked irritated, but his voice was rather bored as he said, "And what loyalty do we owe to you?"

Clare blushed, but said bravely, "It's not a question of loyalty to us. It was a question of fighting totalitarianism."

"Well, perhaps it seemed to us that there were greater dangers in allying ourselves with the West than there were in totalitarianism. After all, we are Asians, and you should remember that to many millions of us the war in the Pacific was the white man fighting the colored." He half closed his eyes, "And when I think of what happened to the unfortunates who did come in on your side. Your country," he said, opening his eyes at me, "or the underground movements of Indo-China and Indonesia, what were your rewards? Simply to have your countries returned to your former foreign governors who couldn't hold them in the first place? It hardly seems worth it."

"Kukrit," Faubion said suddenly, "why do you hate the white man so?"

Kukrit looked interested. "Hate is too strong a word. I haven't time for them. The white man comes to the Orient for one of three reasons: he is in love with the women; or he is in love with the men; or he sees the opportunity of making money. I am not interested in sexual neuroses any more than I am in tradesmen. It is only very recently, don't forget, that we have the chance," he bowed to Faubion and Clare, "of meeting intelligent tourists or impartial journalists." He added very softly, "And even then, only if we know *their* language."

57 Our second introduction was to Jim Thompson, an American who had worked with the anti-Japanese underground in Laos and Cambodia while he was with the O.S.S. during the war. He had returned to Bangkok after the war as a businessman. He introduced us to a side of Siam that tourists relatively seldom get to know—it was the Siam of exiles. Like London during the war, Bangkok was, in Asia, the home of the governments in exile.

Through him we met Thao-Oun, a Laotian, a pleasant young man who spoke beautiful French and seemed deceptively calm and nonchalant. He had been the foreign minister in the brief free government of Laos between the time when the Japanese left and the French returned to possession. He was then living in exile in Bangkok along with thousands of his countrymen who were also refugees. Jim and he had revived the weaving industry of Laos to keep them alive in their exile. He was still one of the leaders of the Free Laos Government, and helped to maintain its tenuous existence. None of them dared return to their own land until conditions between the French and the subject peoples were stabilized.

When he heard that we had just come from Cambodia, he invited us to dinner to meet not only his family, but also Prah Pisett, the leader of the Free Cambodians in Bangkok. It was a strange evening. The dinner was at the house of Mme. Peng, Thao-Oun's sister-in-law, though actually the house was the final inspection office for the silk cloth from the weaving sheds and Mme. Peng and her family merely lived in a couple of rooms left free.

It was a typical Bangkok home, wooden, with little furniture, and built up on stilts against the annual floods which make the many canals a danger as well as a beauty of the city. We had dinner in the garden because there wasn't room indoors. It was cool there. The palm trees rattled overhead, the lanterns caught reflections on our clothes. And it was an unfamiliar life—that of exiles, moving underground, continuing their anti-French resistance movement, determinedly ignoring the fact that they maintained the most precarious of existences on the silks they wove and which an American helped them to sell. Since only Cambodians or Laotians were present, the conversation was all in French, which was not only humiliating (because they spoke so educatedly), but lent, too, a further note of weirdness. It seemed so odd that all of us Asians should have as our only common language something as far removed as French.

Mme. Peng was a short, pretty woman with great vivacity and, one imagined, a command of any situation. She wore an incredibly lovely embroidered skirt which she had made herself, and a heavy, gold brocade scarf which was wrapped around her waist, across her breasts, and thrown over one shoulder, leaving the other bare. She commented on the fact that the design of her brocade, and the design on the border of my sari were almost identical.

Mme. Peng was the first Laotian girl to receive a school and college education even though her family's friends were shocked beyond protest. She returned from Saïgon to her own province where she worked as a schoolteacher. At twenty-five she married a young liberal. Her husband, Thao-Oun's brother, looked very

[188]

much like him but was much quieter. He moved silently about seeing that their guests were comfortable and gave us each a drink of a local whisky called Mekong—the name of Indo-China's famous river. Then he said, "Unfortunately this is the best that we can offer you—the water from our river." He said it as a joke, but nobody laughed. They all held up their glasses solemnly, and Mme. Peng said, "To the time when we can return to our land."

With the whisky were served little cakes on a bed of lettuce leaves. They were made of tapioca stuffed with meat, peanuts and spices. You wrap the cake in the lettuce and eat it in one mouthful—that way you get the taste of all the spices at once.

In the unreal evening, the gentle French voices took up the conversation and told us about their experiences during the war. "The evening that the Japanese came I will never forget," Mme. Peng said. "We had our dinner as usual, and soon after we heard one or two detonations. We thought they were fireworks. By the next morning it was all over. They were not fireworks, they were a defeat." She added with some bitterness, "We Laotians were never permitted to carry arms because the French were going to protect us. Does no responsibility go with government? If they had not fled, if one Frenchman had died with us or for us things might have been different now. Later we saw them drinking champagne and shouting Banzai! for Japanese victories."

Her husband and Thao-Oun, like many other Laotians had eventually joined the anti-Japanese resistance movement that had co-operated with the American O.S.S. people. "In those days," said Thao-Oun, smiling in a friendly way at Jim, "we thought the Americans came as liberators." After the Japanese defeat there were a few glorious months of independence when the Free Laos Government was set up and Thao-Oun and his brother were elected ministers. "Then?" said Thao-Oun, "then the French returned. We couldn't believe it. I asked an American friend of mine and he said, 'The war is over, we must get back to peacetime conditions.'"

The Free Laotians fled to Siam because the French had placed a fifty-thousand-piaster price on their heads. For months they lived on the edge of starvation, trying to make a living in this foreign country. Eventually with Jim's help they had managed to establish the Laotian silk-weaving industry in Bangkok to keep themselves alive.

Thao-Oun shrugged his shoulders and said with less excitement, "Now I change my mind about Japan. Here it becomes plain that if it had not been for the Japanese the independence movements of all Southeast Asia would have taken much longer to get started. We have a lot to thank them for. They showed us that Asians can govern themselves and defeat the West. They showed us how to fight—perhaps Asia would have been worse if they had won, who can say? But that, at least, we must thank them for. In those days, of course, we were so inexperienced that we believed what the Westerners told us. Now we know better."

Prah Pisett and his wife arrived. Thao-Oun sprang to his feet and introduced them. He was a square, well-groomed man, and his wife was lovely, but spoke only Cambodian. Thao-Oun told me quietly, "Her father is almost legendary among Cambodians. He was the chief man and virtual owner of Pratambang Province." With his voice he took me into a sort of conspiracy, "In our part of the world people understand nobility. People still talk about the amazing journeys he used to make from Cambodia to Bangkok with his elephant train. With him he would take his concubines, his wines and all his luxuries. The trip would take him well over a month. Once," Thao-Oun's voice sank to whisper, "once, twelve concubines were delivered of children along the way." When the provinces of Battambang and Pratambang were returned to the French, Prah Pisett and his wife fled to Bangkok to continue the Free Cambodia Movement from there.

We sat down to dinner, and Prah Pisett began the meal with a long speech to me about what an honor it was to meet an Indian and how India was the hope of all of Southeast Asia. From this he progressed into a long and scholarly discussion of the ruins of Angkor. I couldn't help thinking of M. Challier's comment that the Cambodians were like children, unaware of their extraordinary past history—"if you ask a Cambodian about these temples and palaces, he will say, 'the gods built them.' "

[190]

Dinner was entirely Laotian and filled with new tastes and unfamiliar combinations. First there was something that looked like vermicelli but was made of rice and was wound into sort of birds' nests. Over that you scatter mint leaves, coriander, banana flowers and chilies according to your taste, and over the whole thing you pour a thin, mild, but delicious curry sauce. The second course was plain rice, served with fat parcels of mushrooms, meat, liver, onions and spices wrapped in banana leaves and steamed. It had a curious, haunting, perfumed taste. The sweet was coconut custard served in baby coconut shells.

Since they all work hard, and had to get up early in the morning, we left soon after dinner, after an altogether charming evening.

58 One afternoon, when we had been in Bangkok only a few days, I found Clare in our hotel room, her hair newly washed and shining, the curls still crisp from her bobby pins, wearing one of her new Saïgon dresses, leaning close to the mirror and putting on her lipstick with a little brush.

"Where are you going?" I asked.

"You know I can't talk when I am doing this." She completed her careful make-up and then sped out of the room saying, "Meet you for dinner."

She arrived for dinner looking pleased and rather pink. Behind her was Michael, still crumpled from the plane ride.

"Good heavens," Faubion said. "What are you doing here? Buying broomsticks?"

"I came as soon as I got your wire," Michael said innocently. "I can break journey here for a couple of weeks on my way to England."

Clare said quickly, "Michael was so sorry that you two were busy this afternoon and couldn't meet him." She gazed piercingly at me.

"It is, as they always say, a wonderful thing," Faubion remarked with resignation. Michael looked puzzled, and Clare turned even pinker.

We saw rather less of Clare for the next two weeks, but we did do a few things together. Michael insisted that we take a boat trip through the Bangkok canals because, he told us, the city is known as the Venice of the East. Faubion seemed entirely bored while we looked at bigger and bigger temples with even more gold and decoration and porcelain on the walls and roofs and yet more enormous buddhas inside. He gazed at the canal life of Bangkok which is lived mostly on the platforms built out on poles over the water. There, in the afternoon sunlight women braid each other's hair, sift the rice, weave the cloth and the children help in the work. Children are seldom idle in the Orient. Men load the boats, carry the wood, shout to each other across the canals, and guide the big barges downstream.

The next day Michael arranged for us to see the palace, the shrine where the embalmed body of Siam's last king—who was shot—is kept in an urn, the Emerald Buddha and things like that. Through him, because he is only really comfortable with his own kind, we saw something of the foreigners in the city, too, and learned some other facts about Siam which rather interested me.

The Siamese have one quality that sets them off from other Asian nations. They have been able successfully to play different foreign nations off against each other. Before the war they played the French off against the English to avoid being swallowed up by the one in Malaya or the other in Indo-China. By offering the British preferential trade agreements in exchange for their willingness to defend Siam against the French should the need arise, they made certain that the need never would arise, and maintained, precariously, their independence. To the British it seemed like a good arrangement because they had what they wanted from a colony anyway—economic advantage—and without the bother of government.

After the war, when France was no longer a menace, Siamese politicians began playing the English off against the Americans in trade matters. The result was that the latent antagonism which is always present between those two nations was, in Bangkok, very much apparent. But everybody loved the Siamese and treated them with kid gloves. Recently they had acquired yet another threat: any pressure from either side would throw them into the arms of the Communists.

It all made for some funny situations. In these days of searching scrutinies at frontiers, of cables from consulates to headquarters before passports can be visaed, Americans need no visa to go to Siam, and the Siamese can enter America any time without a visa, too. Bangkok operates an open currency market with everybody's approval, although it benefits nobody but the Siamese. It means serious losses to both British and Americans. For instance, one can buy Straits dollars (the Malayan currency) very easily and cheaply in Bangkok and transfer them quite legally through a bank to Singapore. In Singapore itself the British are very severe about black-marketing in currency, but they are helpless against the flow of cheap dollars from Siam.

Most of the foreigners smoothly ignored the fact that Siam supported Japan in the last war; nobody mentioned reparations, or the matters of occupation and trial of war criminals. The prime minister at the time, whom people often called "that brilliant man," was the leading collaborator with the Japanese. Siam received economic aid from America and was already a member of the United Nations.

Michael, with one of his flashes of acuteness, said to me one day, "It must be rather pleasing to you to see an Asian country *making* terms instead of simply accepting them from all of us."

He was right, of course, though I'm not sure that I would have admitted it.

59

To see Kukrit's casual, rather lazy walk, one would never think that he was an accomplished dancer. He was, as well, that rare thing, an artist who is also a scholar. He advised us to see the Khon dances—the ceremonial dances that are so rapidly dying out in Siam.

The story of the dance we saw was, as usual, from the *Ramayana*, the part that shows Sita, already captured by the king of Lanka, and his attempts to seduce her. It was partly danced and partly spoken, and fairly close in style to the Cambodian dances.

He told us that Siam is one of the few countries in which the government supports the arts and suggested that we go to the Fine Arts Department and see what they have done with the classical dances. So one afternoon we went over to the large building, with its theater, music rooms, dance studios and pleasant gardens. We saw a curious adaptation of old and new styles in a play put on by the students. The story was legendary, the dances old, the dialogue modern, and there were a good many comedy scenes.

Afterward, some of the students had arranged a program for Faubion to show him the principles of classical Siamese dancing. All the main steps and postures of Siamese dancing are taught through a "foundation dance." It is considered the alphabet of dancing, and the girls begin with it when they are eight years old. For a year they practice nothing else, because every gesture is in it. Each section is named rather attractively: "the making of the tassels in the garland," "the swan in flight," "Princess Mekala showing her gems," "the wind sways the top of the plantain leaf," and so on.

After the girls finish their training they teach or join troupes, but Siamese dancing in its traditional form is dying out in spite of the efforts of the government to keep it alive. It is only on state occasions or for religious ceremonies that it is still needed.

Kukrit also introduced us to Kumut Chandruang, Siam's most successful theatrical director, so that we would have a chance to see the modern "socially conscious theater," and meet some of the people who work in it. We found the plays lavishly presented and full of brilliant colors. On their stage as well as in their daily life, and even in their architecture the Siamese love a lot of gold and glitter. It is like living in a perpetual Hollywood musical.

After that Kukrit took Faubion and me to the "lower" type of theater—*likay*. The theater, one of five devoted to *likay*, was in a poor part of town and the audience was mostly servants, vendors, etc., and a number of old people who were absorbed in the play, crying in the beautiful parts and laughing madly at the clowns. All the comedy was played in verse with many puns and tricks with words, and the serious part was in verse or song.

On our way back the car was stopped several times by army people, and searched. Several times there were road blocks and detours. All that night from the hotel we heard gunfire, and once the unmistakable sound of tanks rolling down the street. Clare and I rushed to the window and stood watching and wondering what on earth was happening.

The next morning the lobby was filled with army men standing about, and several higher-ranking officers were huddled in conference in one corner. Kukrit came to call in the morning, and we asked him what was up.

"Another coup d'état," he said casually. "Some say it is Pridhi's party trying to get back into power. But that doesn't seem likely. Four of his chief men were murdered last night, the news came through this morning." He looked across at the army men and raised his eyebrows, "And more trouble to come, apparently. Perhaps it will be my turn next."

"To be killed," Clare gasped, "or to stage a coup d'état?"

Kukrit smiled, and said to tease her, "Who knows?"

"Well," Clare said, "I must say, I still don't know what it's all about."

"I'm not surprised. It's not in our usual tradition of coups d'état at all. Normally, nobody is killed in a coup d'état. A certain amount of firing, yes, but over the heads of the crowds, just to show people they are serious." The present prime minister, it seemed, had got into power by a series of such maneuvers, and by rallying his ex-pro-Japanese troops. Thus he had the army behind him and could take over. In the new coup, the marines and the royalists were trying to break his hold on the government. The navy was split between both sides. The Pridhi complication was a subsidiary thing. Some people said that since there was currently a case against him for the assassination of the last king, he wanted to resume office and get the case shelved. Others said that the present prime minister needed a scapegoat but actually had no case against Pridhi, and that was why his four chief advisers had been killed—they were also the lawyers for the defense.

[195]

The upset in the city continued for a couple of days, then calm was restored. The *coup d'état* had failed, and Pridhi remained underground.

60 Kukrit had invited us one evening to have dinner with the present regent for the King of Siam and his wife, Princess Pon-Thip. We all dressed up in our grandest clothes, only to find that the regent, who is also the heir presumptive, and his wife live with great simplicity in a small and charming house, Western in style except for the library which is arranged to suit the very beautiful old Siamese pictures in it.

The princess is a tiny, witty woman whose quality could only really be conveyed by one of those early movies in which the actions are all very quick and everything seems to move at an intensely speeded-up pitch. She was sitting on the terrace outside the library when we arrived, but ran to the door to welcome us in with a stream of chatter and introductions. She got our names right at once, and said, "I'm so glad Kukrit brought you isn't it a heavenly night will you be too cold on the terrace oh dear I'm sure the cocktails won't be strong enough for you, Kukrit, but do mix some more yourself. What a beautiful sari that is! Do let me introduce you to my husband, my dear wouldn't it be lovely if Siamese women had a charming national costume—" She stopped suddenly like a guilty child, and then said, "I'm afraid I'm talking too much as usual."

The regent is quiet and tolerant, and lives in dread of being king. "When I think that my future is in the hands of a lively youngster who likes to tear around Switzerland in fast cars, my blood runs cold."

"Miss Harris," said the princess, unable to keep silent any longer, "Kukrit tells me you are interested in politics. Have you enjoyed our game of musical chairs?"

Clare looked baffled and said, "I—er—"

"The *coup d'état*, I mean. It's wonderful, isn't it? Leaders fight with leaders, cabinets stagger and fall (or not as the case may be) but the country goes calmly on—with only a temporary inconvenience to the citizens of Bangkok."

"Is there," Clare asked of the regent, determined not to be intimidated by royalty, "a *Leftist* movement in Siam."

The regent turned a polite face to Clare, "If by Leftist you mean antiroyalist, I don't believe there is. But then, of course, we would be the last to hear of it, I dare say. We do have liberals, however," Kukrit had moved to the drinks table, and the regent regarded his turned back, "of whom Kukrit is the best sort because his motives are unimpeachable. He is not in it for the usual reasons—but then, it isn't difficult to be honest if you don't need the money. He is the kind of man that can tap the lion's head, and the lion loves it."

"But is there a labor movement, or anything like that?" Clare asked firmly.

"Well," said the regent with a perfectly straight face, "we have two unions, the Central Trades Union and the Siamese Labor Union. One is government sponsored, and the other is a Chinese organization. Neither has ever been on strike."

"It is," said Kukrit, returning, "a maddening country for the revolutionary. Our nature is to be happy. There is a famous Siamese story which illustrates what I mean: Once upon a time there was a woman who was energetic and ambitious. She was married to a lazy man with expensive tastes, but nothing she could say would make him work because he always answered, 'There must be an easier way to make money.'

"In despair she went to her father, a very wise old man and asked him what to do. He said, 'I have discovered a magic formula. Tell your husband that if he brings me ten pounds of the dust that falls from banana flowers onto the leaves, I will turn it to gold for him.'

"The wife and husband were both delighted with this scheme. She set all her energy to work, prepared the ground, and planted banana trees. She tended them carefully until they grew and prospered. Every morning her husband spent an hour collecting the dust, and spent the rest of the day idling about in his usual way and chatting to his friends.

"At the end of ten years he had collected ten pounds of the dust, and took them to his father-in-law. 'Now,' he said, 'turn this to gold for me.'

" 'Ah, my son,' said the old man, 'it has already been turned to gold. For ten years your banana plantations have prospered. Your wife has been selling the fruit so that it shall not go to waste. You are already rich. Go home and enjoy it.'

"So you see," Kukrit finished, "as in all Siamese stories, everyone was happy. The wife worked and prospered. The husband was lazy and prospered, and the father-in-law was saved the trouble of supporting his family."

The dinner was Siamese, highly spiced, hot and delicious. Afterward we sat for a long time in the tepid Bangkok night listening to the princess' flow of amusing gossip and comment, and the regent's occasional and sensible remarks.

61 One day, soon afterward, we drove through Bangkok's crowded streets to lunch with Prah Pisett. The street names all sounded slightly familiar because, like most of Siamese culture, they are Sanskrit in origin and come from India. Thao-Oun and Kukrit were both there, and all of them listened patiently while Prah Pisett made speeches about India's helping the subject nations of Asia. "We need protection, and we cannot look to China for it. Only India can save us now. We wish to form a league of Southeast Asian nations that will protect the small states when we have acquired our independence. For that we need the support of at least one big nation."

Thao-Oun said softly to me, "We have all been taught to think in terms of blocs these days."

"Tell me," I said, "if you were to get your independence, wouldn't you be afraid of being swallowed up by the Viet Nam or Viet Minh?"

"If you take chickens out of the nest and put them in the street, won't the hawks eat them? It is for that protection that we need a league, and need you people."

After lunch Thao-Oun took us to see the Laotian weavers at work. He led us through a maze of interconnected wooden buildings, constructed out over the water of one of the canals. There the weavers were working on old-fashioned handlooms to produce the magnificent silks of the north.

"The main trouble," Thao-Oun explained, "is that American designers need perhaps one hundred yards of the same fabric, but our weavers are apt to get bored of the same design over and over again. They feel it would be so much more fun for the Americans to find something entirely different in the middle of a bolt of cloth."

Their favorite colors are green and peacock, which they call "firefly wings in the garden at night." The women at the looms stopped work and smiled at us. You can tell what part of Laos a woman comes from by the way she knots her hair. The designs of the silks she wears will give you a clue as well. "In the north all women make their own clothes. It is a matter of prestige. A woman wouldn't dare show herself to her friends in a skirt that she had bought." The women usually wear embroidered or flowered silks, and the men wear solid colors or checks. "Isn't it strange," said Thao-Oun, "that American women seem to prefer the masculine silks?"

Michael flew off to England a few days before we left Siam, and Clare seemed a little distraught, and was without her usual bounding energy. "How about moving on to Malaya?" she said one day when we were having a drink with Kukrit. "This has been the most extended two months I ever spent." It had already been six since we left Shanghai.

"No," I said. It was one point on which I was firmly selfish.

"Singapore?" Kukrit asked with more than his usual drawl. "The color bar there is so strong I am ashamed to get in the bath with myself."

"Besides," I added, "I have seen quite enough of British colonies for one lifetime."

"It isn't the heat," Faubion said dimly, "it's the stupidity."

In the end we decided to travel by train down the Malay Peninsula, stopping for a couple of days at Penang, Kuala Lumpur, and Singapore. As usual, people warned us that bridges were mined, trains attacked by revolutionaries, the project altogether fraught with danger, and as usual they turned out to be entirely wrong.

When we said good-by to Kukrit, Faubion said, "Do give us your address so we can write to you."

Kukrit said, "This sounds ridiculous, but if you write, 'Kukrit, Bangkok' on the envelope, it will find me. Anyway, you'll never remember the address." Later we did write and it did reach him.

Early on the morning of the day we left, Thao-Oun came to say good-by. We in turn wished him good luck with the Free Laotian Movement.

"Thank you," he said, "I will try to keep myself optimistic. There are so many people all over the world who have joined the fight for freedom of various sorts, and who come to it with diseased minds. We must try to avoid those cancers. We must stay healthy." He suddenly turned to Faubion, "I wonder, do Americans realize what a store of bitterness there is in Asia?"

Indonesia

62 In the four months that Clare, Faubion and I spent in Indonesia, we all changed a good deal. To all of us the changes were important. Indonesia meant to Clare the reorganization of ideas which were so deep a part of her nature that she wasn't conscious of ever having learned them. To Faubion it meant not only the climax of his book on Asian dance and drama, but also a deeper concern in something he calls "abstract esthetics."

For me Indonesia was my first experience of what I think is a healthy society. In all the months of travel through Asia—superficial as my observations had been—I had retained an impression of the growing consciousness of being Asian that was accompanying the death of colonialism in Asia. In Bali, for the first time, I felt myself a part of that Asian identity, and acquired a greater confidence in our way of life.

The resistance movement against the Dutch was in one of its more violent phases, and when we arrived in Batavia (Jakarta,) we found that it was virtually impossible to travel in Java or Sumatra. Faubion had been in Indonesia before the war and had learned Malay at that time. He suggested that we go to Bali for a few weeks until the Republican leaders were released from jail and we could get some idea of whether it would be possible to travel more extensively after that.

"The only thing," Faubion said, "is that I refuse to stay in the Dutch Hotel in Den Pasar." It was his usual refrain, "We must get out of the town at once."

Fortunately a friend of ours in Batavia gave us a letter of introduction to a Balinese chokorda (a title denoting both caste and social status—the chokordas are the layer of aristocracy immediately under the rajas). Chokorda Agung, we learned, occasionally took paying guests. We decided to take advantage of this letter and left for Bali immediately.

I had heard so much about Bali that I was not too surprised to find it a beautiful country, in a tropical way, with narrow roads winding between coconut groves, a brilliant sparkle from the sea on one side, and the neat rice fields stretching away on the other to where the hills began. The people, however, did come as something of a shock. I have never seen a race as universally graceful and lovely to look at.

Faubion said, "It's something to do with the light. The Balinese skin acquires a glow and a color that diminishes all imperfections of feature or complexion."

Clare said, "More likely something to do with the diet."

But I think it is due to the extraordinary charm of the Balinese, a charm that you feel even if you don't speak to them There is a security in their way of walking, an ease and directness in their conversation, great tolerance and humor in their general approach. It is one of the few countries of Asia where a foreigner cannot make the popular mistake of assuming that Oriental manners and politeness are due to obsequiousness or subservience.

We made arrangements as soon as possible to leave Den Pasar, Bali's capital, for the small village of Ubud where we were to stay with Chokorda Agung.

63 The *puri* of Chokorda Agung in Ubud was a series of interconnected courtyards. The big entry gate from the road opened into the first courtyard which was given to Faubion. It had a living pavilion on one side, built of stone with big decorative panels in the walls sculptured from the soft local sandstone. It had a little veranda and a porch, and inside, a living room, bedroom and bath. The rest of the courtyard was empty, kept as a place for dance performances. Three open pavilions in the other three corners were for spectators.

It opened on both sides into more courtyards. In one of them Chokorda Agung's uncle, the old Chokorda Ngura, lived, and that courtyard in turn, opened on to the courtyard which Clare and I shared with one of Chokorda Agung's wives, who acted as our chaperon. It was a particularly beautiful part of the *puri*, with two living pavilions in it. On one side was the tooth-filing pavilion, which was used at other times as a dining room, a rehearsal room, art gallery or anything else one wanted to make it. In the middle of the courtyard was an open pavilion, higher than the others, from which orchestras played during formal dinners. All the buildings were of whitewashed adobe, with thatched roofs and magnificent wooden pillars carved by the Chokorda's craftsmen, and decorated with gold and paint. In every room were a few samples of his fantastic collection of Balinese paintings.

The first morning Clare and I woke at about five o'clock to the most extraordinary racket in the courtyard behind ours. After daylight, when we got up, we looked out and saw that the old Chokorda kept his fighting cocks behind our pavilion, and as soon as one started crowing, all the others started, too. Within a few days we scarcely noticed the noise, and in any case our hours had changed completely. There was, of course, no electricity so we fell into the Balinese way of rising at daybreak and sleeping immediately after dinner. Oil lamps are not precisely the thing to read by in bed.

There was no hot water either, but in that delightful climate it was no hardship. Our bathroom was across the courtyard, and the first night we were there Clare fussed about trying to find a dressing gown. In the morning we noticed that most of the people who trotted across the courtyard were so scantily clad that our modesty couldn't hold out very long. The bath itself was Indian in style. You pour water from one of the huge urns over yourself, soap yourself, and wash off the soap with more water. At first Clare used to come out rather miserably with damp curls and a feeling that she wasn't really having a bath, but soon she, too, like the Balinese, began to find the idea of a tub dirty. Fancy sitting in your own dirty water! Aren't Westerners dirty in their habits!

Clare and I had, as a servant, Agung G'dé, a high-caste boy who was serving a sort of apprenticeship in Chokorda Agung's *puri*. He was a most graceful young man, light-skinned, and with shaved eyebrows which he kept very carefully trimmed. His manners were perfect. He brought coffee to us on our veranda. We sat there feeling too peaceful even to talk, and watched the morning sunlight blaze on the cannas and hibiscus in our courtyard. The gold paint on the pillars glittered, and under the thatched eaves were deep-blue shadows.

Chokorda Agung came to sit with us for a few moments. "I wish you to be happy guests," he said. "And you," he said to me, "are the first Indian to stay here. As we are all Hindus we should have much in common. Yours and mine are the only two Hindu countries left in the world." He then produced an extraordinary and beautiful carving of two men with a fish, with their arms up and their knees bent. He asked us to put it in our room as an amulet against thieves. Finally he said, "May I ask what caste are you?"

"I am a Brahmin."

"Ah a Brachman! Then I will call you Daiyu from now on. That is what we call an unmarried Brachman girl among us."

Eventually we wandered through the flowers and the many decorated gates to Faubion's courtyard. We found him sitting with Gusti Agung Ngura, the cook. They were talking earnestly. Gusti Agung Ngura was very elegant indeed, and high caste. Because his language was so beautiful, Chokorda Agung had suggested that he help Faubion to recapture his Malay, much of which he had forgotten during the war.

That first day we were not used to the magical air of Bali, and the extraordinary way that it slows you down to an easy, gentle pace of living. We wondered why we were content simply to sit and watch people walk through the puri or, perhaps, stroll along the one road of the tiny village, smile at the people or stare at the sky reflected in the flooded rice fields.

Ubud has about two hundred people living in the immediate village area, in the little compounds enclosed by mud walls opening off the road. The population would be about five hundred if you include all the Ubud area. Always in the village there is a faint smell of coconut oil and perfume from the hair of people who have just passed you, and when that vanishes you can smell the freshly ground coffee and the spices in the cooking from the various houses. That first day we thought of Ubud as the perfect place for a quiet couple of weeks' holiday. Later we realized how wrong we were. By then we were mixed up in all the village activities and saw that, far from being restful, it was the busiest and most time-consuming life imaginable. But we didn't leave Ubud until months later when we finally left Bali altogether, because we entirely lost interest in a quiet holiday when we found that we had stumbled on the most complete and satisfying life that any of us had ever known.

64 Within a couple of days Chokorda Agung decided that we should start meeting the village and learning about its various activities. He was a plumpish, jolly man, of enormous kindness, and with the most devoted love of his village. Hearing that Faubion was a musician, he took us first to see where the rehearsals of the music society were held—the courtyard of Gusti Agung Ngura's house. There we found Chokorda Agung's nephew, Chokorda Mas, sitting by himself, tinkling on one of the instruments. He immediately played for us some of the old music, the special music that accompanies the *Ramayana* stories, and after that some modern music and some of his own compositions. He was famous as a musician in all the neighboring villages, and loved to compose.

Walking back to the *puri*, Chokorda Agung said to Faubion, "Tell me, what is American music like?"

Faubion said, "It is hard to describe like this, in words, but I can tell you this—I don't think it is as vibrant or magical as Balinese music."

"No, I agree. I have never heard American music, but I have a feeling that Balinese music is better."

In the afternoon he walked with us to a place about a mile from the *puri* where a waterfall had been channeled to make a small swimming pool. "We bathe in the river when we want to wash. This pool is for pleasure, not for washing."

That evening Chokorda Agung's uncle, old Chokorda Ngura, came from his courtyard to where we were sitting on Faubion's veranda. He felt that we were sufficiently settled, and had come to call on us. He was a tall, severe man, most fastidious in dress and

[207]

formal in manners. He wore a brown and white printed *kain* (as opposed to the commoner and cheaper sarongs which are tubular pieces of material) wrapped round his waist and falling in flawless pleats to his ankles. His headband was elaborately folded and decorated with a scarlet hibiscus. His nephew, Chokorda Agung, sat with us, too. His manner in front of the old man was entirely different. Deferential, quiet but, as always, exceedingly polite, he recounted everything he knew about us, so that Chokorda Ngura should know exactly what guests were under his roof. He called Faubion's servant, Kunter, and ordered *brum*, Bali's sweet, rather heavy rice wine, and served it to all of us.

After a while, the old man said, "Perhaps these young people would like to go and watch the dance rehearsal." That was our dismissal. We all bowed, wished him good night and went to the music society's pavilion. There in the half-light of Gusti Agung Ngura's compound, I saw my first Balinese dancing, and it was a remarkable experience. In the flickering lights and shadows of the little oil wicks, eight girls were dancing a *gabor*, the dance of the attendants of Kali, the goddess of death. I had expected something rather languorous and South-Sea-Islandish, instead of which the dance held more vitality than any I have seen. It was brilliant, angular, and infinitely powerful. It had the grace of great discipline and perfect technique, and none of the soft prettiness of less developed dancing. The music, too, was almost electric in its strength, with an extraordinary combination of precision and emotion. We walked home in the starlight to the receding sound of the flutes and bells. The deep note of the gongs reached us even after we were inside the *puri*.

65 Within a week our days began to take on a more regular pattern. Faubion, with constant practice, was already speaking Malay fluently again, and Clare and I found that we had to learn it, too, as nobody in Ubud, with the exception of Chokorda Agung, spoke English. Even Clare's firm prejudice against foreign languages began to break down, because Malay is simple to learn, and there seemed so much to talk to the Balinese about. Neither of us ever spoke it really well, but we learned enough to be able to conduct simple conversations and to get through the everyday details of life without appealing constantly to Faubion for help.

Mornings were busy times. While we were dressing and having breakfast, the little girls of the puri would come through carrying baskets on their heads. The baskets were filled with small dishes made of strips of banana leaves woven together. Each dish held a few grains of rice, some flowers and sometimes a chili. They would place them on the steps of the various pavilions or in the gateways. In each courtyard there are special pillars, about five feet high with a tiny shrine at the top, especially for offerings to the good spirits who live above. In the evenings the little girls would come again with more offerings, and this time they would be placed on the ground and in odd places about the puri. Those were to appease the bad spirits who live below, and were immediately eaten by stray dogs, or the puri hens if they happened to reach them first. Usually the girls would stay and talk for a few moments in the morning; they were the children of various retainers or relations who lived in the puri. Then they would hurry off saying they had to get ready for school.

A little later we would see the old Chokorda's two daughters, very neat and clean in their blue jackets and tightly wrapped kains, with flowers in their hair, walk through our courtyard on their way to school. They were the teachers.

Then the boys would come to clean the rooms and wash our clothes, and the clatter and the fragrance of the cooking would begin. When Gusti Agung Ngura had the food for lunch organized, cleaned and ready to cook, he would come and talk to us in Malay for a while in the morning. Clare and I were interested only in the conversation, so after we had finished Faubion would continue with the reading and writing. Meanwhile, since in Bali one always takes the shortest and most sensible path from place to place, flocks of geese would be driven through the *puri*, odd cows, pigs or hens would stray about—sometimes with a small boy watching them, and sometimes not. The fighting cocks would be brought out into the sunlight and be groomed, massaged and fed. Everybody, as they walked through, would stop to exchange a few words, relay a piece of gossip or ask some questions.

By eleven o'clock everyone was busy either in the fields, or with their animals, with work in the *puri*, or on errands to neighboring villages. The children were in school and the women did their household jobs. Faubion was studying, and Clare and I went for walks and explored the country around Ubud.

Light in Bali is like no other light that I have ever seen. It changes colors to curious Balinese versions of themselves, it gives a special radiance to skins, it washes over the land with a strange and beautiful distinctness. The landscape around Ubud is hilly, intensely cultivated, and with many trees. In any one view one sees very little of the sky. The curved, terraced *sawahs* (rice fields when they are filled with water) form great brilliant steps down the hillsides, so that much of the light is reflected from them, shining upward on trees and faces, instead of from more familiar angles. We used to spend hours walking along the ridges dividing the fields, and found new streams, different ravines and bathing places, little villages and temples, and never got tired of the *sawahs* themselves at all times of day and in any light.

Lunch, which Clare, Faubion and I ate in whichever courtyard happened to please us that day, was at about one o'clock. The food in the *puri* was Balinese, with slight concessions to Clare's and Faubion's foreign taste. With the usual chilies and spices we would have plenty of rice, of course; vegetables that we had never tasted before; and a great variety of meats, steamed in banana leaves or made as a sort of shashlik; eels, roast suckling pig, and many other things. Agung G'dé had caught an enormous bat, which he exhibited proudly to us one morning. Clare recoiled, and said, "Do take it away quickly."

We thought no more about it till that evening when Clare had an argument with Faubion about its size. She asked Agung G'dé if he

[210]

still had it to show Faubion. He looked most surprised and said, "But you ate it for lunch. Didn't you recognize the taste?"

The early afternoon was one's time for privacy. You could take a siesta if you felt like it, type notes or read, or merely sit in the courtyard and meditate. About half-past three or four, Ubud came to life again with a renewed burst of energy. The children came back from school and played in the courtyards or in the road. The men came back from the fields. The football society started its daily game on the village green. The girls went to their dance rehearsals. The women, with the day's chores behind them, visited each other, sat on their steps and talked with passers-by. The young men bought their jars of tuak, the local palm beer, and laughed together or gambled. Everyone was friendly, eager to discuss the day's events, full of plans for the next day, with the prospect of an amusing evening ahead.

Almost every evening there was some sort of entertainment, dances or a concert, or a play. In a social unit as small as Ubud, the people must contribute to the entertainment of the village, just as it is essential that they help each other with their work in the fields. Occasionally there was the excitement of dancers from another village coming to give a performance or a traveling group of players who would act all night in Ubud.

Faubion christened that time before sunset the "violent hour" because all of Ubud was so energetically engaged in one activity or another. As soon as it was dark, however, it was time for the quiet gossip, the timeless conversation, and the casual exchange of information. We had evolved our own cocktail from arak, which is distilled from rice wine, smells dreadful but tastes divine and is very strong, mixed with brum which made it sweet and milder. Tuak cost the equivalent of one American cent a bottle, and arak and brum were about twenty cents a bottle each. All transactions had to be in silver because in the villages of Bali they didn't trust paper money.

We ate dinner by oil light whenever we wanted it, depending on what time the dancing started afterward. The day ended either immediately after dinner or as soon as the entertainment was over.

[211]

Then we would walk back to our courtyards shouting to friends, "Safety in sleeping!" or "Safety in going home!" if they lived far from the *puri*.

66 One morning Kunter, one of the servants, sat in the sunlight gazing at what we thought was a lovely piece of Balinese carving. His round charming face was creased in concentration. He was a low-caste boy, with a bewitching smile, and was the most appealing of the young men in the *puri*.

Faubion pointed out to Clare and me, "Where in America would you find a servant so absorbed in the study of a work of art?" He called to Kunter to bring the carving over to us. Inexplicably embarrassed, Kunter walked slowly to the pavilion. Then we saw that he was holding a small mirror in a wooden frame. He had been gazing most intently at his own face, counting the pimples on it. He was very worried by them, he said; nobody else in Ubud had pimples.

We had ordered a taxi from Den Pasar that day to go down and buy some supplies, since we had decided to stay in Ubud. To cheer Kunter up, we asked if he would like to come with us.

"To Den Pasar?"

"Yes."

"In a car?"

"Yes, would you like to come?"

Chokorda Agung, who came in for the end of this conversation, told him to go and put on a shirt and borrow a sarong. He vanished almost before the Chokorda had finished speaking. Then we were told that Kunter had never been to Den Pasar before, and had never ridden in a car, so naturally he was incredulous.

We stopped at the Bali Hotel, and told Kunter that he could go off and explore the town and meet us at three oclock. But that was a little too much for him, and he crouched uncertainly on the steps of the terrace not knowing which way to go. Faubion called a *jongos* (room boy) and asked him to take care of Kunter. We gave him five guilders for his lunch, and fifty with which to buy us cigarettes

[212]

—really to give him the courage to go to the market and see how the big city operates.

He met us again at three with considerably more assurance. He had met a friend from a village near Ubud, had exchanged news in the market, had ridden in one of the horsecarts, and had had the enormous prestige of spending fifty guilders on cigarettes without a second thought. He could hardly wait to get back to Ubud because he wanted to tell the other boys about Den Pasar. He asked if he could go again the next time, and then suddenly decided that that might be selfish and added hurriedly that perhaps *after* the other boys had seen it. . . .

If you ask a Balinese how far away a certain place is, he will always give you the distance in terms of how long it takes to walk there. That evening Chokorda Agung told us that he was walking to Sayan, "which is one hour's distance from here," to find out precisely when the Sayan temple festival would take place. He wanted to tell the Ubud people what they could expect by way of dances at it. He took us, at a speed which left us gasping, across the *sawahs* to Sayan. There we went to call on the old and famous Chokorda Rai. One of the few Balinese who had ever been to Europe, a dancer so brilliant in his day that the older Balinese still compare young dancers with Chokorda Rai at his height.

He was a startlingly beautiful man, with sharp, experienced eyes. Tall and straight-backed he received us with the usual graciousness of the Balinese. With a liquid sweep of his dancer's hands he indicated that we should consider his *puri* our home. The servant at once brought fruit and *tuak*.

Faubion made a formal speech to the old man about how honored we were to meet so great a dancer.

"But now I am so old," said Chokorda Rai, "I have even lost the excitement of music, and that is the last thing to go."

"One can still tell from your walk," Faubion said, "that you must have been a prince among dancers as well as by rank."

The old man laughed with delight, and the wrinkles on his face showed for the first time, "I see that Tuan Bowers understands our dancing. Until one learns to walk like a Balinese, one can never dance like a Balinese." He turned politely to Clare, "And you, Miss Harris, are you happy in Bali?"

"I find it very beautiful," she said in her still uncertain Malay. Chokorda Rai looked cozily round his courtyard. "Yes, it is very beautiful. You must find it very pleasant after your own country," he said conversationally.

Clare began to bristle, "Have you ever been in America?"

"No, indeed. But I have been to Europe. I went with the dancers which the Dutch sent from here to the Paris exposition—ah, that is some years ago. I, too, found Bali very beautiful when I returned."

"Didn't you like Paris?"

"How can one like Paris? The cold is so barbaric that it freezes all feeling. One can neither be happy, nor can one—as young boys do—enjoy one's miseries. And besides it is such a dirty city. Can you believe it, Daiyu," he appealed to me with that Oriental solidarity I had come to expect, "the streets are so filthy that one would not consider walking barefoot there!"

But it turned out that he hadn't seen very much of Paris because the Dutch hadn't allowed the dancers to go anywhere. They were shuttled between the theater, rehearsals, performances and their hotel rooms, with no time to see Paris in between.

More *tuak* was brought in, and we sat and talked until after sunset. Finally Chokorda Agung asked the details he wanted to know about the festival.

"Is it something very special?" I asked.

"It is the usual six monthly festival that every temple in Bali has. It is very convenient. Since each temple is built at a different time, and every village has one or more temples, there is nearly always a festival going on somewhere near by. So we are never without entertainment."

At last we said good-by. We had hoped for the light of the moon to find our way back through the fields, but it had clouded over. Chokorda Rai sent one of his servants along with us. Carrying a big bamboo flame, he sang quietly as he walked ahead of us all the way home. The flame reflected and shivered in the water of the *sawahs*.

67 One of the characteristics of the Balinese which appealed most to me was their great chattiness and their complete willingness to sit down at any time and gossip for a while. Kunter would walk through the courtyard carrying two huge tins of water suspended on a bamboo pole across his shoulder. He would pause for a moment and watch Faubion studying Malay, and announce, "I am very happy."

"Why?" Faubion sounded startled the first time—unhappiness is usually the thing one comments on.

"I like living here and working here."

One can't say, "Why particularly today?" because after a while, "Why?" becomes a silly question, only to be answered with "Why not?" So one says, "That's nice."

And Kunter walks on saying, "I knew you would be pleased," or something of the sort.

As you go for a walk, almost anyone you pass might say, "Where have you been?" the standard Balinese opening.

You answer, "In the *puri*."

"And now you are going to the river to bathe?"

"No, just for a walk."

"I see you are seeking a black skin," this was usually said to Faubion who went about without a shirt trying to get sunburned.

Or, when we sat in the courtyard in the evenings, people always gathered around to talk. When one of them left to go and have his food or to do some duty, we would only have to ask of the group in general, "What is his name?" to hear his whole story, where he lived, what his parents were like, the fact that he used to be a thief when he was a little boy, but grew out of it, or that he could have been a good dancer but was too lazy, or that his fighting cocks were the best in Ubud, and so on until we changed the subject.

In the same way, everyone knew everything about us in a very short while, and Clare was considered most inhibited because she wasn't willing to discuss any detail that they happened to bring up.

One morning I went into the tooth-filing pavilion to watch a man who was painting gold designs on dance costumes for the music society. He smiled at me and said, "Are you well again?"

Rather startled I said, "Yes, quite well now." I had stayed in bed the previous day trying to get rid of a sick headache.

"That's good. I heard you were sick in your head and in your stomach."

"Yes, that's right."

"But you took medicine and are quite well now?"

"Yes, quite well."

Clearly it had been an item of gossip for the village.

Quite casually one morning, when Kunter was sitting on the steps of Faubion's porch listening to us practicing Malay, he started talking about himself. He worked for Chokorda Agung for nothing except his meals and a place to sleep. For a few hours every afternoon he worked in the rice fields and earned a little money from that. He did all this because his father had married again and the new wife was not kind to Kunter, so he didn't want to stay at home. He supported his mother who lived in a tiny shack in the village, and sometimes went back there at night so that she wouldn't be too lonely.

Some weeks before, one of the Chokorda's guests had given Kunter seventeen guilders as a tip and, suddenly rich, he went out and bought himself a new sarong for twelve guilders.

"Is that expensive?" Faubion asked.

"Oh, no!" Kunter smiled his wide charming smile at Faubion's ignorance. "That is a very good bargain. I only got it as cheap as that because it was secondhand, and a little torn." With the rest of the money he bought staples for his mother.

Faubion gave him a shirt that he had worn only once because it was too small for him. We never saw Kunter wearing it, and for days we couldn't decide whether it was because he had had sense enough to sell it (he would have got fifteen or twenty guilders for it in the market), or whether he was saving it for a special occasion, or whether he was afraid to wear it in case the Chokorda thought he had asked Faubion for it. Much later we discovered that he didn't wear it in the *puri* because he didn't want the other boys to feel left out.

Kunter didn't smoke or drink. His chief amusement seemed to be sitting on the steps—carefully at a lower level than us, always, because he was low caste—and watching us and smiling whenever he caught anyone's eye.

Clare asked him once, "Why do you smile at me?"

Kunter said, "Because I am happy."

68 The dance performance for which the music society had been practicing was held in the outer court of Chokorda Agung's *puri*, in front of Faubion's living pavilion. The village crowded in, and perched themselves on walls, in the watching pavilions, on the steps, ground, wherever there was room. Immediately several little stands selling peanuts and biscuits and fruit were set up outside the big gate. There, by lamplight, the infinitely fine texture of Balinese skins in their many shades of brown showed up with sudden beauty. The orchestra began the "entrance music" which signals to the village that the show is about to begin, and then progressed to the music for the *baris*, the first part of the dance, a section taken from *Gatojatya Seraya*, a Hindu-Javanese historical dance of the thirteenth century.

It is the story of Prince Abhimanyu, the son of Arjuna who is a page at the court of his uncle and has fallen in love with the Princess Siti Sundari. When he hears that another marriage has been arranged for her, he goes at once to Siti Sundari to tell her the bad news.

First, attendants appear to announce the arrival of the prince, then Abhimanyu himself, a magnificent and terrifying dancer, arrives, and dances in anger while he waits for the princess to keep the tryst.

Siti Sundari was played by the most beautiful girl in Ubud. When she appears there is an enchanting love dance between her and the prince. Suddenly one of the servants gives an alarm and the prince is forced to take flight with his servants following after.

On their way they are caught in a thunderstorm and take shelter in a graveyard. The prince falls asleep in a sort of bower made of bamboo and banana leaves which the children had helped to build in the courtyard that afternoon.

The graveyard belongs to the goddess of the dead, Durga. She has sent six of her handmaidens to look for corpses for her to eat. Then comes the dreamy, and incredibly lovely gabor, which we had watched in rehearsal.

During their search, the girls find the prince and his attendants, and call Durga's chief handmaiden, Kalika, to come and see. Kalika arrives in the terrifying form of a witch. Enormous, dressed in billowing rags and horrid bits of cloth, with her long gray hair flying wildly about, and great claws on her hands, she brings with her several attendants—dogs, monkeys and other animals. She wants to kill the prince, but she can't because he is a descendant of the gods and only Durga can do such a thing.

Instead she wakens the prince and leads him to Durga. In this dance Durga takes the form of Bali's most important and most frightening witch, Rangda. Even larger than her handmaiden, with streaming white hair and a hideous mask, enormous teeth and long wicked nails on her hands, she threatens the prince.

The children in the crowd sat with fascinated eyes (although they must have seen this dance before), still uncertain whether this was a real witch or make-believe. There was dead silence while Rangda advanced on the prince.

In terror the prince calls out the name of his father, Arjuna, and suddenly the witch stops, because in the past Arjuna has done her a great favor so she cannot kill his son. But Rangda is not sure whether this really is the son. She tells the prince to prove his parentage. Arjuna was a magnificent dancer, one of the greatest in the old legends. If the prince can dance as well as Arjuna, and prove his parentage in that way, then Rangda will spare him.

This, of course, is the moment for the dancer to show his greatest virtuosity, as indeed he does, and satisfies Rangda who then shows him a safe way to return home.

The whole thing is a combination of dancing and drama. The

dance of the *gabor* girls, the love scene and the final exhibition are the high points of the dance side of it. The moment where the prince goes to sleep in the graveyard is a great place for comedy. The timid attendants start at every noise, frighten each other while they are trying to keep watch, and fumble about in what is supposed to be total darkness. The arrival of the animal-servants of Kalika were an eternal delight to the children, while the courtiers in the beginning have plenty of opportunity for ad-libbing and general fooling about.

The costumes, gold-painted and very rich looking, showed up beautifully in the lamplight, and all the headdresses were made of flowers. The girls had, as well, flowers entwined in their hair and streaming down their backs, mostly frangipani, jasmine and hibiscus. It took about an hour for each girl to construct her high, elaborate headdress of flowers. It could only be used once.

Faubion, naturally, had been going to rehearsals every evening, and had already made friends with most of the dancers. Iruju, the stocky, brilliant one who danced the part of the prince, came to talk to us after the performance.

He perched on the steps in the usual way, smoking the strong, conical Balinese cigarettes which smell of cloves and cinnamon. "Tomorrow," he said, "I must leave Ubud. I must go to Sakti."

"Where is that?" Faubion asked. "Is it far from here?"

"No, only about half an hour. But I must go for several days and I am unhappy to leave Ubud. I like to live here and dance in the evenings."

It seemed that there was to be a temple festival soon in Sakti, and of course they had to have dances for it. Iruju, whose reputation as a *baris* dancer was greater than anybody's in that area, had been asked to go to Sakti to train the dancers. They had always been too poor before to have a music society, but now they had just started one, and Iruju was to go and give lessons.

"But if you are so unhappy at going," I said, "why not send someone else. Why should you go?"

"Oh I couldn't do that. Everybody must have a time to show off, and this is the time for Sakti to show off, so of course I must help to teach them."

"It sounds very interesting," I said, "I would love to come and watch."

He looked very pleased. "Really would you? I will come at seven tomorrow evening to take you. Will you come?"

"Thank you very much. I will be ready at seven."

The next evening he came. Faubion who had hurt his foot (a tragedy which in Bali means complete loss of movement because one walks everywhere), was unable to go. Clare and I went with Kunter and Iruju, walking across miles of sawahs, extraordinary and lovely in the starlight. Iruju, walking in front, caught fireflies and put them inside his shirt so that their flashing and flickering gave us a dim illumination to see the narrow path. Kunter, walking behind us, shouted out to people across the sawahs, or to people who passed us on the way, to tell them who we were and where we were going.

Sakti was a very poor village. It could afford only a very small gamelan (orchestra,) and very poor clothes. Clearly the people had to work so hard that they hadn't time to practice their music and dancing. Iruju must have told very grand stories about his foreign friends who were coming to watch, because the entire village had turned out to welcome us. The chief men of the village solemnly took us to their rather battered practice shelter where a bench had been placed for us to sit. Somehow the village had scraped together a couple of plates and spoons, and they served us sliced papaya with sugar on it (a great luxury), and coconut milk for which they had one glass and one cup without a handle. An extra lantern was brought for us to see the dancing better.

Iruju was a good teacher, severe, but understanding. All the teaching was done by imitation, a considerable contrast with the intellectual teaching of the West. After the children have learned the whole dance, they may improvise, add frills and special things of their own. The little pupils worked very hard, small brown faces intent, all their concentration on watching Iruju—and of course watching Iruju was an eternal pleasure—they were clearly conscious of what a great privilege it was to be taught by him.

Faubion is in the habit of saying that rehearsals are much more fun to watch than finished performances because you get a clearer idea of the construction of the dance. In Sakti I began to agree. Leg and body movements which are apt to be covered up by the grand costumes of a formal performances. That way, with the boys dancing in just a sarong hitched up high, and the girls scantily clad, one could see the whole moving line of their bodies, and it was really beautiful.

Several hours later we thanked the Sakti people and left. Iruju stayed on to complete the rehearsal. All the way back Kunter sang the gabor music to us, and led us, in his casual sure-footed way, along the sawah ridges.

Thinking about the rehearsal, Clare said, "It looks so difficult, I would never be able to learn dancing."

Kunter said, "If you are happy you can always learn to dance."

69 Chokorda Alit, was a slender busy young man, with a vaguely tired manner. He lived behind Chokorda Agung's puri and we used to see him quite often hurrying through the courtyard. He would nod and smile at us in an abstracted way, but seldom stopped to talk. One evening we discovered what it was that occupied his time so fully. He kept fighting cocks and crickets. He came up of his own accord and sat on the porch with us.

"Yesterday," he said, "I was so depressed I could scarcely eat my dinner because I lost two hundred guilders in the cockfights. But today I am very pleased. Not only have I won back the money, but I have made sixty-five extra!"

"How very exciting," Faubion said, "I have never seen a cricket fight."

Chokorda Alit produced a little bamboo tube and removed from it the wad of banana leaves which acted as a cork. Out of it marched his prize fighting cricket. "It is very fierce," he said, his face lighting up with affection. "With this one I will surely win." He stroked back the wings of the little insect, and gently put it back in its bamboo tube. "You have no cricket fights in America?" he asked.

"No, unfortunately."

[221]

"No cockfights either?"

"Not even cockfights."

"But then, what do you do with all your chickens?"

"Well, we keep them for eating, or for eggs."

"How strange," Chokorda Alit said, his voice full of sympathy.

After that, the ice seemed to be broken and we saw him often, and got to know him almost better than anyone else in Ubud. He was the first to ask us to stop using his title and call him Alit, and the one we always turned to with our eternal demands, questions and requests for explanations. I always felt it was something of a triumph for us because he was by nature a retiring and a lonely person and had, to an exaggerated extent, that peculiarly Balinese quality of gentleness and grace which foreigners often mistake for softness.

70 A few days after our visit to old Chokorda Rai of Sayan, he came to repay the call, and to invite us to a dance in Sayan the next night. He had been too polite to ask me questions about India and Hinduism the first time we met, but this time his full interest came out and he exhausted my feeble knowledge of Malay with his questions. What happens in India when a Brahmin marries a low caste? What is the caste of the children? What happens if a raja marries a low caste? How is the head wife chosen? The best I could do was to turn the questions back to him and ask, "How is it in your country?"

"Ah, if a daiyu here marries a low caste, then she must be made dead to her own caste. To do that she is driven three times round the temple by the priest and then hit three times with a special kind of leaf, and that means that she is dead to her caste and must always live as a low caste. After that people must address her in the low form 'you,' and she must speak low Balinese for 'I,' but she must address others in high Balinese for she is no longer a Brahmin. It is a satisfactory system because then she can stay in the village and continue her life in a new status. Otherwise she would have to leave because she would belong to no caste and," he said as though it were an accepted fact, "one is always sorry to have to live in a new village."

The old man sat easily upright, his back never touched the back of the chair. Occasionally he leaned forward on the cane on which he rested both his hands. He looked particularly elegant, in formal dress—a *kain* with a *saput* (a folded waist cloth) over it, flowers in his hair and perfume on his forehead. His thin, precise hands, made none of the nervous and meaningless gestures of our own more hectic civilizations. And he had a poise and a dignity for which one could only be thankful because it lent us some of his restfulness. He never left his village without a servant so, as always, one of the Sayan boys sat on the steps of the porch with Kunter and Agung G'dé and some of the other boys from the village had drifted in. Our conversation was conducted with the complete lack of privacy which makes the Balinese feel cozy, and disturbs them not at all.

We had sent out for *arak* and *brum*, and occasionally Chokorda Rai would speak to his servant who would hand him a cigarette. Then he continued his questions. We were talking about Gandhi when Chokorda Agung came out from one of the inner courtyards and joined us.

"What do you think made Gandhi a great man?" Chokorda Rai asked.

I gave a few ordinary, rather dull reasons.

Chokorda Agung sprang to his feet, "No! The thing that made him great was that when the most important people came to see him they found him dressed like a peasant, sometimes without sandals, with only a banana leaf to keep the sun from his head. To be as humble as that, you must be great." He sat down and added rather sadly, "If I were to do that my people would not respect me. You must have a great spirit to be both humble and respected."

We had a charming moment when Chokorda Agung looked round his *puri* in a pleased way and said, "Do the princes in India have such houses?"

I stared at the pavilions and thatched roofs, growing shadowy as the last of the evening sun left the courtyard, and said carefully, "I have never seen one as beautiful as this. . ." unable to describe the obviously unimagined splendor and lavishness of Indian palaces.

"But," he insisted, "are they *like* this?"

I replied finally, "No, they are not built in courtyards like this."

Chokorda Rai leaned forward on his cane and asked, "Which is the richest raja in India?"

"The Nizam of Hyderabad, I should think. He is the richest man in the world."

"In the whole world?"

"Yes."

"He has more cars, more money, more wives?"

"Well, he certainly has a good many."

"Is he also," Chokorda Rai asked me with his tone of voice to consider the matter carefully, "a good man?"

"I think he is a bad ruler because he is unfair to his people and does not put his great wealth to help them, although he gets his wealth *from* them."

"Indeed. And he is a Hindu?" The old man sounded severe.

"No, Moslem."

"Ah! Islam. . . ."

They went on with their questions until I said, "I wish you could come to India. I am sure you would love it."

"Oh no, no," Chokorda Agung said quickly. "That is not possible. I cannot leave Bali. Once I went to Java, and I was never so unhappy. There everything is different, it is not beautiful, and the people look so lonely as if they had no friends. I missed my home very much and came back as soon as I could."

"Wouldn't you like to travel at all," Clare asked with surprise. "What about America?"

"Never, never. I do not want to go to America. The only thing that would persuade me to go would be if I could share our beautiful dancing with them. But where would I ever find a Balinese dancer that would be prepared to leave Bali?"

Later in the evening, when we had all had a good deal more *arak* and had sent Kunter out for yet another bottle of *brum*, and Chokorda Rai had sung us a little song, we somehow got on to the subject of abduction, which Chokorda Agung told us was a fairly ordinary part of life in Bali. Laughing merrily he told us how he had abducted his second wife, and had even abducted wives for his servants.

"Of course," he added, "it depends on whether the servant and the woman he wants are good people, otherwise I would not go to all that trouble to do it."

"How do you abduct people?" I asked, not quite certain whether or not he was joking.

"Well, these days one does it in a car. Suppose you want a village woman, you take a car and park it under a tree on market day. She comes to market carrying things on her head. Then as she passes the car you reach out and pull her in. She doesn't even have time to shout. Usually she thinks first of the things she is carrying, and by then it is too late. We drive off."

"Suppose she doesn't want to come?" Clare said, her feminist instincts well to the fore.

Chokorda Agung looked puzzled, "But of course she doesn't want to come. Why else would we abduct her?" Then, by way of explanation to a rather stupid foreigner, "How can she protest when it is a chokorda that abducts her? If I am of a higher caste, she should be pleased."

"Can you kidnap a high-caste woman that way?" Clare found it hard to believe all this.

Chokorda Agung burst out laughing and pointed to Chokorda Rai. "Not so long ago his niece was abducted by my nephew. She is happy now."

"But can't the girl run away? This is a small island. She could go back to her parents."

"No, no, how could she? If after three days the man has not made her happy, she may return. But longer than that, and she must stay with the man."

"Well," said Clare, pink with indignation, "that's very barbaric. The girl you kidnaped for your servant, for instance, what happened to her?"

"She cried a greal deal at first and came to me and asked me to send her back, but the next day she stopped crying, and now she lives in the puri with her husband."

"But why can't you arrange a proper marriage? Why not give the girl some choice?"

"I told you," Chokorda Agung said patiently, "that way she would not come. In the end she is happy, why should she not be kidnaped? Only because of some childish whim or preference? Besides, it is less expensive. There are not the before-wedding feasts."

"I see," said Clare, not seeing at all. "But in that case, why don't you kidnap every pretty girl you see?"

"What would I do with so many girls? How could I support them?"

"Don't the parents ever object?"

"No. Usually they know about it and are quite pleased. Specially if it is a high-caste man that takes the girl."

"Well," Faubion said, "I must say, I call that a sensible system." Clare turned on him, "Oh Faubion! How can you joke about it? It's terrible!"

"I am not joking," Faubion said, "it does seem sensible to me when I think of all the silly nonsense that goes on in our country, Clare. Before you get married, for instance, you go to considerable time, trouble and expense to fool a man into thinking you glamorous, intelligent and worth supporting for the rest of your life. He, meanwhile, tries to make you think him attractive, successful and worldywise. In short, you are both pretending to be a higher caste than you are. Here, at least they don't do that. Here, at least it's straightforward and honest. And in the end you get married with only a slightly better knowledge of your husband than an abducted Balinese girl has."

"I call that," said Clare grandly, "very specious reasoning. The point is that you do it of your own free will."

"That's not what the psychologists would have you think in these compulsive days. And anyway, how many American husbands and wives discover, after all that fuss and bother, that they don't like each other after all."

"But it's their own choice—" Clare began desperately.

"Oh God!" Faubion interrupted. "I'm all in favor of a system that saves you from the idiocies of your own choice."

Chokorda Agung, rather bewildered by this conversation, was turning his face from Faubion to Clare as though he were at a tennis match.

Clare appealed to him, "Suppose it were to happen to your own daughter?"

He smiled, "I hope not."

"But it could happen, and what would you do?"

"If the man were the same caste, then I wouldn't mind too much. If it was suitable, that would be all right."

"But if he were of a lower caste?"

"That couldn't happen."

"But if it should?"

"No, I do not think that will happen."

71 The next evening we went to the dance in Sayan. Faubion borrowed a bicycle because he couldn't walk that far on his injured foot, and Clare and I went along with Chokorda Agung and Iruju who had no lessons in Sakti that day.

The joget, which is the name of both the dance and the dancer, is really simply a flirt dance. There is some slender story about a girl who becomes possessed of an evil spirit and acquires an extraordinary and seductive beauty. She calls men from the audience to dance with her, they cannot resist her, but she turns them all down. However, the one she allows closest to her during the dance is the one she likes best. The men can choose what style they will dance in, some are funny, some passionate, some cold, some warlike, and some just bad dancers. Naturally it is a terrific opportunity for the young men of the village to display their prowess; equally, it requires great virtuosity on the part of the joget; she must follow the dancing of the man she has called, but she must never allow him to touch her.

The music, which was my favorite of all Balinese music, is played on an all-bamboo gamelan of xylophones and flutes. Mostly it is very gay, but in parts of the dance there are strange, attenuated passages where the melody becomes almost too faint and wandering for recognition, then suddenly snaps back into excitement as the *joget* calls another man out of the audience.

After some of the Sayan boys had danced, we insisted on Iruju's going in, too. He was very shy because it wasn't his village, and he didn't want the other young men to think that he was usurping their territory. Finally we did make him go in, but he was still too shy to do more than circle widely around the *joget*. Chokorda Agung lost his patience in the excitement of having a boy from his village compete with the Sayan boys, and shouted, "Get closer! Get so close that you can smell her!"

The crowd was delighted and screamed with laughter, but poor Iruju was so embarrassed that he ended the dance at once and came to sit down with us. At that moment the *joget* came whirling up to Faubion with that extraordinarily suggestive trembling of an eyebrow which represents the invitation to dance with her. The crowd, of course, was on her side and shouted to Faubion to get up and dance. He said he couldn't because of his hurt foot. Luckily for him he had a reasonable excuse, because to the Balinese it is inconceivable that *everyone* should not know how to dance. Whether you do it well or badly, naturally, depends on your talent, but they simply don't understand somebody who doesn't dance at all—as surprised as an American would be if another American didn't know how to read. Any part in any village dance performances, for instance, can be filled in by a member of the audience in case the best dancer for that part is ill or away. You must, in Bali, be as well trained to entertain your neighbors as you are to work for your living. It is a necessary part of community life.

Bali is really a country of amateurs, which I think is ideal. Their artists are amateurs only in the sense that they paint or dance because they love it, not because they lack proficiency. If they can earn something by selling a painting or teaching dancing, that is just something extra to be thankful for. Their real job is cultivating the land and tending their animals. Art is important in their

[228]

lives because it is their greatest pleasure, and their chief spare-time occupation. Everybody is an artist of some sort because it is considered a necessary part of their normal development. Patronage of the artist by the chokordas and the rajas is an important part of the system, too. Other Balinese very seldom buy a picture, for instance. Either one of the family paints one, if decoration is required in the house, or a neighbor will come in and do one for them in exchange for a bunch of bananas or some coconuts.

There are, perhaps, half a dozen painters in Bali who can earn their living by painting full time. Among them, one of the best-known and brilliant artists was Idé Bagus Madé who lived in Ubud. Idé Bagus is a title meaning that a man's caste is Brahmin. Chokorda Alit brought him to call on us one day, and we sat all afternoon talking about his painting.

"What," asked Faubion, "in your opinion makes a good artist?"

Idé Bagus Madé, in his timid way said, "His thoughts must be good."

"If you were to teach a child painting, how would you begin?"

"I would teach him first to draw animals because that is what a child thinks about and likes."

"Which do you think is more important, drawing or painting?"

"Drawing, of course. By that you can tell how a man thinks. Color is his feeling. To be an artist at all his heart must be good, so color will be easy for him. But to the *real* artist, it is the discipline that makes him great."

"But when you use a color, why do you never use oils?"

"I use Balinese colors [tempera] because oil is like a motorcar—too shiny."

"Do you prefer to paint landscapes or still life?"

Idé Bagus Madé looked confused, "I do not understand. A picture must have life in it, and life is the people and the country. If I draw trees or a *sawah* there must be men in the fields or animals under the trees. That is how life is."

"How did you begin to paint?"

"How? Well I just started." He had occasional lessons from a local teacher in between his appointed work in the village, and

[229]

happened to excel in such a startling way that he had enough orders from chokordas and foreigners to spend most of his time in painting.

Alit, laughing at Faubion, said, "You ask such Western questions."

"But it's important," Faubion said, "to know how an artist functions."

Alit shrugged his shoulders, "It's his nature. What is there to ask about?"

"You're probably right," Faubion agreed thoughtfully. "I wish I understood why one makes such a song and dance about it in the West—books of criticism, essays on esthetics, what is good and what is bad, and heaven knows what. Every magazine must have a certain space devoted to criticism of art recently produced."

"That is very strange," Alit said. "Can't people judge for themselves?"

"Apparently not. They are afraid of being accused of bad taste."

"If you will forgive me," Alit said extremely politely, "I only bring this matter up because you seem worried by it, but I think I understand why it is so. In the West you cannot understand your own art because your artists are always the people who cannot fit normally into their society."

"Yes," Faubion said eagerly, "they are the maladjusted ones— sexually or socially or someway."

"So," Alit continued very gently, "is it not the art of frustration? To produce art, or to appreciate it should be the normal function of a man—in a normal society. It should be a part of one's daily living."

"How do you suppose it has happened that art has become abnormal in the West?"

"I have never been there so I cannot really tell. But I should think it is because your children always seem to have so much that they must do, and so much that they mustn't do, and they do not understand why. After such a childhood it becomes impossible for them to express themselves naturally. I say this very lightly because I have seen only a few foreign children. I may be mistaken."

[230]

72 One afternoon I was sitting on the steps in the outer courtyard of the *puri* watching the children play a rather involved game with sticks and stones. Several of the young girls who dance in the *gabor* were sitting with me trying to explain the game. They heard someone address me as Daiyu. One of them said, "Are you truly a daiyu?" puzzled that I am a Hindu, but not Balinese. The outside world is apt to mean only Java.

"Yes," I said.

Another girl moved over next to me and said, "I am a daiyu, too." The others moved respectfully down a step.

Chokorda Agung came up and asked me to pay a formal call on his wife. I followed him rather nervously to the courtyard where his first wife lived. I had seen her before, but I had never had the courage to do more than greet her as she seemed rather distant.

Anak Agung Rai was small, slender and with enormous elegance. Apparently it was to be a very formal occasion because she was wearing Javanese clothes—an exquisitely draped *kain* with many tiny pleats ironed into the folds in front, all sharp and precise, a well-cut jacket, and high-heeled Surakarta slippers of green leather embroidered with gold, very unusual for Ubud. Her face had the sort of distinguished ugliness that immediately intimidates servants and foreigners, and puts children on their best behavior. Her hair was smooth, lacquered and very simply dressed. She seemed to have none of the ease and graceful casualness that I had come to associate with Balinese women, although she was exceedingly polite—without warmth.

She offered me fruit and coffee, and asked to be assured of our comfort in the *puri*, and then there was a frightful pause while I tried to think of polite phrases in Malay. At last I said, lamely, that her clothes were beautiful.

"I seldom wear these," she said, "as I do not like clothes bought in the market. I prefer to wear *kains* that I make myself. It is the

[231]

great pride of a Balinese woman to be able to weave her own *kains*. I make all my own, and even some for friends as presents."

All the material used as upholstery and for cushions in the *puri* was woven by her. "I like all my linen, sheets and tablecloths to be handmade, too," she said, "that is why there is always work. I never have time to sleep in the afternoons." She attended to the making of the offerings, too, though the lesser offerings are delegated to the second wife. "People in Bali," she told me severely, "can't stop their work even if it takes them until late at night."

She tried to get to bed by nine o'clock, though when there was dancing "it is considered proper that I go. My husband is much interested in those things." She continued in a politely explanatory way, "In Bali, women are under orders from their husband. Even for my pleasures I must follow his wishes. Foreign women do what they themselves please, is there any joy in that?"

As long as we were on the subject of husbands and wives, I ventured a question about her own marriage, and learned that she was a cousin of Chokorda Agung's, and that their marriage had been arranged by her parents. Though she had seen Chokorda Agung, "I did not think it right to look in his direction."

"In India," I said hopefully, "the dowry and the trousseau are an important part of the marriage." (What my Malay actually managed was, "the money and the clothes are number one. . . .")

"Here, too," she said, "a girl's father must give her cloth to take to her husband's house." With a touch of pride she told me that she had come with ten full sets of special clothes, and many sarongs for ordinary wear. Her in-laws gave her money and jewelry. After her marriage, all the money in the house was handled by the chokorda, although the running of the *puri* was entirely in her hands. When you get married you must think only of your husband's family, and regulating his household is your highest duty.

Anak Agung Rai's day started late for a Balinese because her husband did not have to work in the fields. She bathed, said her prayers, and every fifth day made offerings. Then she made breakfast for her husband—rice and a full meal, although she herself had only coffee. She saw that the food for the day was prepared and the vessels cleaned, gave orders to the nine servants of the *puri*, did her weaving and any other work that might come up. Only on festival days did she pay calls at other *puris*.

"You must," I said at last, "find foreigners like us very strange. Our manners are so different."

For the first time during the visit she smiled, "Foreign manners are good—for foreigners."

73 A minor scandal happened in Ubud. One of the little *gabor* dancers had been kidnaped by a man from a near-by village. Kunter told us about it when we were walking to see the work of some wood carvers. He said it was a pity because Ubud had lost a very good dancer. "Besides," he said, "it is very bad because she is still young, she hasn't become sick yet."

We were all shocked. "Can't her parents do something about it?"

"Well, she is the daughter of a lover, so naturally her mother's husband will do nothing."

"But her mother? Surely she must want to rescue her child."

"I don't know about that. She pretends she knew nothing about it before it happened."

"What is the point of kidnaping such a young girl?" Faubion asked. "I mean, surely, er—can one . . ." his sentence trailed off.

"Sleep with her?" Kunter said. "Yes, why not? But it is not good, because it means she will have a baby too soon, as soon as it is possible. Such a child is weak and thin, and never healthy."

We were all silent at this unexpected point of view. Clare said at last, "Poor child, she must be very miserable."

"For a few days she will weep. They have a house to themselves, and I think when they are alone in the evenings, then she will be happier. They will sit together, outside in the night, and then they will go inside. In the end she will be happy again."

That evening Sakti had its festival for which Iruju had been training the dancers. We were all invited to go, and many of the Ubud people went with us to see how effective Iruju's training had been. Sakti danced quite well, but Ubud was scornful and apt to titter. The girls said that the Sakti gabor had no grace, and all the dancers were very nervous. They had borrowed extra instruments from Ubud for their gamelan and were clearly proud, though shaky, over their dance festival.

Iruju said that there was talent there. One boy might turn out to be very good indeed, and most of the others would, at any rate, be adequate. Clare came away very cross, saying that Ubud was smug and irritatingly pleased with itself. It was a difficult point to accept that in Bali it is perfectly all right to laugh when you think something is done badly. There is no coddling and flattery of children. If they don't like to be laughed at or criticized, let them learn to do it well.

74 We had been in Ubud about a month when Chokorda Agung suggested that we accompany him to Singaraja, which is in the far north of Bali, a five-hour journey from Ubud over the mountains. He said, "Daiyu, I want you to meet one of the most famous men of Bali, Anak Agung Wayan Panyu Tysna. He is the elder brother of the raja of Singaraja, which is the richest of all the eight provinces of Bali. He renounced his throne and gave it to his brother because that position kept him from living as he wanted —with his people—and gave him too many duties so that he had no time for his real work which is education and village reconstruction. I want you to meet him because he studied in your country."

Driving north to Singaraja the scenery changed gradually from the terraced sawahs and orderly coconut groves of south Bali to the dry areas and pine forests of the mountains, and back again to the plains of north Bali. The tiny island contains within its hundred miles of length the most complete variety and sufficiency that nature and luck could have provided: mountains, lakes, rivers, plains, the ocean and useful luxuriant vegetation and an easy, semitropical climate. Commercially it has been fortunate in the absence, in an

[234]

otherwise exceptionally endowed island, of gold, spices, precious stones and petroleum—none of the lures for an exploiter, and none of the causes of money becoming overimportant in the social order.

Anak Agung Wayan Panyu Tysna turned out to be a middle-aged man. He was eager to talk about his work and to show us some of his projects. I asked him how he came to study in India, and he replied that to do his work effectively he thought he should collect new ideas abroad. He had heard that the place to study was Europe, so he decided to go there. On his trip he landed in India, met some people that interested him, thought that probably conditions in India were closer to conditions in Bali, came in contact with people engaged in rural reconstruction, and so he spent all his time in India. He had not yet managed to get to Europe.

When he returned to Bali he began putting his schemes into practice. He built schools in the city of Singaraja as well as in the villages. In these, the concentration was on agricultural improvement and practical education. Dutch was not compulsory. He built, as well, libraries and experimental farms.

He told me that he wanted to go back to India for a few months "because I have heard that your new government in concerning itself very much with such problems," he said in English. "You come here to learn, I go to your country to learn. Is it not strange?" He saw the rise of Bali's population leading to an eventual dearth of food, so he had a sense of urgency about getting his work well begun and if possible spreading it to other parts of Bali to counteract this menace of the future. "But a rich country is often lazy."

He showed us around his primary school. It was eight months old and was built very cheaply because much of the work was contributed free. "The people are glad to help build schools." There were eighty students in the school who came mostly from the villages around Singaraja. The school provided them with a place to stay, and that is why the numbers were limited.

From his new teacher's training school, girls were to be sent out to village schools after they graduated. It had fifty-eight students between the ages of seventeen and nineteen, and the requirements for entering it were that you have six years schooling and must come from a village and eventually teach in a village. The school undertook to find them employment afterwards and to arrange for their living in Singaraja.

Talking to one of the instructors later, Clare said, "Are your students interested in politics at all? Do you have classes in current affairs?"

He looked startled and said, "About politics we cannot speak to the students." After a pause, "It is too dangerous."

"But do they read newspapers, and show an interest?"

"I suppose," he said cautiously, "that they read the papers of both sides, but I do not dare to ask the students."

"Why? Is there pressure from the Dutch Government?"

He wouldn't answer that, but after a moment he said explosively, "Please understand, all of us, students and teachers, are for independence. Every child is for independence."

As we were spending the night in Singaraja, we went to the *pasar malam* (a combination of a bazaar and dances which takes place in the evening), and saw the north Bali versions of dances we knew from Ubud, and gambled in the little Chinese stands. In Singaraja, Bali's biggest port, the Chinese control 90 per cent of the shipping, most of the business, and are the moneylenders because they have a sense of capitalism and a business acumen which the Balinese entirely lack.

We drove back to Ubud the next afternoon, and immediately were surrounded by people asking questions about our trip. Then they told us that because Alit had been lucky at the cockfights he had decided to give Ubud a treat. That night there was to be a wayang wong, an early Hindu form of dance drama performed by strolling companies of players. The stories are the usual ones of Rama and Sita, Arjuna who appears often as the embodiment of all male grace, and the very popular part about the army of monkeys and their king, Hanuman. They play in masks and there is quite a ritual connected with these masks because they are sacred. They are kept on golden sticks dug into the ground behind the orchestra, and as the masks are needed in the action, little boys go behind the orchestra, put on the required masks very solemnly. Then they walk slowly in a curious rhythmic step across the dance floor and present the masks to the players. The conversations between the leading characters are half sung and half spoken, while the comedy parts are almost all ad-libbing.

The performance began at ten in the evening and ended at about four the next morning.

75 We had been in Chokorda Agung's *puri* for nearly five weeks when we decided that since we were clearly not going to leave Ubud, we might just as well rent a house there and settle down for a few more months. We asked Chokorda Agung what we should do about it, and he undertook to arrange the whole matter for us, and to engage servants.

"But we mustn't put you to so much trouble—" I began.

"No," he interrupted, "it is better that I arrange it. The village must not think you are leaving the *puri* because there is any breach between us."

That afternoon I went down to the swimming place and spent a couple of hours with some little boys who were playing there. They showed me how to slither down the hillside over a sharp drop straight into the pool. In return I showed them how to swim what Wellesley used to call "the six-beat crawl." They learned in about ten minutes, and then complimented me on this efficient Western style of swimming.

By the time I got back to the *puri*, Chokorda Agung had made all the necessary arrangements for our house. His cousin Chokorda Raké had a small house which he didn't use. Servants had been informed. In a couple of days it would be cleaned and ready for us. He had never before rented the house, but since we were so happy in Ubud he didn't want us to leave and had made an exception. Then with no warning Chokorda Agung turned to Faubion, "I have talked to so many people in the village and they like you because they feel you are one of them. You understand this pleases me very much because, since you are a friend of mine, if they did not like you I would have to tell you."

It took no time at all for the news that we were renting a house to be all over Ubud. That evening Faubion's porch was crowded with people asking questions and giving advice.

About the middle of May we moved into our new house which was charming, white-washed and furnished in an offhand, comfortable way. It had a bathroom (a great luxury), three bedrooms, two sitting rooms, two verandas, a well in the courtyard which everyone in the surrounding houses used, trotting casually through our cannas, a private path down to the bathing place in the river, two chrysanthemums (very rare), and an enormous stuffed lizard for good luck which our landlord, Chokorda Raké, had hung in the living room. In front of the house there was a terrace, with a balustrade decorated with rather lovely stone figures, which gave on to the road, and a separate paved sitting-out place in the front garden. In the back courtyard there was a thing which Faubion, in some sort of an architectural seizure, called a belvedere. But the best thing of all, Kunter assured us as we were leaving, was that the house had the most splendid view in Ubud.

I looked carefully for the view as soon as we got there. On one side of the house was Chokorda Raké's puri, on the other a high wall to give us privacy from the people going down the ravine to the bathing place. The back veranda opened on to a walled courtyard in which were family shrines, the well, and the belvedere, while the front garden was bounded by the main road which led to Den Pasar.

"Where," I asked Kunter, "is the view?"

"But, of course, here," he pointed to the main road. "You can see any car go by, the people go to market along this road, any stranger in Ubud must pass here. And then your house is exactly across the road from the alun-alun [village green] so you can watch all the games, dances, and fights and anything else that happens there from your own front steps."

I saw his point. The only problem was to find room on our front steps, as the entire village, of course, knew of their convenient location, so they were eternally covered with serried ranks of children during the day and adults in the evenings. This was very pleasant and friendly as we heard all the news and gossip, and had, besides, a constant source of messengers to run errands. ("Buy me some peanuts if you are going that way," "We have run out of matches," "Are you going through the *puri*? Take this message to Chokorda Agung.") We had all become used to the lack of privacy in Bali, and I used to feel quite lonely if there wasn't a little gang of children sitting on the back veranda watching me type.

Chokorda Agung had hired for us a cook, Wayan Pandé; his son who was to be our *jongos*; a young cousin who carried water, cleaned the rooms and generally helped out; and a gardener. He had fixed the salaries, supplied us with linen and with initial household supplies, so we had the curious sensation of moving into a perfectly running house with none of the attendant headaches.

Our first evening there we sat out on the paved place in the front garden and looked dutifully at the view, feeling important but a little nervous at being householders. We saw for the first time what was to become a familiar and friendly sight on subsequent evenings. Every morning a little boy came by with a flock of ducks, guiding them with a long stick with a flag on the end. Very solemnly they marched down the main road and turned off into the *sawahs*. There the boy used to stick the pole into the earth and leave the ducks to graze in the flooded rice fields until evening. They were trained not to leave the field where the flag had been placed. In the evening the boy picked up the flag and walked his ducks back to his home where they slept. There was something very pleasant about the idea of taking ducks to pasture every day, and we got into the habit of watching for them at dusk.

Chokorda Agung and old Chokorda Rai of Sayan came to call on us. Our first visitors.

"Now that we are really friends," Chokorda Agung said, "and you are living in Ubud, please call me Agung instead of Chokorda. May I do the same, Daiyu?"

"Of course," I said, very flattered. He asked me what my name meant, and Chokorda Rai gave a long dissertation on the Sanskrit meaning and the festivals connected with it. He suddenly ended it with, "It is a beautiful evening, you are happy in your own house, but I am unhappy."

"What has made you unhappy?"

"I have not words for this sadness. It is inside me."

[239]

"It's a sad world," Faubion said sententiously.

"Only at this time. First, as Daiyu knows, there is God. That is the period of Kerte which lasts two thousand years when man is at one with God and can speak to him directly. Then comes the period of Traite which lasts five hundred years when God ascends out of man and man must search for God. It is a time of mental inquiry. Next comes Duopare, the period in which desire enters man when mankind is split into men and women, a period of vacillation and precarious balance. Lastly comes Kali which lasts two hundred and fifty years and is a period of corruption, fighting and general upset. We are in that period now, and even I, old as I am, hope to live to see the end of it and of this four thousand-year span. Then we can again enter the first period and be at one with God. Perhaps this is what makes me sad."

76 In the morning the girls from Chokorda Raké's puri came around with specially fancy offerings to bring us good fortune in our new house. The servants had decorated the back veranda with flowers and sprays of bamboo leaves, and as we sat there having coffee the stream of boys and girls from the neighboring houses began to give us their good wishes and to get water from our well. Kunter arrived with his two big water cans, and stayed to chat for a couple of minutes. "I have left my cow to graze on your plot of grass in front of the house."

"I didn't know you had a cow," I said.

"It isn't actually my cow, but the man who owns it has promised me the first calf if I will feed the cow until it is born."

"That's a very cheap and clever way of getting a calf."

"Ye—es," he said doubtfully, "it is now three years since we made this arrangement. I am afraid she may be barren."

After that, whenever we saw Kunter we used to shout, "*Sudah?*" meaning "Already? Is the cow pregnant?" and he would shout back, "*Belum!*" "Not yet!"

Our cook, Wayan Pandé, came to Clare and me with a little book in which he wrote accounts, but life in Ubud was too busy to spend time on accounts, so I said, "Wayan Pandé, how much does it cost for us to eat every day?"

"About five guilders silver."

"Does that include the servants?" Clare asked.

"Yes. I have told them that you are not wealthy." Clare looked startled, and Wayan Pandé added, "Don't be sad. I have told them that here they will eat well, but they must not expect extravagant luxuries. For instance, they mustn't buy fish or things of that sort for themselves."

"Well, that's very reasonable," I put in quickly.

"I have heard that you all like hot food, just as we eat it, so it is cheaper to cook for all at the same time."

"Good. I will give you thirty-five guilders every week and—"

"Daiyu, market day is every third day, so give me fifteen guilders every three days."

"All right. We don't want to look at accounts. Once a week one of the boys can take the bus to Den Pasar if we need other supplies. And for everything else, manage it all your own way."

"Good."

Wayan Pandé was one of the nicest and wisest old men I have ever met. He was as straight and graceful as all Balinese. As Clare once pointed out, if you walk along behind a Balinese you often think, "What a beautifully built young man!" Only when you are in front and can see the face do you realize with a shock that it is often an old man.

He was enormously protective of us and our interests, advised and helped and kept us from making mistakes of etiquette or judgment. He had great tolerance and a wide smile showing all his teeth blackened with betelnut. His son, Madé Jawi, our *jongos*, was very like his father, except that he was extremely high-spirited where his father was retiring. Kompiang, the second *jongos*, and Tugog, the gardener, were higher in caste than the father and son, but they all ran the house and garden as though it were some enormous game. It was impossible to think of them as servants.

One of them, in turn, always managed to stay near the front of the house or out in the garden, and would yell out names from time to time to the others in the courtyard. On inquiry we found that they were shouting the name of every unmarried girl as she passed the house on the street. Then the ones at the back would nod wisely and discuss her chances and whether or not she was pretty. On market days they were especially busy as girls used to come in from other villages with their vegetables or cloth to sell in Ubud.

The second day we knew we were established because Tugog brought us a present of some goldfish which he put in a bowl in the lizard room along with a piece of white coral and some vague green things. The belvedere, it turned out, was a chicken coop, and two chickens appeared in it. A black and white dog adopted us and we tentatively called him Rover, and we acquired an enormous white cock which did nothing much except look decorative and scare the chickens.

"Now," Clare said, "if we can only persuade Madé Jawi not to use the coffee percolator as a flower vase, and explain that lysol is *not* a perfume to be scattered gaily through the house, I think our household duties are at an end." And, indeed, they just about were.

The third night we had our formal housewarming dinner and invited Chokorda Agung, Chokorda Ngura and Chokorda Rai. We couldn't ask Alit, Wayan Pandé told us, because a matter of seniority was involved.

Before dinner there was a meeting of the music society. First, Agung gave them a stiff lecture about not practicing enough. Then he told them that they had been invited to play in Gianiar for the festival of *Galungan*—a great honor—but their playing was so much lower in standard than the dancing that he was ashamed to have them perform in another town.

The society had raised some money to send one of their talented dancers to study the *kebyar* with one of Bali's best known *kebyar* dancers, Idé Bagus Blangsinga. He had returned to report on his progress to the society, and to show them how he was getting along. They watched him very critically, and then said he should go back and study for another month or so.

After the meeting we came back to dinner to find the servants had borrowed dozens of little earthenware bowls which they had filled with oil and wicks, and had decorated the garden and the house with lights. We got in and sat down just in time to receive the chokordas as they arrived. They all looked very grand indeed, although I had told them that it was informal. They were wearing beautiful batik *kains*, brilliant *saputs* around the waist, were bare-bodied, and had elaborately tied headcloths with flowers. Seniority was established by Chokorda Ngura who sat on the highest level. Madé Jawi and Kompiang scurried about, plainly scared by such grandeur so soon, but acquitted themselves magnificently.

They had all done everything they could to make us proud of our house. There were flowers in every room, and the boys wore them in their hair, too; they had perfumed themselves and borrowed new sarongs. Dinner was rice and roast suckling pig—with the skin served separately in very crisp strips which you ate with your fingers—chicken curry and a sort of cross between paté and sausage. The vegetables were cabbage cooked in coconut milk, very young peas still in their pods, steamed, a kind of squash with peanuts, and a salad. After that there was fruit—papayas, bananas and mangosteens—and in the lizard room, after a delay to give the servants time to wash the wine cups, coffee with condensed milk. We, I think, were much more impressed than the chokordas.

After dinner we had arranged a dance on the village green so that all of Ubud could celebrate with us. It was a *janger*, which is both sung and danced by young boys and girls and is very gay. They had come from the next village and were not particularly good dancers, but the Ubud people enjoyed it anyway because they could congratulate themselves on the beauty of the Ubud girls in comparison.

77   Our courtyard was apparently a very good place to catch dragonflies because it was near the river and had the well, too. So there was always a little trickle of children coming through, led usually by Agung's little girl by his second wife, holding long sticks on the end of which they had put some sticky stuff. With these imple-

ments they caught the dragonflies, and when they had caught enough to cover the entire stick, they took them home to be cooked. They taste something like bacon, fried very crisp.

Since I spent most of my mornings in the back courtyard, I came to know some of the children quite well. In particular there was a little Idé Bagus who always used to stop by on his way to school and exchange a few words.

"Daiyu!" he would call from on top of the wall.

"Yes?"

"Watch me jump as the cock jumps!" He would spring down, flapping his arms, and come and sit on the veranda step. "Good morning."

"Good morning Idé Bagus K'chil."

"I have decided to learn English. Will you teach me?"

"All right." He asked me how to say various phrases in English: "Where are you going?" "Give me a match please," "What time is it?" and wrote them all down. Impressed with his writing I asked how old he was.

"Thirteen," he said.

I was very surprised because he was so small, and said, "Oh surely not, you must be nine or ten."

He looked at me, his round charming face entirely unconcerned, "Yes? All right, ten." He picked up his notebook and got ready to go to school. "In a few days it will be Galungan. On that day may I use some of your perfume? It is a great day, and I would like to wear it for my friends."

"Yes, if you want."

"Thank you. Safety in remaining." He trotted off.

In the afternoon he usually came back and sat on the front steps to watch the football on the village green. At dusk he would go off for his evening meal. It was a curious thing, but I never saw a Balinese child that needed to be called to meals or to do the various jobs assigned to him. Sometimes, casually in the middle of a conversation, they would trot off. If you said, "Where are you going?" they would answer. "It is time to work in the sawah," or "I must bathe," or "My food must be ready." You would say, "Then safety in going,"

"Safety in remaining!" they would yell, already halfway down the road.

I never saw a child cry except when he was physically hurt. And in Bali, as in most of Asia, the older children are made responsible for the younger ones. A girl of thirteen, say, like Alit's daughter who danced in the *gabor*, does not feel imposed on if she has to take care of her two-year-old sister. She comes back from school in the early afternoon, feeds the child at the same time as she eats herself, and then takes her along when she plays with her friends. If she has a dancing lesson the child either sits—(without whimpering or needing attention)—and watches, or is put in charge of one of the girls who is not dancing. She will bathe her baby sister in the evening at the same time that she herself goes down the ravine to the river and when the child is put to sleep her evenings are free, just as her mother's whole day except for the few morning hours has been free to conduct her own activities.

Little Idé Bagus returned later in the evening and announced that he had eaten his food, but his house was empty.

"Then how could you have food?"

"I don't eat in my house. I eat with Chokorda Raké and sleep there, too."

"Then who lives in your house?"

"My mother and her husband. They are away for a few days. But it is still my house. It will be mine when my mother dies."

"Who do you mean by her husband? Your father?"

"No, Daiyu." He shook his head at my silliness. "My father is dead. My mother married again, she is very happy with this one. He is young and very handsome. She used to be a very beautiful dancer, but now she is old."

"How old is she?"

"She is already old."

"But why do you live with Chokorda Raké? Why not with your mother?"

"The Chokorda summoned me, so of course I had to go. If he wants me in his *puri*, I must be happy to go."

I didn't question him further because I thought he might have been glad of the Chokorda's support because he was poor. I had seen him often doing odd jobs about the *puri*, although as a Brahmin his caste was higher than a chokorda's.

At last I said, "You'd better button up your shirt, it's getting cool."

"This shirt," he explained as though I were really too stupid to be believed, "is a little small for me and does not button easily. It is the only one I have, otherwise I would wear one that *does* button." He went on without pause, "At *Galungan* we will have a house festival, and you must come. My mother will be here then."

"I'd like to very much."

"We will also have a cockfight. You will see my cock fight."

"You have only one cock?"

"Yes, but a very strong one."

"What happens if it loses?"

"Then we eat it. If it wins, I get money." He got up, "Good night. I must go and sleep."

78

Wayan Pandé said one morning, "It is very expensive to have bread sent up from Den Pasar. I know how to bake bread, but we have no oven."

"It will be much more expensive to buy an oven than to buy bread," I said.

"No, it should cost about eight guilders for an oven." That was about two American dollars.

"Really?"

"I think I can get one for that."

He returned in the afternoon with a large, square, kerosene tin which had one removable side. It was the oven. Wayan Pandé baked two samples loaves for us first, one with raisins. He mixed the dough out in the sun, used *tuak*, the palm beer, instead of yeast, to make it rise, and baked it in the tin which was placed over a low fire, and had smoldering coconut shells on top of it.

The first loaves were such a success that Wayan Pandé said it would be good to bake a lot more the next day so that we could send them to our neighbors as presents. That evening we were all sitting on the paved place in the front garden when the return presents came in, a pomelo and some rice cakes from Chokorda Raké, corn on the cob from Chokorda Agung, a colored basket from another friend, and a decorated flute from Alit. Madé Jawi and Tugog were particularly pleased with the flute because they already knew how to play the small Balinese sort, and now they could learn to play this larger one.

Kompiang, who was the least communicative of our boys, suddenly leaned back where he was sitting, and gazed up at the tree above the paved place. In his voice there was the need to convey something to us—a mood, or a pleasant day, or the slight tiredness of the evening, anyway something comforting. He said, "This place is very beautiful now, but wait until there is a full moon. Then you see the light through the leaves and hear the wind in the tree. It is really beautiful then."

Inexplicably moved, I said, "Yours is a beautiful country altogether."

"Yes," he said, "whenever I am tired, I know I can always go look at the *sawahs*."

Faubion said, "This life of yours is very nice, too, as long as something doesn't happen to interrupt it."

Wayan Pandé asked, "What do you mean?"

"Well," Faubion said, "suppose I lived here. One day I decide I am not rich enough, and if I go to Den Pasar and open a shop I will have more money. So I sell my *sawahs* and go off to Den Pasar. After a few months I find that my shop does not make money. In Bali without land you cannot live. What am I to do? Shall I become a beggar?"

"Of course not. You would walk back to Ubud."

"But what would I do here? I have sold my *sawahs*, remember."

"Your friends," said Wayan Pandé, "would look after you."

"Suppose I am a terrible person and have no friends and no family either."

"There is no one in Bali that has no friends. You would always be fed and looked after."

[247]

After dinner there was to be a very famous *joget* in the village. The Joget of Bungkasé was the best in Bali. We had seen the instruments being carried into Ubud past our house that afternoon, and had asked who the people were, as the musicians were strangers to us. In the evening the instruments were lined up neatly across one end of the dance area in the big shelter where the cockfights were held. All around the other three sides the villagers stood watching the *joget* who sat on a plain kitchen chair in front of the elaborately carved and gilded instruments. She wore a costume of a dull, faded gold, like the costumes of all successful dancers in Bali. They save their money to buy new costumes, but their popularity and frequent performances soon fade them again. She was young, but not as beautiful as I had expected—until she started dancing.

The orchestra began the haunting, persistent theme of the flirt dance. Suddenly, without rising from the chair, the *joget* tensed her body into position. Her feet flung out asymmetrically, toes upturned. Her left hand, holding a green and red fan, sprang out level with her shoulder; her right, with empty fingers, fluttered at her side. Her eyes spread open wide, staring into that dream world of Balinese dancing.

With a burst of music she rose and began circling round the dance floor in her search for a partner for the dance. After the first couple of boys had danced with her, all the *gabor* girls and our boys started shouting for Faubion to dance. This time he had no excuse, and got up looking most embarrassed, but danced rather well. The crowd, of course, was ecstatic, and when he did an imitation of the *gabor* dancers, they screamed with joy until we couldn't hear the music. Even the *joget* herself, who was supposed to retain her poise and coldness toward all the men who danced with her, couldn't keep from laughing. After that, Faubion's stock in Ubud shot up.

79 Only one thing about our boys produced its moments of irritation. We had, perhaps foolishly, asked them to correct our Malay whenever we made mistakes. This seemed to them entirely sensible, but they could never understand that our wish to learn might be tempered by moods of any sort. One of us once said, rather crossly, "Madé Jawi, where is the drinking water I asked you for?"

He said calmly, "You should say ayer, not ayar. I will get it."

"*Don't* correct my Malay when I'm angry!"

"If you are angry you are quickly old," he said brightly. "That is a Balinese proverb."

One couldn't then help laughing, and found rather to one's surprise that all trace of irritation had gone.

There were compensations, too, in their way of working. They seemed to find it all so amusing that involuntarily we were drawn into their good spirits. One morning we showed the boys how we wanted the bathroom scrubbed with lysol and a brush. We explained that the walls as well as the floor must be cleaned. Most of that morning they seemed to have enormous fun sloshing around with buckets of water. Gales of giggles issued from the bathroom because they thought it very funny to use a brush for the floor. Normally, they only used a brush for washing clothes in the river.

When they had finished they came and asked us to inspect the place. When Clare pointed out a shelf that they had missed, they chorused, "Thank you, thank you!" and sloshed happily on for a while. They were clearly rather proud of their work, afterward, and kept dashing out of the kitchen or the front of the house to ask if one of us had bathed yet so that they could clean it again. In the afternoon when Faubion was on his way out to watch the football game, Madé Jawi said, "You haven't had a bath," accusingly.

"I had one this morning."

"You should have another before you change your clothes."

"But I've already changed."

"You should have a bath. We bathe twice a day."

"Oh all right. . . ."

80 Little Idé Bagus turned up one morning to tell us that there was a three-day festival in Batuan. He wanted to go to it, and would take us.

"We will go for the middle day because that is when they will have the best dancing. The Raja of Gianiar will be there. It is a beautiful temple, even bigger than the Temple of the Dead in Ubud."

Batuan was a strange village, populated almost entirely by Brahmins with only a few Kshatriyas—the second highest caste. The dance that Idé Bagus wanted to see was called the gambuk, a very old dance, indeed, accompanied by chanting and an orchestra of flutes, stringed instruments and some percussion. It was quite late at night when the long, mystic, very lovely performance began, by oil light, against the ranks of Balinese faces absorbed and delighted.

"This is a religious dance," Idé Bagus told us, "some part of it must be performed at festivals and holy occasions. That is why Batuan always keeps gambuk dancers, although many people think it is old-fashioned. Everything borrows from this dance because you can't make gambuk modern." He darted away into the crowd and returned with sweet potatoes for us to eat because we were his guests.

Most of the night was gone by the time we got back to Ubud, but Idé Bagus said, "That was only a short section of the dance. Do you not see now that it is the heart of all Balinese dancing?"

81 Desa Kutut was a plump, graceful girl with magnificent eyes. She was very free and talkative and full of fun. We found her sitting in our courtyard one afternoon when we came back from swimming. She said she had nothing much to do that day and had come over from Chokorda Raké's puri to ask if she could look at Clare's and my clothes. Rayon rather puzzled her, she couldn't decide if it was silk or cotton, and she asked if we had any cloth that we ourselves had woven.

"No," I said regretfully, "I don't know how to weave."

She was always on the edge of laughter, and it was always spilling over into her conversation. "How your parents have neglected your education!" She added consolingly, "I, too, never finished my education. I only got almost to the fifth class, and then I had to stop. You see I went on a visit to a cousin of mine who lives in another village, and after I had been there only three days I was kidnaped."

"How awful!" I said, alarmed. "Who kidnaped you?"

She suddenly looked reserved and said, "My husband."

I thought that perhaps it was more of an elopement than a kidnaping, and said more carefully, "Did you know him? What was he like?"

"I didn't know him," she said casually.

"Why didn't you stay with him?"

She said very quickly, "I had no intention to. It must be settled in three days whether a girl stays or goes, but I stayed in his house a month because that was the time when the Dutch were returning to Bali and I wasn't brave enough to go out." Eventually she did get back to Ubud, and came to live in Chokorda Raké's *puri* because he was a relative, and helped with the household work and the weaving in return for her keep.

"Was your husband bad to you, is that why you left him?"

"He wasn't either good or bad. The real reason was that I was not attracted to men at that time although I had already been sick. I was happier at school."

Clare asked Desa Kutut about marriage ceremonies, and she explained that first a coconut husk is put on the threshold of the house to which a bride is to be brought. Incense is burned inside the bark, and a chicken is killed and the blood sprinkled on the ground. But the main ceremony comes when the chief man of the village gives the couple food, which they must eat "with good heart." Then they are married, and burning incense is put under the bridal bed.

I was much more interested in Desa Kutut than in marriage ceremonies, so I asked if she could marry again.

"I have no such intention at present. If I feel like it I can. Then I will have children." She raised her eyebrows and smiled, "I have not yet found anyone attractive."

"Can the Chokorda order you to marry anyone?"

"Not if I don't want to."

"How about your parents?"

"My mother is dead, but my father is alive." She burst irrepressibly into laughter, "No one is brave enough to order me to marry. I have resisted a man for a month!"

Soon afterward she had to hurry off to do her evening chores, and Clare and I joined Wayan Pandé, Faubion, and the usual group in the garden. I said that I couldn't understand why Desa Kutut didn't get married, she was so good looking and so full of spirit.

Wayan Pandé said, "Men are a little afraid of women who live in a *puri*. Balinese men are born to work and they die by it. The land gives them their life, so they must live for the land. In the *puris* of the chokordas you have a different kind of mind. The men and women who live there feel no strength in their work because they know that if anything goes wrong, the chokorda will take care of them. It is his responsibility.

"So unless Desa Kutut marries a man from another *puri*, she will remain unmarried."

"How sad," Faubion said.

"No," Wayan Pandé said, "she remains chaste only by her own choice."

"But what would happen if she got pregnant?"

"Sometimes a girl can persuade a man to marry her, but if there is more than one man involved, all the men must go to the temple with her, and the gods choose which one is the father. He must marry her or support the child."

"Do people think badly of a girl like that or a marriage like that?"

"No, it is natural."

"Are people scornful of a woman who doesn't marry at all?"

"No," said Wayan Pandé, looking quite bewildered by these questions, "because people know that it must be from choice. Balinese men can have several wives so there is no reason why a woman who wants to get married, shouldn't."

Clare asked how long before her child arrives a woman stops working.

"After the fifth month she does only very light work."

"Who does the work for the last four months?"

"The last four months?" Wayan Pandé said, startled. "The last two months, you mean."

I thought I had misunderstood. "It takes nine months to have a baby," I said carefully.

Wayan Pandé looked at me as though his conviction of foreign idiocy was at last confirmed. "If a woman were pregnant for nine months she would produce a child that already had its teeth!"

"You mean," I insisted, "that Balinese women have their children after a seven-month pregnancy?"

"Yes, of course. We are not animals to have such long pregnancies. The third day after the baby arrives the woman is allowed to get up, but she does not work for a month."

We asked several other people who had joined the group, but they all said the same thing—a seven-month pregnancy was normal.

Faubion said in English, "A Balinese month has thirty-five days."

Clare and I did a little mental arithmetic, she came out with the answer first, "But that still doesn't work out right. It takes a foreigner two hundred and seventy days to have a baby, and a Balinese only two hundred and forty-five."

"Well," Faubion said, "they are just cleverer than other women. That's all."

82 In the third week of May preparations for the *Galungan* festival had already begun, although *Galungan*, itself, came on the first of June. When I was walking through Chokorda Raké's *puri* I noticed that the women were making great numbers of rice cakes and drying them in the sun on palm mats. There were thin sheets of something that looked like toffee, and I stopped to examine them. One of the women, a most engaging relative of Chokorda Raké's, asked me if I would like to taste some.

It was a sweet made from rice, cocoanut, and palm sugar, a little like chewing gum in consistency. "Do you like it?" she asked.

"Very much."

I noticed my little Idé Bagus sitting with Chokorda Raké in a separate pavilion. He was busy plucking the hairs out of Chokorda

Raké's chin. He used two coins, gripped the hair between them, and yanked it sharply out. I waved to him, but he only raised his eyebrows at me in that curious and attractive Balinese greeting.

In the evening, however, he came over with a large plate of the coconut sweets for us, and asked if I would like to go for a walk. Taking a walk with a Balinese child is one of the most humiliating things I know. They are so wise in the things that matter. Little Idé Bagus, like most children brought up in the country, knew such important things as how rice grows or what trees have leaves that can be used in cooking. He showed me how to climb and get a coconut when I was thirsty and wanted something to drink. He caught beetles to amuse me with their pretty coloring, and others which he put in his pocket for eating later. He knew how to catch eels in the sawah water, and which ones to throw back as too young or too thin. He could tell from the flight of a bird whether it should be scared away because it would eat the grain, or whether it was a bird of prey and should be left alone because it would eat the vermin in the fields.

He introduced me to a little friend of his, a cowherd. He had two cows and looked after them most affectionately. He told me that a couple of weeks before the young calf had fallen down a ravine, and when he started down to rescue it, the mother cow, in a panic, gored him in the leg. He was still limping and had a bandage on his leg.

"How cruel," I said, "when you look after her so well."

"Cruel?" he said blankly. "That is her nature."

I came back to the house rather appalled at my ignorance and clutter of insignificant knowledge, particularly as Idé Bagus kept saying, "Have you such trees in India?" or "Do you catch them this way in your country?"

The next day a barrier was put up across the road in front of Chokorda Agung's puri, because there were to be cockfights in Ubud for two days while the work in the village almost came to a standstill. Old Chokorda Ngura was there as soon as the fights started and nothing would move him until it was all over at four o'clock. Everywhere in Ubud the young men were taking the birds out of baskets, stroking the feathers and massaging the muscles on their

[254]

legs. Some were smearing the feet of the cocks with cow dung, which is supposed to strengthen them.

Betting had started the night before, and in the morning our boys drooped about the house, but cheered up at once when we gave them twenty guilders and told them to take the morning off. Clare and I were not allowed to go because Wayan Pandé said it wasn't a suitable sport for girls. Faubion went off with the others, discussing odds, and wondering how many people would come from Pliatan, Maas, Sakti, Sayan and other near-by villages. He came back to lunch and reported that the cocks have spurs attached to their feet. They fight to kill. If a cock turns coward—even after it wins—the other owner gets the winnings. If both turn coward, all money is refunded. Only old cocks fight. The whole thing, Faubion said, is a remnant of the old days when blood sacrifices were a necessary part of religious festivals.

In the afternoon one of the boys from the village came to see us, very pleased because two of his cocks had won. Faubion congratulated him and said, "Please put some money on your third, for me. If two have won, yours must be very good cocks."

"No, no," said the boy. "My third cock mustn't fight. If two have won the third mustn't fight."

"Why is that?"

"It would be tempting the evil spirits to want so much. If two have won the third must fail."

83 Wayan Pandé, knowing by now that Faubion was writing about Balinese dancing in his book, told him that in Badang Tagal, a small village near Ubud, there was a very famous *legong* dancer. She was so good, that she could make her living by teaching alone. She had trained some of the *gabor* girls and had "many other pupils in many *puris*, as far as Gianiar and Klungkung." She was called Lamon, was a Sudra—the lowest caste—and was married to a dancer.

We asked the Ubud gamelan if they would play for us one afternoon, and Wayan Pandé went to fetch Lamon. The Balinese have something that they call *jam karet*, "the elastic hour," so the gamelan didn't arrive until fairly late and we had a chance to talk to Lamon. She was a startingly beautiful woman, fair in complexion and with great serenity in her face.

Faubion asked her many technical questions about the dance which she answered, smiling and showing her even, filed teeth, and then, because the Balinese are never embarrassed by a discussion of money, we asked if she made a good living from teaching.

"Oh, enough to buy food, and a little to spend on my daughter. I have only one sarong and this yellow jacket. This *kain* I am wearing is borrowed because I wanted to look nice when I came here."

"When you teach children," Faubion asked, "can you tell from the beginning whether they will be good dancers?"

"You can tell what *type* of dancer each will be by her face. You can tell from her eyes whether she will be good."

"From the expression, do you mean?"

"No, from the way she sees."

The Ubud gamelan arrived, and Lamon got up. "I haven't brought a *saput*," she said, "but I can't dance in this jacket because I must have my shoulders bare. Can you lend me a towel?" She peeled off the jacket, wrapped the towel quickly round her, and began to dance the long, exquisite *legong*.

The fifth day before *Galungan* was a very important day. School closed for ten days and the children came racing across the village green to tell us that the holidays had begun. The little Idé Bagus sat with me—(always on the same level, because we were the same caste)—and asked a lot of questions about how "great days" are celebrated in India, whether the ceremonies are the same, how many priests officiate and so on. Then he picked up my matchbox which had a Dutch flag on the cover, and said, "You should have matches with the Indonesian flag. Red and white, for strength and purity."

I started to tell him what the Indian flag was like, but he interrupted, "I know, I know. There is a picture of the Indian flag over the picture of Gandhi which hangs in our school."

Later in the morning a priest came from the temple by the river and sprinkled the house with holy water. Afterward he asked for some money for the temple. Like everything else in the house the matter was referred to Wayan Pandé who said, "Yes, you should give him five guilders. You live in Ubud, and so you receive the protection of the temple. You must then take the responsibilities, too."

He told us, as well, that the markets would not be held for nine days so we should buy supplies. The boys sat in the courtyard making special offerings to take to the temple—intricate designs of woven bamboo and palm, decorated with hibiscus. The girls in Chokorda Raké's *puri* were busily at work on the looms finishing up the *kains*. Everybody has to wear new clothes for *Galungan*.

In the evening Chokorda Raké sent us one of the most delightful presents we have ever received. Four musicians in their formal dress brought their wooden instruments with metal keys to our house. All through the evening, and while we were having dinner, on the veranda, they sat in the court yard and played us the music of the *wayang g'ndair*.

Bare-bodied, with red *kains* and gold headbands, they sat straight and serious in front of their four decorated instruments performing the especially beautiful music which accompanies different scenes of the shadow plays: the mystic, thin "arranging of the puppets," the rattle and thunder of the "battle music," the liquid and brilliant love music, and some rather jolly music turned out to be "when good people are crying." They had a rather clever trick of tuning one instrument about a sixteenth of a tone higher than another which is playing the same notes because, they said, this gave the music resonance. If you play exactly the same note exactly together you get a "dead sound."

As our part of the *Galungan* celebrations we decided to ask the wonderful Joget of Bungkasé to dance for us again. Alit had fallen into the habit of visiting us for a short while nearly every evening, so we invited him to dinner that night. He was in a talkative mood, in his own gentle way, and greeted us by saying that if we were celebrating *Galungan* we must be Balinese already. "And you, Faubion, are my brother. Are we not the same temperament? I will give you my son as a present." Faubion thanked him in some confusion, and Clare looked nervously at me, wondering whether we had inadvertently adopted a small Balinese boy.

I told him quickly that we were having the *joget* that evening, and he should dance with her.

"Oh no," he said, suddenly shy, "I would never dare."

"But you must have courage," Faubion said.

"There are three kinds of courage, and I have none of them."

"What three kinds?"

"One is the courage of hot-bloodedness—for instance, I have crickets to whom I feed hot red peppers so that their feelings rise and they must fight. That is one sort. The second is the courage of duty. And the third is the courage of friendship, so that if a friend says, 'Die with me,' or if you can help a friend only with your death, you do not hesitate. That is the highest kind of courage."

"I am sure that's the kind you have," Faubion said.

"I hope. A little. But that is because I no longer have any great love of life."

"How old are you?" Faubion asked.

"Thirty-two. And you?"

"The same."

Alit took his hand very warmly and said, "You see, I told you we were brothers. We may have different mothers and fathers, but we are brothers, not only in age, but in feeling. The only difference is that I am growing old."

"What makes you say that? I don't think you are old."

"When you can no longer take pleasure in looking at a beautiful woman, then you know you are growing old."

"But you have other pleasures—"

"Ah yes, my fighting cocks and my crickets," Alit said affectionately. "Do not think I am sad to be growing old. To have memories rather than experience is a good thing because they cannot be spoiled. In fact," he said, rather laughing at himself, "they improve as you grow older."

Faubion said, "But that is almost like death, to take no pleasure in your senses or your experience."

"Yes," Alit said casually, "I am ready for death. Now I need only purification because life and death are the same thing."

"Do you *want* to die?" Clare asked explosively.

"No," he said thoughtfully, "but should I need to die for a friend or for any other reason, I am ready."

"Aren't you afraid?" Clare insisted.

"Afraid of what?"

"Well, I mean, perhaps there is no life after death."

Alit looked puzzled. "If your thoughts and your life are happy, then after you die you will be happy. If you fight and are angry here, then you will fight after death, too. So it is our duty to be happy now. For those that do not seek for purification there is no light after they die. If they cannot see they must exist in darkness afterward." Suddenly apologetic, he smiled at all of us. "Please forgive me. These are the thoughts of a child. I know nothing except my cocks and my crickets." He clasped his thin hands on his knees in an indescribably elegant gesture, and smoothly changed the subject.

The *joget* was lovely, as always, and already her reputation had spread so there was a great crowd from other villages. We asked her to spend the night and dance for us again the next morning so that we could see some of her other dances. Her repertoire consisted of several dances requiring extraordinary versatility. She danced as a princess, an attendant, a *garuda* (a mythical Hindu bird), a king going to battle, Rangda (Bali's fiercest witch), and of course the flirt *joget*. She danced for two hours without pause, giving us bits out of each dance.

[259]

84 The festival of *Galungan* was something vaguely comparable with All Soul's Day. It is the day you take offerings to the dead who are buried but not yet cremated, and also to the happy spirits who have already been cremated and now live in temples rather than cemeteries. But *Galungan* also had some of the aspects of the Indian *divali* or the Chinese New Year. Debts were paid, gambling was unrestricted, people appeared in new clothes, and everyone must eat pork on *Galungan*.

The evening of May 31 there were great festivities. Chokorda Agung gave a huge dinner in his *puri* to which all the neighboring chokordas were invited, and we, too, were included. Before the feast there was a dance, a *kebyar*, which provides probably the greatest opportunity for the display of virtuosity in an individual dancer. The dance itself was created by Mario who, thirty years ago, was the greatest dancer that Bali had ever seen and also one of its most beautiful men. He was now too old to dance, but he had come to Ubud for *Galungan*, bringing with him his best pupil, Gusti Raké.

"Gusti Raké," Mario said, "is a truly great dancer. These days the boys think that they can learn the *kebyar* in a month. But in dancing, as in everything else, the children are in a hurry nowadays."

Gusti Raké was, as Mario said, magnificent. We had seen the *kebyar* danced before only by adolescents, and watched, that night, a mature man and a finished artist perform it. For the first time we were conscious of the almost electric tension which the *kebyar* produces, the enormous vitality and strength of the dance.

The dinner itself was huge, with two turtles, chickens, pigs, many vegetables, rice and fruit. All through it a small gamelan played from the central pavilion in the inner courtyard, and afterward the Ubud music society danced the *baris* and the *gabor*.

Galungan morning the girls from Chokorda Raké's *puri* came around with the most elaborate offerings we had yet seen. Big woven palm trays contained the usual rice, spices and flowers, with coconut, vegetables, cakes and meat added. One tray was put in each

[260]

room in our house, and each room was sprinkled with holy water. Outside the house our boys had put up tall decorated bamboo poles, and on each side of the front door there were intricate designs of animals and people made from different colored palm leaves. All morning the boys decorated the verandas with pine branches and gardenias. I tried to help them, but they told me, "Daiyu has not intelligent fingers." We had given them each a sarong as a present and Wayan Pandé had given them a little lecture on working hard, so the house was a ferment of activity.

Then the *Galungan* presents came pouring in—rice cakes, slices of meat, trays of liver sausage, turtle sticks, paté made of chicken heart, wine, fruit and many other things. It was all far too much for us to eat. We tasted some, and gave the rest to the boys.

My little Idé Bagus came to see us and to use my perfume. He looked very dignified in a new sarong, and with flowers in his hair. He asked if he could borrow my watch for the day. He would bring it back in the evening because it wouldn't be good to keep a borrowed article overnight.

The girls from the *gabor* came in to show us their new clothes. They had yellow temple flowers in their hair, and little wads of a sweet-scented variety of moss tucked behind their ears. I gave them a couple of bottles of nail varnish because they loved decorating themselves. Sayu Madé Rai, the beautiful one, opened her incredible eyes very wide, "How wonderful to be rich!"

"What would you buy if you were rich?" I asked.

"Clothes," said Sayu and Alit's little girl at once.

Warsi, Kunter's sister, said, "A bicycle because then I could go to the dances even in faraway villages."

Purni, tall and self-possessed, thought a moment and said, "If I were very rich I would buy jewelry."

Then they told me that the girls in the Ubud *gabor* were to learn another dance that none of the music societies in the neighboring villages could do. Iruju's young sister was now considered accomplished enough as a dancer to join the society, too. They went off, calling out wishes from the road, their fingers held well apart to allow the varnish to dry.

[261]

In the evening the girls went in procession down to the temple, all dressed in their best *kains* and carrying offerings on their heads. All evening in the neighboring villages there was dancing and music. Ubud had a shadow play and a concert.

On the way back to the house, Madé Jawi and Kompiang were walking with us, and Kompiang said that he liked the shadow plays best.

"Best in the world?" Faubion asked.

"The best thing in life," Kompiang said seriously, "is mankind."

"The best, though not always good," Faubion said, making a rather feeble pun in Malay.

"Of course not," Madé Jawi said. "It is so much easier to be bad than good."

"How do you mean?"

"If I wish you evil I could hit you now and it would all be over. But to be good to you would take years."

"Which," said Faubion, "would you rather have, health or wealth or beauty?"

"If you have health," Kompiang said, "you have also wealth because you are strong and can work and live well. But beauty is a matter of the heart."

"The heart is important in understanding people, too," Faubion said. Kompiang looked puzzled.

"Well, do you think it is possible for one person to understand another?"

"No."

"But you have friends. Who is your most intimate friend?"

After some thought Kompiang said, "The tailor's son is my best friend."

"Well, do you understand each other?"

"Oh yes. But since we are fond of each other it no longer matters."

85 We had two chickens in our belvedere for several days after *Galungan*, and meanwhile our meals were very fancy—duck, goose, slices of beef roasted on spits. Eventually I asked why we never ate our chickens, and Madé Jawi told me that they clucked so much he thought they must be happy and it seemed a shame to part them. We finally compromised by buying two baby chickens to keep in the coop until they grew up so that Madé Jawi would not be lonely while we ate the other birds.

The whole of June seemed to be a time for celebrations and entertainment. Everybody had more time on his hands, and several of the *gabor* girls and even some of the women from Chokorda Raké's *puri* would come and visit us in the afternoons and drink lemonade, try on my clothes and show me the different ways of tying a *kain*. In the many conversations that we had with them a number of things struck us as worthy of consideration. One of the first points that impressed us was the extent of the employment of children in Bali and, in fact, in all Asia—not in the context of fair labor standards acts, or child employment legislation, but in the context of their place in the family, and their part of the community life.

Along with the considerable freedom, lack of parental bullying, and absence of silly compulsions, Balinese children have a good deal of what I like to think of as *reasonable* responsibility. The *gabor* girls, for instance, who were all about twelve years old, were entirely competent to attend to their own needs, their schoolwork, their dancing, to look after the younger members of the family. They all knew how to weave their own sarongs, and even had cloth left over to sell; they could all cook and manage the household if they needed to, even though the numbers ranged from the fourteen that Alit's daughter would have to look after, to the four members in the family of Sayu Madé Rai, the exquisite girl who danced Siti Sundari. This had nothing to do with the financial status of their families. Both Alit's girl and Sayu were well off; Purni, another of the *gabor* girls, fairly well off; and Warsi, Kunter's sister, rather

[263]

poor. Yet they still seemed to feel that they had enough time to play with each other or to talk to us of an afternoon.

And that brought up another interesting point. There seemed to be none of the irritated boredom that Western children feel in the company of adults. They showed a few marks of deference, but otherwise were as interesting and entertaining to us as they were to their own friends.

Clare one day made the ordinary comment, "Really, childhood is the happiest time of one's life."

The Balinese sitting on our veranda looked politely puzzled because the cult of the "happy childhood" doesn't exist in Bali. Finally Sayu said, "Yes, it is a time for learning, and learning is always interesting. But one is happy when one grows up, too; it is the quality of the happiness that changes."

Clare said to me in English, "It would be no use writing 'a pursuit of happiness' into a Balinese constitution. They'd think you were mad."

Something else that rather startled Clare were the Balinese's very straightforward inquiries about sexual matters, and the extent of the information that the children had. It often puzzled me that even though Clare had read Freud with her usual care, and herself attributed many Western neuroses to confusion and lack of directness about sex, still she continued to feel that Western standards and attitudes are the best. To Eastern cultures that recognized polygamy she attributed the morals not even of an alley cat. She found the "pornography" of the Indian *Kamasutra*, or the Japanese *Bride's Book* revolting in its directness about matters veiled, secret and rather dirty in the West. She was exceedingly embarrassed by the easy Balinese inquiries about whether or not a young girl had menstruated. She could not understand a pride in pregnancies, and really felt quite sick when she learned that a husband in Bali is not only present when his child is born, but helps in its delivery.

One afternoon the very pretty girl who used to sell us vegetables from time to time joined the usual group on the veranda. She walked to Sayan every day, bought vegetables there because they were cheaper, and then returned to Ubud to sell them at a small profit. I asked whether she would be considered good looking in Bali.

"Oh yes, very," Madé Jawi said.

Kompiang added rather wistfully, "She has not had a *kotor kain* yet." (Literally, "a dirty cloth.")

"How do you know?" Clare asked sharply.

"Well, her mother washes her clothes here by the river, that is how I know. But it is never a secret. Within a couple of months everyone knows which of the girls has been sick."

Another afternoon I at last got a chance to talk to the woman I liked so much in Chokorda Raké's *puri*. So far I had only exchanged greetings and a few words with her. I had asked Wayan Pandé about her and discovered that her name was Anak Agung Ngura, and that her husband was supposed to have been killed in Java fighting for the Republicans. She was about thirty years old, the youngest of a very famous family. She had five brothers and five sisters, all children of Chokorda G'dé Sukawati. One of her brothers was the president of the East Indonesian government in Macassar, and both Chokorda Agung and Chokorda Raké were relatives.

"He had thirty wives," Wayan Pandé said solemnly. "He is still remembered as one of the most magnificent people in Bali. He was the greatest, loved by the people. Whenever he heard that the people were not eating, he said, 'Take whatever you want from my *puri*, even if there is nothing left afterward.' " He looked sad and added, "I was a child at the time, but I remember it."

Her own story was enthralling, and very funny in parts, although her husband's fate was tragic. Four years before, her husband had gone to Java to join the Republican Movement. He had fought in an unsuccessful engagement in west Java but had eventually managed to escape the Dutch. But when he was embarking on a boat for Bali, the Dutch opened fire on the boat and he was shot and very badly wounded. Somebody who saw the incident reported that much. The probablity was that he had been killed, but it was not certain. He might have escaped again, or he might be in hiding.

Before he went to Java they had lived in Den Pasar where he was

[265]

working, although his family home was near Ubud. Anak Agung Ngura, herself, was born in Ubud, but while she was still a child her father had died, and she, along with Chokorda Agung, had been brought up by old Chokorda Ngura. Since her husband went to Java, she had been living in Chokorda Raké's *puri*, as he was her uncle.

"Do you like life in the *puri?*" I asked.

"Oh yes. I sit and sleep and eat. That is real freedom isn't it?" she said, laughing. She was a tall woman, with a mature and lovely face. "After I eat, I sleep. After I sleep I eat."

"But will you do that for always? Won't you marry again?"

"As soon as I have definite news that my husband is dead, I will marry again. But until then I don't think about it because, really, it would be too embarrassing if I did and he came back."

She sounded so offhand that I asked, "Was yours an arranged marriage?"

"Oh no. And not a kidnaping, either. We were in love. I met him while I was at school in Den Pasar, and we were married within three months."

"That sounds very nice and free. Are all Balinese women like that?"

"We have a good deal of freedom here, but it is not always a good thing. It leads to promiscuity among the women, and that is very bad."

I was impressed by her high moral tone, and said soberly, "I see. But even though promiscuity is not a good thing, the freedom does mean that love marriages like yours can come about. Is there any restriction about how long you must be engaged?"

"Well, we did get married rather suddenly, but that was because I was pregnant at the time."

"Oh yes?" I said, trying not to laugh, "By your husband?"

"Of course. We loved each other at once, so I was already happy when we were married. But my family was furious."

"I can imagine."

"Oh not because we had slept together, or because I was pregnant," she corrected me. "We were the same caste—Kshatriya—but you see, he already had a wife."

[266]

"Oh," I said faintly, "where was she?"

"At his house in Singapadu. You mustn't be embarrassed for me," she said twinkling, "I'm not shy about it—everyone around here knows." She looked thoughtful, "You know there are women who marry four and five times, and I must say, I can't approve of that—though it is mostly low-caste women who do that. We have a saying in Bali that if a woman has more than three men she is worthless. And really, I do think that if you are not kidnaped (which of course does excuse you) once is enough. Or twice at the most, if you have a very good reason."

"What was your husband like?" I asked, consumed with curiosity.

Her beautiful face collapsed with laughter, "Oh, as ugly as I am!"

Clare interrupted, trying hard to be serious, "Do women in Bali play any part in politics?"

"Well, in this way," Anak Agung Ngura said. "When my husband goes to fight, I do his work and manage the land. We work together. If a husband and wife do not see together what good is anything?"

Clare said instructively, "Foreign women are getting more and more interested in politics."

"Oh I have seen foreigners. There was a chokorda who went to Macassar and came back with a Dutch wife. She was so ugly! Like a peasant, with thick hands and feet. But I have seen some French women, and they are very elegant."

"Is it considered bad for women here to have a career and earn their living?" Clare persisted.

"Oh no. There are many women of all levels of society who do. The peasant's wife takes produce to the market and sells it, so do his daughters. Some of my relatives are teachers. . . . On the whole I think Balinese women are more free than foreigners, because when I see foreign women who come through Bali so many of them are working at something or other, usually like you, Daiyu, writing things. But think of the life of a Balinese woman of my caste. Can you think of anything more free?"

"But," Clare said, "foreign women can travel; if they don't like their husbands they can get a divorce—"

Anak Agung Ngura interrupted, misunderstanding Clare, and incidentally giving too clear a picture of how foreign women appeared to her, "Yes, yes, in Bali, too, you can leave your husband, but you go back home, then, where you belong. What is the charm of traveling about the world and looking unhappy in every new country? Stay with your people, that is better."

And there, as usual, we ran into that perpetually puzzling barrier of the Balinese. Travel holds no glamour for them. They simply do not want to leave their island. The explanations we got for it varied from, "Many foreigners come to Bali, and if they are willing to leave their own country, we can only suppose it is because Bali is better," to, "The family is the center of life, and how can one leave one's family?" Once one of us had said to Madé Jawi, "Don't you ever get tired of this lush scenery and this temperate climate?" and he had replied quickly, "I will never get tired of the Balinese land until the day I die."

"Well," Clare said, bringing her firmly back to the point, "even if Western marriages aren't entirely successful, you have abuses here, too, kidnaping and things."

Then Anak Agung Ngura said a most instructive thing that explained a good deal of the psychology of kidnaping, and why it persists even though the penalty for taking a woman by force can be imprisonment. "I find it a bad custom, too, but you must understand it saves the reputation of the woman. A kidnaping cannot be her fault. But it is terrible for a woman to be openly seductive. Here, men marry often, and that makes the women wicked, because then they have jealousy in their hearts and to hold their husbands they become seductive. That is why a woman who sleeps with many men is bad, too, because it is understood that in every case it could not have been the man who was the aggressor."

Faubion, who had been sitting with us and helping us out of the tangles of language, burst out laughing. The boys came over to join us and find out what the amusement was about. The *gabor* girls were sitting on the edge of the veranda step, half listening to us, and half playing a game called Tigers and Mice which is played with stones on a sort of checkerboard that you mark out on the ground. I asked what would become of them when they grew up; would they marry whomever they pleased?

[268]

"Yes, if their love is returned and if the caste is right. Sayu's elder sister married for love, but Warsi's sister had an arranged marriage."

"Suppose," Faubion said, "Sayu fell in love with Madé Jawi, and he didn't like her?"

"Then she must love by herself." A low-caste man can't kidnap a high-caste woman, but high-caste men can marry into lower castes. "Because, just think, our men marry sometimes ten times; how can he find ten Kshatriya women to marry him? It is very sad," she said teasingly to our gardener, "Tugog cannot marry *his* girl, he can only go to her bed like a thief!"

The boys laughed, and Tugog shrugged his shoulders and said, "Then she will marry someone else, and I will marry someone else, but for now we are pleased."

"Will that be easy for her?" I asked. "In India the in-laws prefer a girl to be a virgin when she marries their son."

Anak Agung Ngura's loud, released laugh broke out again, "Oh, that would never do in Bali! You should match yourself before marriage, both should be happy on the night of the marriage."

"Don't the men mind?"

"In a way," said Tugog, "it is a compliment because it means that after experience she has decided that she likes you best."

"Caste," Faubion said, "is a very strange thing. It seems to restrict only the people that are most privileged by it. A high-caste woman can only marry in her own caste, but a low-caste woman can marry anyone."

Wayan Pandé said, "That is because in Bali a woman doesn't fight the wind."

They all nodded wisely, but Faubion said, "What do you mean?"

"If the wind is hot, you are hot; if it is cold you are cold. If a woman marries high, she is high, and there is nothing she can do about it."

It was, by then, early evening, and Madé Jawi brought out the brum and arak. We offered Anak Agung Ngura a drink which she refused at first, but finally accepted.

"Does a woman get a bad name if she drinks?" I asked.

"No, she just gets drunk," said Anak Agung, and drank her brum.

After she left, Wayan Pandé told us that she was one of the most envied women in Ubud because her independence was not only a matter of character, it was also a matter of money. Her father had left her forty sawahs and many coconut trees, and she hired eight men to work the fields, managed the estate herself, and at harvest time went down to watch the rice being cut. The money from all this was entirely her own, and when her mother should die, she would get more fields. Her expenses were few—clothes, hair oil, small luxuries—so she was a wealthy woman. Her pleasures were watching the entertainments around Ubud, and singing. She used to be a janger dancer when she was a girl.

Wayan Pandé's opinion of her was, "She is very brave, she will face anyone. Also her family is very good."

86 All through the last days of Galungan various barongs from the villages around used to come through Ubud, and at intervals all through the days one heard drum beats and the bells which announced their coming. The barong is a strange mythical animal, huge, with long shaggy fur, its back and head decorated with tinsel and gold, mirrors and flowers, and an enormous fiercely painted mask. Two men, inside the skin, make the barong dance in the manner of a pantomime horse. The barong is the strongest force for good in Bali, the only thing that can fight the wicked witch Rangda—although the battle is never concluded. The villages take their barong out, and for a couple of cents it will dance in front of your house and bring you good luck.

The Ubud children soon learned that I could never resist these performances, so as soon as anyone heard a barong coming, they would rush to the house yelling, "Daiyu! Daiyu! A barong is here!" Then, naturally, they would seize the best places on our steps and wait for the show. The musicians would put down their instruments on the side of the road, and perform any music you asked for because the *barong* could dance in any style. The other men who traveled with the *barong*, carrying flags and high decorated umbrellas, would take up their positions on either side of the *barong*, marking off the dancing area, and then the *barong* would begin. If any cars came along, which was not very likely, they just had to wait until the performance was over.

The *barong* can be a tiger, with a bright red face and snapping jaws that click loudly together to frighten away the witches, or an elephant or other animal. The men under the *barong* dance, and the movements of their legs and the swaying rhythm of the animal's back are beautifully worked out in dance steps. Sometimes masked attendants will dance with the *barong* in a rather fanciful version of the *baris*. The *barong* moves about in its ponderous graceful way, the musicians play, the children shout with delight, and after some minutes, the *barong* moves on to the next house.

Wayan Pandé and the boys were always pleased with the *barong*, too. It made them feel safe and protected from *leyaks*, which are the ghost-demons of Bali. Clare, who was all against superstition of this sort, used to tell them severely that it was all nonsense.

"You only say that because you have never seen them," Madé Jawi assured her.

"Have you ever seen one?"

Wayan Pandé said, "Oh yes. I have seen them just here on the village green."

"What did they look like?"

"Like ordinary people, but you can tell from their faces that they are *leyaks*. That is why they usually walk with their face down so that you cannot see."

"In India," I said, "you can tell them by their feet. Their feet are always turned backward no matter what the rest of them looks like."

"Ah yes? But that would be no good here because our sarongs are shorter. But one certain way of telling is by the hair that grows all down their spine. They are very clever at hiding it, though." He turned to Faubion, "If you meet a beautiful girl walking in the evening, you must be very careful, you might not recognize the face of a *leyak.*" Wayan Pandé continued seriously to Clare, "Only a few days ago I heard *leyaks* walking down the road to the east. I didn't see them, but I heard their laughter."

"But why didn't you call us?"

"You would have seen nothing, they would have gone by then." He went on to tell of an experience he had once had with *leyaks* when three of his friends were ill, and the *leyaks*, knowing they were in a weak condition, came around the house every night. "For a month I hardly slept at all, guarding against the *leyaks*. The first time I heard them they woke me with their laughter, and I ran out of the house and turned a flashlight on them. They were in the shape of wild pigs, and fire came out of their heads. I picked up a bamboo stick, and because I was strong they ran away. But I kept watch every night until my friends were well."

As a celebration for the last day of *Galungan* we asked Wayan Pandé what other dances we could ask for in Ubud. He said we had never seen *pentchak*, and since the boys all enjoyed it, that might be a good thing to have. We asked what *pentchak* was. It turned out to be a dance evolved from the movements of wrestling, stylized and set to music. "I thought about learning it myself, once," Wayan Pandé said, "but it is the art of self-defense, and what should I defend myself against? If you learn *pentchak* it makes your heart hard and your thoughts large, and what use have I for that?"

"Have the *pentchak* dancers in Ubud hard hearts?"

"Of course. You can see it in the way they play football. When they miss the ball they get very angry."

The Dutch, until recently, had banned *pentchak* dancing because it wasn't considered right that the Balinese should study the art of self-defense, even when it remained only in a dance form.

The *pentchak* was, without exception, the most dramatic dance I have ever seen. Not as beautiful as the *gabor*, not as brilliant as the *kebyar*, for power and excitement it was unequaled. It was danced by one or two men wearing only a short, tightly wound sarong, and a gold and scarlet headband with flowers. The music was only drums and cymbals which kept up an undercurrent of complicated rhythms, with a clash of cymbals for climactic moments. The village stood around our little strip of lawn watching the dancers through the flames of the oil lamps in dead silence. When it was finished, we all let out our breaths in a gasp of relaxation.

87 Any tourist that goes to Bali is told about the trance dances and in particular the kris dances, those fantastic, mystic performances in which men stab themselves with daggers and no blood comes, and they do not even hurt themselves. We had thought that like most tourist stories this was probably exaggerated if it existed at all. Consequently, when we heard of a kris dance that was to take place in a village called Kesiman we went to it with only half-hearted interest. Perhaps for this reason the kris dance, when we saw it, was all the more astonishing.

The temple at Kesiman was built in the usual way, of a courtyard within a courtyard, and was, for this occasion, exuberantly decorated. Enormous pennants flew all around, and the inner courtyard was marked out with tall bamboo poles flying long black and white streamers. The shrines were piled with offerings and flowers. Long processions of women, chanting as they walked, brought the gods to the temple from their houses. The women were as magnificently dressed as any I had seen in Bali, all in formal costume, with bright silk or cotton sarongs, and a long strip of brilliant brocade, silk, or embroidered material wrapped tightly around their bodies from armpits to hips.

Hundreds of people were milling about in both courts of the temple, and after the gods were put in their shrines the ceremonies began. First the performers must be put into a trance, and that is done in front of the main shrine with a priest in attendance to sprinkle them with holy water and to chant the incantations. Women keep up a background of chanting, too, which gives the ceremony a strangely anesthetic air. Incense and the sacred fires keep them all in a mist of smoke.

The "story," as far as we could gather from the performance, concerned the battle between Rangda (the force of evil) and the barong, which is the great protective force. The dancers are men who are going to eliminate the force of evil, and draw their krises with the intent to kill Rangda. But her magic is so powerful that they cannot touch her, and she makes them turn their krises against themselves. Then the barong, whom these men were trying to protect, and who in turn protects them, cannot undo the magic of Rangda, but it has strong magic of its own. It makes the men impervious to their krises, so that under the spell that Rangda has cast they are compelled to stab themselves, but under the barong's protection, the krises do not pierce their skin. All the characters in this dance, the three incarnations of Rangda, the two barongs, and all the men and women perform in an entranced state. As in most forms of Hinduism, the connection between religion and the dance is an accepted thing, and this particular dance, which must always be performed in a temple and under the auspices of the priests, is particularly holy. "Unless," as Alit once said to us, "you have had either a mystic or great artistic experience, you can understand only dimly the connection."

When the process of putting the witches into a trance was complete, they screamed and began to rise from the mat in front of the main shrine. They were held down forcibly by a couple of men to each incarnation of Rangda until the necessary headdresses and masks were put on them. They turned with their hands spread wide in horrible claws, and came screaming and screaming through the main courtyard of the temple while the crowd backed away from them. They all clutched their magic cloths and made menacing movements toward the people. One Rangda was almost falling, so deep was his trance.

The barongs were sprinkled with holy water, and they too came out swaying wildly through the courtyard. Before the Rangdas could engage them in battle, the men and the boys who were sitting, entranced before the shrine, bare-bodied and wearing only a tucked-up sarong, sprang to their feet and clutched their krises for the defense of the barong. The krises were turned on the dancers and they started to stab themselves. The curving daggers were sharp but they did not enter the skin, although the muscles of the men stood out with the force they were using. Their faces were contorted with pain, and they screamed as they swayed backward and forward forcing the kris into their neck or chest.

The entire procession of Rangdas, barongs, and kris dancers went slowly through the main gate into the outer temple, and there walked three times around the big shelter where they usually had cockfights. Some were in deeper trances than others and on that tour several of the kris dancers fainted completely and had to be brought out of their trance.

Meanwhile, inside the temple, many of the women and some of the men were being put into a trance by the same means as before. Eventually the women got up and staggered to one side, holding fans, flowers and flags. Suddenly there was a great wailing from them. Most of the women were in tears, and stood together with their eyes closed or half-closed, weeping and moaning. Their voices swelled with bitter laments. In an absolute abandonment of grief they wept with each other. While they stood there the procession of the Rangdas, barongs and kris dancers reappeared and was led back to the main shrine.

Then the women in their beautiful ceremonial clothes made the same pilgrimage in the outer court. They were followed by attendants and the chief priest who was himself deep in a trance and stood on the steps of the main gate, his face turned to the women, but his eyes wide and glazed.

All at once, the women broke into a dance, still weeping, and performed with exquisite grace and beauty snatches of the legong, gabor and others which I didn't recognize. We were told that when they were not entranced those women couldn't dance with anything like that proficiency.

Eventually they, too, returned to the inner court where the dancing and the stabbing with krises continued. The gamelan played and the crowd moved closer. At one point we were so close to the kris dancers that we could see the saliva in the corners of their mouth, and their arms trembling as they pushed their daggers with all their force.

When a dancer is actually pointing the kris to his body it is forbidden to take it away from him, but eventually all the dancers were brought out of their trance. They were calmed down. *Tuak* was poured into a banana-leaf cup and put into their hands. They poured it on the ground as a libation to the gods, and gradually came out of the trance. Then they joined the crowd quite naturally, wiping the sweat from their faces and smiling at the foreigners.

At last we tottered out of the temple, extraordinarily moved and shaky. Someone asked me for a cigarette, and I opened my hand to find a mashed and crumpled package of what had been cigarettes earlier in the afternoon.

Although this was one of the most impressive, it was not the only trance dancing that we saw in Bali. We saw it quite often, casually in the villages where there had been bad health or misfortune and purification was necessary.

One week end we decided to go to the beach. Kuta, which is near Den Pasar, is one of the most spectacularly lovely beaches I have ever seen—wide, curving, white sands with coconut palms behind, and good breakers to surf-ride in. The Balinese from the fishing village came down to the beach morning and evening to bathe with us. They had a very neat way of undressing. They walked right down to the edge of the water in their sarongs, dropped them, and quickly ran into the waves, modest and sensible. One person was left behind to keep the sarongs from getting wet. The men bathed on one side and the women and children on another, and they played as though they were all children, splashing each other and laughing, but always washing, which was the real purpose of the sea bathe.

In the evenings we used to walk into Kuta to listen to their gamelan. We thought it very good, but the leader of the orchestra said that they had been practicing for two years but still did not consider themselves good enough to perform outside Kuta.

One evening we heard music coming from the beach and went down to listen. There was some sort of ceremony going on, with many offerings to the evil spirits of the sea, people chanting, music, and in the middle of it all two women and a man being put into a trance. Attendants lit incense in front of them, and as the sun went down the chanting intensified.

The women rocked back and forth violently, making strange, painful noises. After a few minutes they got up, and to the sound of music began a slow, lovely dance, still entranced, down toward the sea.

Until nearly dark they danced on while little girls took the offerings into the water. At last they sat down and were brought out of the trance by the attendants. Evil had come to the village from the sea, and the spirits were being pacified.

88 In Ubud, one evening, the boys were all excited and told us of an amazing play which was to be held near by. It was a play of great mystical significance, and it had not been acted in Bali for fifty years because it was so dangerous. It was to start at midnight and continue till morning, and they wanted permission to go. We very stupidly decided that the ordeal of standing up all night was too much for us and did not accompany them.

In the morning they told us what they had seen, and it was, as they said, an extraordinary story. The woman who played the leading role (the part of a man) was the wife of a man who had been put in prison for his anti-Dutch activities, and she vowed that if he came back safely, she would do this very dangerous part.

The story was of a raja who adopts a little child which is lost, and which he thinks is a Sudra, the lowest caste. He brings the child up in his puri. The little boy is actually the son of a Kshatriya, high caste, but the raja does not know this, nor does his daughter, the princess, who falls in love with the Sudra retainer. The prime minister tells the raja that his daughter loves the young man, and the raja, furious that his hospitality has been so abused, orders him to kill the retainer. Then comes the exciting part when the retainer is supposed to be actually killed with a kris. It was unheard of for a woman to attempt such a role.

Since she was a woman, they did not use a kris, but they beat her with a stick, "really beat her," Wayan Pandé said. "We were close and saw that there was no pretense. Then she stopped the prime

[277]

minister's men and said, 'You cannot kill me this way,' so they threw *sirih* at her and she died." *Sirih* is the betelnut that the Balinese chew; it is supposed to have magic qualities.

Kompiang said, "I saw the whole thing as close as from here to the wall and I saw her die. She was so pathetic and the play was so beautiful that we all wept. Everyone there—a thousand people—all wept."

Then a god comes down and says that the man is really a Kshatriya, and brings him back to life. He marries the princess. "We were so happy because she had really died, and the magic brought her back to life."

Wayan Pandé's comment was, "She is old and has four children, but she looked as beautiful as a goddess."

89

One morning the little Idé Bagus came along and sat rather dejectedly on the veranda with me, and said his usual courteous "Good morning." Then he told me, "I have no elder sister and no younger sister. I have no elder brother and no younger brother. So I think you should be my elder sister. It is quite all right because we are both Brahmins, aren't we?"

"Yes, we are."

"So will you be my elder sister?"

"Thank you, I will."

"Good. I shall call you *Kaka*, or *Ka* for short."

"All right, *adit*." (Younger brother.)

He jumped up, laughing very hard, "Now that you are my *ka*, I ought to tell you that I kissed Chokorda Raké's little girl."

A little uncertain of what my role should be, I said carefully, "Did you really?"

"Are you angry?" he said quickly and seriously.

"Well, I don't know. Was the little girl angry?"

"No. She liked it just as much as I did."

"In that case I'm not angry."

[278]

"Good." Then he showed me how you blow a kiss in Bali. You touch your nose and then touch the other person's nose. He announced informatively, "If you kiss a man with your mouth it means you are willing to sleep with him."

Trying not to laugh, I said, "Thank you for telling me. How do you know all this?"

"Every child my age," Idé Bagus said with surprise, "knows these things."

Then he took me for a walk to the sacred spring across the *sawahs* from Ubud. He told me that if you pick any leaves or flowers there you forget your way home and are lost forever. If you bathe in the waters under the spring the spirits will be angry and give you a fever.

The better we got to know Chokorda Alit, the more surprising we found him. Listening to the Ubud gamelan rehearsing for their performance in Gianiar, one evening, we saw that Alit was instructing the orchestra and playing from time to time himself. Old Chokorda Rai of Sayan was sitting with Madé Jawi, Kompiang and us. We asked if Alit often played with the gamelan, and were told, "He is the best player in Ubud. When he was younger he used to play a great deal. He and Chokorda Mas together won the competition for the best in Bali."

When the *gabor* dancers came on, Chokorda Rai directed the proceedings and corrected the girls from time to time. We asked which he thought was the best dancer.

"Yes," said the old man, "it is important to know. A girl when she dances must attract men. If she is a great dancer people must forget their reason when they watch her. But a man should dance with his blood and know the meaning of what he does. Sayu Madé Rai is the best dancer because she thinks straight toward the dance, and she has the best dancing position. Purni's movement is the most fluid, and Alit's little girl has good eyes. But Warsi's smile is the best, and that is very important in Balinese dancing. There must be just that slight turning up of the lips which is not enough to make folds in the face."

"But when anyone is as beautiful as Sayu," I said, "it scarcely matters whether she can dance or not."

[279]

"Sayu?" said Chokorda Rai. "She is quite pretty of course, but her mouth isn't good."

"But her eyes are simply lovely, aren't they?"

"Yes, but if a girl has a beautiful mouth, her eyes must be beautiful, not necessarily the other way around."

"Then which do you consider the best looking?"

He pointed out a plump little girl who was not a particularly good dancer. "That one," he said, and his handsome old face lit up with pleasure.

"But she has big hips," Clare protested.

"That is good," said Chokorda Rai.

"In America," Madé Jawi said, "don't they like big hips, and tall women? Here we like them because they are strong."

"Well, in America they think a woman's figure is good if she is fairly tall, and has a small waist, narrow hips and long legs."

"Beh!" Madé Jawi said, that explosive little Balinese expression of surprise. "With all that thinness underneath, how would she ever carry loads on her head?"

"No American woman is as useful as that," Faubion said firmly.

After the rehearsal Alit came back with us and we asked him why he so seldom played music now.

"I think," he said in his gentle, weary voice, "that a man should study a little of everything. I studied music and such things when I was young because those are the first of the things a man should know—the world about him. Then he should study religion, and finally he should study himself."

"And what do you study now?"

"Oh I?" he said laughing. "I study how to die."

We looked startled. Alit explained more seriously, "All their lives people are beset by fears. Bali, in her great good fortune, is saved some of these fears. We are lucky because we have a sufficiency in our island, and we are lucky that we have no money, for money is the prelude of desire. But we, too, have fears of hurt, and fears of misfortune. And what do all fears come to in the end? What is it that none of us can really accept? I think," he said with a question in his voice, "it is the idea of death. That is why I study how to die. If I can live without desire and without fear, then I can ask for nothing more. Already I have no more desire, and so," he turned slightly to Clare, "I study death."

90 Naturally, since we saw so much of them, we came to know Wayan Pandé and his family rather well. They were of the lowest caste, which did not prevent Wayan Pandé's being one of the most respected men in Ubud. He adored his two sons, and never made excuses for them. Madé Jawi, and his elder brother who worked in the *sawahs*, both had, as a result, the kind of unshakable security and directness that such a home life gives. They were the most refreshing people to have as friends because one couldn't blackmail them with affection, gratitude, dependence or any of the accepted ways. There is a great dignity that comes with independence of this sort, and for the first time we saw that human relations can be straightforward and satisfactory without the irritations of possessiveness.

Wayan Pandé's elder son, Togog, was the best-looking boy in Ubud. Once when I commented on this, Wayan Pandé said, "He is recently married and is happy. That is why you think him beautiful."

Faubion asked Togog, "Were you in love?"

"Oh yes!" he said most emphatically.

"Do you love your wife more than she loves you?"

Togog answered with great delight, "*Sama sama chinta*." (The love between us is the same.)

He took us to see the family's fields, one day. There were five *sawahs* and he worked all year in them, especially hard at that time because Madé Jawi and Wayan Pandé could not give him their usual help. They got three crops a year, but that meant only enough rice for the family because there were nine people to feed. On our walk back home he asked if we would like to come to their house and meet his wife.

Rigig was a small, plump, rather shy girl, a year or two older than

[281]

her husband, who was about nineteen. She didn't know exactly how old she was and told us, smiling, "If you do not count, then the years do not worry you."

The entire family lived in one compound where there were five small pavilions. They were poor, so their pavilions were mud-floored, thatched and open on three sides with a mud wall on the fourth. The sides could be closed with palm mats, and the pavilions themselves were raised a couple of feet as a protection against the rain and the animals. They were built around a central courtyard where the animals were kept—two pigs, one cow, seven hens, one cock and many chickens. Behind the pavilions there were ten coconut palms and some banana trees. They had a vegetable garden, too, but it was in one of their sawahs because in the compound the animals would eat the vegetables.

The best of the pavilions belonged to Togog and Rigig. "When Rigig came here as a bride," Wayan Pandé explained, "she liked this one best, so my wife and I moved into the next one because we are old and such things no longer matter to us."

In the compound Rigig's day was a very full one as it started about six in the morning and continued, with its jobs of cooking and looking after the household and Wayan Pandé's two small children by his second wife, until nine in the evening. "It sounds like a lot of work," she said, "but I have time to see my friends and to go to the dances. And since I am married, I am happy to look after my husband's family, and the work in the house pleases me."

She and Togog had known each other since they were children. Wayan Pandé said that he had always assumed that they would get married, but he had to wait until they found it out for themselves.

The whole family, although it was almost the poorest in Ubud, enjoyed a curious deference in the village itself and in the surrounding area. Once Clare had borrowed Chokorda Agung's bicycle to ride into Pliatan to see some wood carvers. On the way she lost her purse, and returned rather distressed to tell Wayan Pandé about it. He listened and said, "I will go to Pliatan and talk to the people. I can only do what is adat" (something between custom and manners), "but perhaps whoever found it will return it."

[282]

Within an hour Wayan Pandé was back with the purse. "I told them that I work for the girl who lost the purse, that she is very honest and not rich. I told them, too, that she is fond of our people. That is true, isn't it?"

"Yes," Clare said, turning red with embarrassment.

"So the man who found the purse gave it to me, and I gave him a reward from the money."

"Thank you very much," Clare said, "I really can't think why he returned it."

"Perhaps if he had not known to whom it belonged. But if he had not given it back, afterward his friends would never know what his thoughts were."

Kompiang told us later what the real reason was. "If Wayan Pandé had not been the person to ask for the purse, perhaps it would not have been returned."

As a result of this, and of many different incidents, Clare came to a conclusion that before the trip would have been a very difficult one for her. "Nowhere," she said, "including the most democratic countries, have I seen such easy association between castes, classes and economic groups as in Bali."

"I thought you disapproved of systems of aristocracy," I said, partly to tease her and partly to find out how far she would follow her previous statement.

"I do," she said. "But every country has some sort of an aristocracy—of money or of birth—but here it doesn't make a barrier. I suppose Chokorda Agung is the richest man in Ubud and certainly he is a high-ranking prince. Yet when he comes here to talk to us, anyone can sit on the steps and listen or join in. The only mark of respect is that they sit on a lower level. He is also the president of the music society, yet before a performance he dashes about fixing lights and costumes with all the others. He and Chokorda Raké and Alit all have big puris, but anyone in Ubud ambles through taking short cuts or picking the flowers, and the children play all over the place. Does all that happen with your Indian princes?"

"No," I said, "I only wish it did."

91

During the months that we lived in Ubud, Clare acquired, for the first time in her life, an interest in paintings. She used to spend a good deal of time with Idé Bagus Madé, the most brilliant of Ubud's painters, and had bought one of his canvases. She told us that she would like to buy more, but he didn't want to sell them. "I paint both to get money and to enjoy myself. If I sell everything I have, what can I buy with the money that will give me as great pleasure as my pictures? So I sell only enough to allow me to live."

Many of the artists in Ubud, realizing that Clare was interested, used to bring us their work, sometimes to ask our opinion, sometimes in the hope of selling them, and sometimes just to show us how they were progressing. Durus, a very pleasant youngster, had once made a drawing of the *gabor* girls which Faubion had liked and had bought to use with an article he was writing. He asked Durus to make a set of a dozen different dance poses.

About a week later Durus brought them, lovely imaginative pictures with a lot of movement, and a certain stylization at the same time. We were all sitting in the garden with Alit when the boy came up, and we looked at the pictures and praised them.

"Why don't they sign their pictures?" Clare asked Alit.

"He can't write, I expect," Alit replied matter-of-factly.

"But I mean nobody signs his work, even if he can write. Someone else could claim their work so easily."

"Then," said Alit, "the artist would be flattered. His picture must be good if someone else wishes he had painted it. Besides, he can always paint another." He smiled in his gentle way, "Anonymity is not important to us. We do not like to keep our art in museums— where is the joy in that?"

"Well, the beautiful things of one generation should be preserved for the generations afterward to see."

"But there will be other beautiful things in later generations."

"Yes, but all the same—" Clare began, and then gave it up.

Durus had brought a friend with him who was holding several of

[284]

the strangest pictures we had seen. Wierd surrealist paintings, strange colors and shapes, and pictures of dreams. Clare held one up to Alit and said, "What do you think of that?"

"I don't understand it," he said, "but that is the way *he* sees."

Clare was most worried when she saw that faintly under the paint on one of the pictures there was the outline of a previous picture. The boy had erased the first one because he hadn't enough paper to paint the next. Clare immediately gave him some money to buy paper with. She never did become reconciled to the artistic extravagance of Bali.

92

I was sitting rather moodily on the back veranda one morning late in June, drinking coffee and watching the usual parade of people through our back courtyard to the well. A couple of children were picking the leaves of a special shrub to crush them into a paste for curing headaches. Desa Kutut, the jolly girl from Chokorda Raké's *puri*, had just finished placing the offerings in the family shrines, and she and our gardener, Tugog, were sitting on our courtyard wall and talking. Idé Bagus slicked back his hair with a tiny brown hand, yelled good morning, and vanished down the path to the bathing place. Wayan Pandé was mixing bread dough in the sun. Kompiang and Madé Jawi were cleaning the oil lamps and trimming the wicks and shouting comments to people at the well. It was a typical Ubud morning.

From the front of the house I heard the voices of Americans, strangers, altogether an extraordinary thing in Ubud. I darted into my bedroom as I heard, "Are you an American?"

Clare's voice, sounding puzzled, said, "Yes."

"Well, so are we. We heard that there were some Americans living up here so we thought we would stop by and visit with you."

I heard them all walk out to the courtyard. Madé Jawi and Kompiang came into my room, looking very correct and indefinably wary. They had put on their shirts. They asked if these were Dutch visitors.

I said, "They sound like Americans to me."

"In that case, shall we buy more *brum* and *arak?*"

"Yes, I think you'd better."

The Americans turned out to be some of a group of journalists who had decided to make a quick survey and tour of Indonesia. They were in Bali for a couple of days as part of their tour. They spent the day with us and asked us endless questions, very few of which we could answer. "What is the average wage of the Balinese?" "Is there any real understanding of democratic principles among them?" "Are they ready for independence?" "What about this feudal system of rajas and caste?"

I kept quiet through as much of the conversation as I could because I have found that while people will go to a European for expert knowledge about Europe, or to an American for expert knowledge about America, the evidence of an Asian on Asia is apt to be discounted as "emotional."

After they all left, the Balinese—who had kept away most of the day—came around to ask who they were and all about them. We, in turn, asked them what they thought of the Americans.

"They look very worried and angry."

"They are tired," Clare said, "they have been traveling a long time."

"How long will they stay in Bali?"

"They leave tomorrow."

"And then they will write about it?"

"Well, they have been in Indonesia for nearly two weeks. . . ."

"Why do they not stay longer?"

"Why should they?" Faubion said briskly. "You don't like to travel either."

"But we don't write about America."

"And besides," Faubion said, "they have jobs to go back to, and probably wives and children—"

"And motorcars and refrigerators," put in Madé Jawi cheekily, and everyone laughed.

Faubion said seriously, "They are trying to help you become free."

"It is sad that we cannot talk to them as the Dutch can."

It was apparently a day for visitors because that evening, while we

[286]

were sitting in the garden and talking to Alit, a Dutchman came up and told us that he was passing through Ubud and had heard that we were having a dance performance that evening; could he stay and watch it? While we were saying of course he could, Alit had automatically risen from his chair and was about to move onto the ground.

Faubion said, "Don't move, Alit," and started to call for another chair when the Dutchman explained to us in English, "It is the custom in Bali for different ranks to sit on different levels. He will be much happier if he sits on the floor."

I was too angry to speak, but Faubion said in his clearest Malay, "Alit, you and Daiyu are the only people present with any caste at all. So if one accepts the principle of rank, in Bali it should be the foreigners who sit on the ground."

93 In the third week of June, Badang Tagal, a small village near Ubud, had a temple purification ceremony. Since the big temple in Ubud, near the river, is the *Pura Desa* (Temple of the District), the people came there to place their offerings and to bathe.

The procession was among the loveliest we had seen. Badang Tagal had the reputation of producing the prettiest girls in the area, and it was easy to see why. The procession was a long one, led by the smallest children wearing very elaborate flower headdresses and their best *kains*. After them came the gamelan, because nothing in Bali can be done without music. They had very beautiful, ancient instruments in Badang Tagal, tuned in a four-tone scale, and the children sang with the music. After the orchestra came a line of girls which made the assembled crowd of young Ubud men gasp. They were all the unmarried girls of Badang Tagal, wearing yellow *kains*, and green and gold brocade wound round their breasts. They carried the offerings in decorated baskets on their heads. As this long line of yellow and gold and green against the clear browns of the Balinese skin came swaying into Ubud, everybody rushed out to watch, shouting that Balinese exclamation of surprise, pleasure or wonder, "Beh!"

At the end of the procession came the men carrying drums and gongs and keeping up the necessary accompaniment of the game-lan. High, on palanquins, sheltered by umbrellas and accompanied by flags, were the gods that were being taken to the temple. None of the men could go into the inner court on that occasion, so Clare and I followed the girls and watched the ceremonies inside the temple, while the boys sat on the bamboo bridge outside waiting for the girls to go down to the river to bathe.

For two nights there was dancing at the temple, the *baris*, and something we hadn't seen before, the *topeng*. It was a different sort of dance-drama, and the leading parts were taken by Iruju, and his father who was even better than the boy. The whole thing was played in huge masks, and the usual magnificent costumes, but by then we knew the individual styles of Ubud's dancers well enough to recognize them even though we couldn't see their faces. The stories of the *topeng* were, for a change, not from Hindu mythology, but concerned, instead, the intrigues and drama of ancient Balinese court life. The characters were fairly standardized—wicked prime ministers, comic attendants, beautiful and virtuous princes, etc., but they told us that the stories were all actually based on Balinese history of various periods, and that some of the plays could not be performed in some parts of Bali because they would offend the de-scendants of the originals.

94 July fourth was, appropriately enough, election day in Bali. The voting took place in Chokorda Agung's *puri*. He was a candidate, and so was our landlord, Chokorda Raké. They were sit-ting outside the *puri* with a couple of the other candidates from near here. From the whole district, there were eleven candidates, of whom nine could get elected. That would make them electors whose job it would be to vote for the people who would represent Bali in the government of East Indonesia, in Macassar.

In the morning the *kul-kul*, a large, hollow tree trunk which has a deep ringing sound that can be heard in the fields around, was sounded to collect everyone to the big shelter where they held the cockfights. There the election procedure was explained to them, and each man was given nine slivers of bamboo. He then walked into the puri where eleven baskets had been placed in one of the pavilions. Each basket had the name of a candidate on it, and the men had to put their sticks into nine of the baskets. A man stood watch to read aloud the names of the candidates for the benefit of the illiterate.

"Nothing secret about this ballot," Clare said as we wandered through peeping into the baskets to see how the various candidates were coming along. Everyone seemed to be enjoying themselves and sat about in little groups chatting and eating peanuts from the stalls.

We met Wayan Pandé coming back from buying vegetables and asked him if he were going to vote.

"I haven't time to sit around gossiping," he said, "I have to go and cook your food."

"But you *ought* to vote," Clare said. "We can eat late."

"No, no. Let the youngsters enjoy themselves. Togog will vote for me. One in a family is enough." He hurried off.

The whole day, however, was filled with political talk. When we got back to the house we found that the boys had been cleaning out the cupboard in the kitchen. On one pane of glass they had written in soap, "You must not steal bread." On another was, "Complete Freedom. Don't weaken until Freedom." Rather surprised, because we had never discussed Indonesian politics with them, we asked, "Are you interested in getting freedom?"

Madé Jawi said at once, "Of course. Were we not all members of the PRI? Haven't we hidden in river beds and fought and gone without food for our freedom?" PRI stands for Pemuda (youngman) of the Republic of Indonesia.

"We didn't know that," Faubion said apologetically.

"How should you? Usually it isn't safe to talk to foreigners about such things." Madé Jawi turned his full attention on us. "Have you never seen the scars across Chokorda Agung's back? Well, those are his souvenirs of the beatings he received when he was put in jail by the Dutch. Chokorda Ngura was imprisoned, too. Many people from Ubud. . . ." Poor Chokorda Ngura, old and gentle and distinguished. We were all shocked into the realization that he had never really got over that extraordinary session in jail with all its accompaniments. That was why he would only see foreigners if they were guests at the puri, and then only with the careful intercession of Chokorda Agung.

The story, as in all Southeast Asia, was the same. After the Japanese were defeated there was a brief period of freedom for the Indonesians, and then the Dutch returned with arms and troops calmly prepared to take back the colony they had lost. It came as something of a surprise to them that even to the "lovable, childlike Balinese" this was a little too much. For several months there was fierce resistance from them, but eventually superior force triumphed and Bali was again subdued. But to this day the Dutch will tell you with a note of warning, "Scratch a Balinese and you will find a savage." I repeated that remark to Madé Jawi, and he burst out laughing and said, "But one does not even have to *scratch* a Dutchman!"

Ubud, like most villages, had its various individual representatives of different ways of thinking. There was the village rake, known for his gambling and spendthrift ways, whom all the girls rather liked, and were rather afraid of. There was the village beauty, Sayu Madé Rai, the village scholar, the fast young woman of the village, and so on. Anak Agung Anom was the village radical. Clare had made friends with him because she said he was "politically conscious"—a rare thing, we had thought, in Ubud.

We had first met him when he sat next to Faubion during a football game and started asking him questions which showed considerable knowledge and canniness. Faubion, who is always in something of a haze over politics, was rather lost.

Anak Agung Anom said, "You have just been traveling through China and Japan?"

"Yes."

"All Japanese conquests have been taken away and the land returned to their owners?"

"Yes."

"But not to their real owners."

Faubion was silent, thinking of Indonesia, Malaya, Indo-China.

Anak Agung Anom continued, "Americans do not wish for colonies?"

"No. That is why the Philippines have their independence."

"If America does not believe in colonies, why doesn't she help us?

"We have tried to help you—"

"Ah, yes. But the only people that can really help us are the Indians. They know how to free themselves from a ruler. Other people will give us promises, but India will give us help. We can learn from them. Isn't that true, Daiyu?"

"I certainly hope so," I said, and made a mental note to write to my father that night.

On election day Anak Agung Anom came to see us, and Clare at once asked him questions about election procedures and particularly about age limits.

He said, "The limit varies in the islands, but here people are so unsure of their ages that it is impossible to say definitely at what age you should start voting. If you feel like twenty-one you vote."

"Are you going to vote?"

His round, serious face took on a slightly sulky expression, "What would be the use? Can there be a free election under colonialism?"

"But surely, one way of changing the conditions would be to vote in the elections and send good men to Macassar."

"The Balinese understand those arguments perfectly well, but they do not bother to vote because they know the elections aren't fair. Even if we elect a good man, the Dutch can say he is not good, and he must go. This may be Dutch democracy, but if it is, let them keep it in Holland." Madé Jawi and Kompiang had stopped their work and were listening, too. Anak Agung Anom continued, "Here in Bali we have an almost socialistic state, we have no great poverty here, and we are happy. But we are apt to look no further than our boundaries, and that is why we will not see the danger approaching."

"What sort of danger?" Clare asked in her brisk, reporter way.

Anak Agung Anom turned to her with a voice full of sadness. "The danger is from you," he said. "Is it not strange that people who are so sympathetic with us should be our greatest danger? In the old days white men conquered us and governed us because we believed that they were stronger both in fighting and in government.

Now we have all seen the white man ignominiously defeated by Asians. With the decay of the colonial system the legend of governmental competence goes, too. We found we were quite well able to govern ourselves, and now when any Dutchman says to us, 'If we leave, chaos will reign,' we think at once of the history of Europe for the last few years. Is there chaos greater than that? And then, if we cannot laugh, we must cry that it took us so many years to find out. . . ."

Clare, moved in spite of herself, said, "And what is the new danger? Communism?"

"Oh no, that is no danger to us. It is this: even if the white man is prepared to relinquish other superiorities, he still feels that his 'way of living' is better, and he will force or cajole us into learning it—though in some cases, like the Philippines, it is eagerly accepted. Is it consistent with either your morality or ours to do such a thing?"

"Don't you," Clare asked uncertainly, "need technology, medicine—?"

"Don't you," Anak Agung Anom said, "think of anything besides making your bodies more comfortable?"

"Don't you want to learn from us?" Clare said.

"Oh yes," he answered in a tone of utter despair, "we shall have to learn from you. Every Balinese can tell the time by the sun, but he will want to wear a watch. He will want the money to buy it. He will forget the importance of his land to search for money. Our isolation and our happiness cannot last forever. But," he said very softly, when it comes to that I do not wish to see my island. If everything I love is dead, why should I live?"

Faubion said, "If we were sensible, we would learn from you."

Anak Agung Anom smiled, "But you, after all, are almost Oriental."

Later he invited us to his house "to see how a poor man lives." We walked along one of the back lanes of Ubud to a part where the mud is so deep when it rains that you have to walk with your sarong hitched above your knees. His little farm had crumbling walls, and one pavilion where he, his wife and child, and the two children of his brother who was still in jail, all slept. The little kitchen was no more than a shelter with only one wall and a roof. He opened the pot on the fire and showed us what was being cooked for the day. Sweet potatoes mixed with a little rice, and that was all.

"This," he said, "is our second pavilion. I started building it when I came out of prison two months ago, but it isn't finished yet because I can't afford to buy the materials."

"You were imprisoned for being a member of the PRI?"

"Yes, a very active member. I believed the Dutch should leave Indonesia even more strongly than many of the others because I had been studying by myself. Before the war there were no schools here. You could only be educated if you had much money and could go to Den Pasar or to Java. Since the war I have spent much of my time in jail, and now I cannot get a job unless I make a promise that I will engage in no more political activity. The Dutch can make it very hard for you. And, naturally, I could not give such a promise."

"Naturally."

His small plot of land could not grow rice, so he raised sweet potatoes and tried to live on them. They had no coconut trees, and no other vegetables; one pig, one goat and a few chickens. Sometimes his wife made a little money by reeling cotton. "Fortunately," he said, in Bali if I say to a friend, 'I am hungry,' he will feed me."

The little naked children played and laughed in the yard. We walked back to our house feeling sad and inadequate, and from the ridge in the path looked back to the poor little plot of land and the sagging huts.

Rather depressed by this interlude, when we saw Alit in the afternoon we asked him what he thought of the encroachment of Western ways and thought on Bali. I tried to explain the point a little bit, and told Alit that in college in America when one studied sociology or education, enormous emphasis was put on the small unit. Socially, one was told, it was healthier, everybody had a part in the community and its life. One learned under what disadvantages city children lived because their schools were not a part of the community; they never knew the other children or their teachers in an enviroment other than the schoolroom. To counteract this trend, Parent-Teacher associations were encouraged, extracurricular acti-

[293]

vities, smaller classes, seminars and so on. At the same time, on the artistic front, strong encouragement was given to Little Theater groups, community enterprises, chamber music so that friends could get together and provide their own entertainment in a world of radio, television and the movies.

Well, precisely the community which the American sociologist yearns for exists in Bali. It is a country entirely composed of such small units. The village, which is all-containing, can satisfy all sides of an individual's life. Would all this be lost if Westernization were to come to Bali?

"Yes," Alit said, "we are fortunate in being rich enough to feed and clothe ourselves, and rich enough in another way, to amuse ourselves. But have you no faith in our vitality? Anak Agung Anom has a heart full of bitterness because he has suffered much, so as yet he can see no further than his own despair. But Bali is a strong country, we have great resilience and power inside ourselves. We can use Western influences as we use the waters from the mountains. They are allowed to flood the land, but they are dammed in such a way that they do not carry everything with them, but flow around the villages, water only the *sawahs*, and the waste runs into the sea. We cannot preserve Bali from the West," he smiled slightly teasingly at us, "it is only the West that would want to preserve Bali as a museum."

95 In the second week of July we finally decided to leave Bali. We had been talking about it for some time in a reluctant and desultory way. Every now and again Clare would say, "Really, you know, Bali is only one small island in all of Indonesia." Faubion would immediately become entirely vague and wander off, and I would nod uncomfortably and say, "I suppose we really ought to go to the Celebes or something."

In the end we never did go to any of the other islands except Java. The thing that made our minds up for us was that we heard that the Republican government was moving back to Jogjakarta under a cease-fire agreement. There was considerable excitement in Ubud. My little Idé Bagus came up and said, "Ka! It is said that Indonesia is to be free!"

"I know. It's wonderful. But does it make any difference to you? You're Balinese, after all."

"I may be Balinese," he said, "but my blood is Indonesian. Now we can sing the Indonesian national song without fear of going to jail." He sat down beside me and taught me the words which were all about Indonesians have one heart and one purpose, *Indonesia rayat, merdeka! Merdeka!* (Freedom, freedom! for the Indonesian people.)

Learning the song, suddenly the idea of leaving Bali seemed terrible.

"Idé Bagus," I said miserably, "*adit,* will you miss me when I go?"

He thought the point over carefully and said, "No. For the first few days I will be sad."

"Well, at least you're honest," I said with irritation.

"But, Daiyu," he was very serious, "how could I insult you by lying to you? It is understood that you must return to your own country."

I thought, it *is* true, one really can't blackmail them. Clare came out of the house carrying a paper and pencil. She said, "We must go to Jogjakarta as soon as possible. With Dutch 'Police Actions' happening so unexpectedly, we never know how soon it may become impossible again."

We wrote out a couple of cables and called Madé Jawi to take them to the bus stop and give them to the driver to send from Den Pasar. As usual he asked what was in them, and I told him in detail because we had all become quite used to the idea that the Balinese sense of curiosity doesn't allow for any of the sillier privacies.

He said, "It is settled then? You leave in five days?"

"Yes," I said. And suddenly it did seem very settled.

The last days were filled with goodbys and presents and a final frenzy of entertainment. My little cowherd, the one that had been gored, brought me a small brown bird with pink legs and feet which he had tamed. It came when you called it and sat on your shoulder.

He also gave me a very large hat which he had woven out of bamboo, the green leaves and the soft white stem. He pointed out that he had given it a particularly wide brim because girls should wear something a little different from the usual man's hat in which he works in the sawahs.

Chokorda Raké, invited us to lunch. We were about to get ready to go to his puri when great trays of food started arriving—rice, many sorts of meat, chicken and vegetables—and finally Chokorda Raké himself arrived smiling and jolly, and announced that the food was from him. "We will all eat here in your house because the puri is so full of women!"

He was really the perfect guest, interesting and amusing and didn't stay long. He told us that as a result of the July fourth elections he had been chosen the elector from this district. "I thought very seriously before taking a public post again. I had been pungawa (administrative head) of this district for many years, but when my sons were imprisoned I resigned, because then I knew that justice was impossible under this system."

"Have you changed your mind now?"

"I hope that something can be done with the government of East Indonesia. And then," he added seriously, "I am one of the few Balinese who is prepared to go to Macassar. It is not a fine job, that. You have to be away from Bali for three months in the year. It is hot. The food is not good. But I love my sons very much and one is there studying engineering, and the other is still in jail in Macassar."

I thought this a very sensible attitude. If only more people could get rid of the idea that political appointments are glamourous.

Kunter came over to give us the good news that his cow was pregnant at last. The three years' feeding had not been in vain. He was very pleased, but couldn't decide whether he wanted a male calf to be strong in working in the fields, or a female that would produce more calves.

Alit joined us in the evening and said that he had asked our favorite joget to dance for us after dinner. She performed again with all the grace in the world. As the last of the men to dance with her came

[296]

onto the floor I realized with a shock that he had only a stump for one arm. He waved it gaily about and I saw that he was wearing my watch on it. His face was covered with Clare's talcum powder, and he was really a grotesque figure. But he was a very good dancer—even in Bali where the hands are so important in dancing. The crowd screamed with laughter and encouraged him to get closer and closer to the *joget*.

Faubion told Alit that such a thing would be impossible in America, that one could not laugh at another person's infirmities.

"But," said Alit, "it was cut off when he was a child."

"Still, one should feel sorry for him."

"Why? He is one of the strongest workers. Besides, he is a very funny dancer."

I overheard this conversation and turned to Kunter who was sitting next to me. "Don't you find him pathetic?" I asked.

"Pathetic? But what can you do for him?"

The following nights were full of dancing, the *pentchak* and the *gabor* of Ubud, Idé Bagus Blangsinga to do the *kebyar*, and a strange dance called *oleg*, a sort of double *kebyar*, danced by girls whom Chokorda Rai had sent over from Sayan. It was a recently composed dance and its popularity had swept the island. During the days we saw people and packed.

Clare said, "Our life in Bali seems to have been nothing but sitting and chatting to people, how is it possible that it should seem so entirely satisfactory?"

Faubion had given most of his things away rather than go through the bother of packing them, so he could sit and chat to people right up to the very last moment. "What will you miss most about Bali?" he asked the evening before we left Ubud. But it was impossible to say, the days were so full of things we would miss.

The little Idé Bagus was sitting with us, and I said to him, "Can you read fortunes?" I held out my hand, "Tell me if I will come back to Bali."

He turned my hand round and held it up in front of my face with the palm toward me. "Do you see a letter M written there?"

I looked, and saw—as there is in most people's hands—an M formed by the lines. "Yes, I do."

"Do you know what it means?"

"No."

"It stands for *Manusia Musti Mati*." (Mankind must die.) "That's all the fortune any of us needs to know." He ran away laughing.

96 The Republican government of Indonesia had moved back to Jogjakarta only a few days before we got there. The big arches of welcome that had been constructed over all roads leading to the city still stood with their brave banners and slogans fading slowly in the sunlight. Huge posters greeted the returning Republicans with SALAMAT DATANG (SAFETY IN ARRIVING). The letter S in flowers, laurels or paper welcomed Sukarno, released at last from imprisonment. Everywhere there were hundreds of red and white Republican flags—the first time we had seen them flown—on buildings, bicycles, cars and held in the childrens' hands.

Jogjakarta had a wildly festive air which contrasted strangely with the shabbiness of a city that had been under siege for so long. Bright letters on a pennant announced that the hotel was called *Merdeka* (Freedom), while underneath on the remaining fragments of the smashed panes of the entrance porch, one could see that it had been the Grand Hotel while the Dutch had held Jogjakarta. There was a bustling excitement on the streets and smiling Youth Army boys in their torn black shirts and red scarves helped the regular soldiers to direct traffic, guard mined houses, organize the streams of returning refugees. In shops, on street corners, in the hotel, in offices, everywhere the greeting was *Merdeka!*

All of us were singularly fortunate to be in Jogjakarta just at that time, because my father had followed up his speeches to the Security Council at Lake Success, presenting the Indonesian case, with more concrete assistance in getting the Republican government back to their capital, so his name was a passport anywhere in the Jogjakarta area. In fact, President Sukarno, whom we saw very soon after our

[298]

arrival, greeted me with, "Even before I say *Merdeka* I must tell you that both personally and on behalf of all Indonesians, our greatest thanks are due to your father for the work he did for us at the United Nations." Then he and his wife, with their charm and informality and extraordinary good looks, proceeded to make us feel that even if they had not been the most important people in Indonesia at that time, they would still be among the most fascinating people we had ever met.

We, of course, congratulated them on being back in their capital, but he turned a worried face on the shabby, faded room of the Residency, and said, "Thank you, thank you, but we are so ashamed to receive you here before we have had a chance to repair the damage. My wife is worried about these covers and this furniture. We have tried to clean them."

Mme. Sukarno, with her exquisite profile and smooth heavy hair held up with big silver hair pins, looked doleful for a second, too, but neither of them could keep the delight and optimism out of their voices for long. She said, "But none of that matters. We have been so cut off from news. Tell us the thing we most want to know —how is Bali? You have just come from there, I hear."

We all raved about Bali for a while, and President Sukarno said, "I know what you are feeling. I am half Balinese, my mother came from there. It is like a slight but perpetual pain to have Balinese blood. You cannot stop thinking about it." He pointed to a bare, discolored patch on the wall. "There used to be a picture of Bali on that wall, of men with their chickens going to market. But that was —what is the word?—borrowed?—when the Dutch left." He spoke without sarcasm. "They took a great deal from here."

"Oh how ridiculous to remember all that!" Mme. Sukarno interrupted. "All of you are back in Jogja, and this is a time for happiness," she said, all the happiness in the world in her voice.

That afternoon President Sukarno lent us a car to take us out to Prambanan, a famous Hindu temple, and assigned an information officer to conduct us there. The trip was an education from more than an artistic point of view. First of all the destruction of the villages around Jogjakarta was far greater than I had expected. A couple of shattered walls might be all that was left standing of a village. In the ruins of tiny towns, all of whose inhabitants had been forced to leave, we saw the remains of the Republican army slogans, WE FIGHT FOR FREEDOM, INDONESIA HAS ONE HEART, and so on. Entire villages had been mined and destroyed until there was nothing left but piles of brick and dust. The road itself was extremely bad, full of holes and craters, and all the bridges had been blown up completely or severly damaged. All along the road, to the north, we could see the great volcano Merapi that guards Jogjakarta.

We dutifully looked at the temple, with our minds still full of the destruction we had seen. Several chidren in tattered clothes followed us around and expained the bas-reliefs of the *Ramayana* to us. As we left we said, *"Salamat tingal"* (Safety in remaining), as we aways had in Bali. But these children immediately stood to attention and shouted, *"Merdeka!"* in reply.

On the way back to Jogjakarta, we stopped the car to take some photographs, and one of the soldiers working on a demolished bridge called out, "Are you for the Republic?"

"Oh yes!" we shouted back, decidedly.

97 Before the war Faubion had spent some time studying and lecturing at Taman Siswa, a teachers' training school and cultural center, run by a magnificent old man, Ki Hadjar Dewantoro. In those days the only education in Indonesia was Dutch, and Taman Siswa was not only the first place to teach in Malay, but also the only school which offered to send teachers to any village, however remote, with the condition only that the village would provide the teacher with food and a place to stay.

Faubion had found one of his prewar friends, a fellow student at Taman Siswa, in a military hospital, wounded. He told us that Taman Siswa had had to close down during the Dutch Occupation because most of the students and teachers had either joined the army or gone into hiding in the hills. Now, it had been opened a week, and already five hundred students had joined, but they were mostly children as the others couldn't yet be released from their wartime work.

On the insistence of Faubion's wounded friend, we went to Kaliurang, which was about twenty-five kilos north of Jogjakarta, at the foot of Merapi, and where there was a large encampment of the student army. The road to Kaliurang was so damaged that only jeeps and trucks could negotiate it. We were escorted by some of the student army people who took us to a celebration of the announcement of the Republic at their headquarters.

98 Everyone in Jogjakarta was so absorbed in the news of the moment and in the return of the government that our conversations of those days seem now to belong to a very remote past, like the newspapers one finds lining drawers in guest rooms.

There was Haji Saleem, who was then foreign minister, a short, oldish man with a white beard, shrewd eyes and a wonderful gift for aphorism, saying bitterly, "I hold the Dutch responsible for each gray hair on my wife's head." She had stayed in Jogjakarta all through the Occupation, and her husband had returned from prison to find her tremendously aged. And I remember her timid voice saying, "The night the Dutch withdrew was so quiet I couldn't sleep. I had become too used to the gunfire."

It was with the optimism that was everywhere in the city at that time that Haji Saleem said, "We are no longer concerned with flags and nationalities, but with the restoration of peace and prosperity, and that can only come with the end of colonialism."

I can remember the contrast that Dr. Hatta, the vice-president, presented to Haji Saleem. Very quiet, modest to the point of diffidence with no violence in his speech or gestures, without Sukarno's dash or Saleem's sharp tongue and touch of grandiloquence, he looked like a successful businessman, a curious type for a revolutionary. He talked in a measured, sensible way about the transfer of sovereignty, the problems of peace. He talked in figures and statistics, and turns out to have been a remarkably sound prophet.

Then there was Mrs. Santoso, Indonesia's famous woman leader and politician, with her lovely complexion and her assured manner, recounting over a cup of tea, the terrible and tragic story of her husband's murder. "The last words he heard before he died were from the Dutch sergeant who shot him, 'I don't care who you are. I don't care that you are a civilian. The whole Republic is rotten!' I am not the only Indonesian woman who has suffered this, there are many, many. . . ."

Many of our conversations were like that—atrocity stories interspersed with politics, memories sandwiched between plans for the future. Before we left Jogjakarta, we had dinner with President Sukarno and his wife. It was like being at home again. We were the only guests, and we talked about everything except politics.

Late at night, when we left, the Sukarnos, looking young and very full of vitality, stood on the steps of the Residency with linked arms, smiling and waving. "*Merdeka* and good night."

"*Merdeka*, and safety in returning!"

99 We might have stayed in Jogjakarta much longer, except that Clare one day said with rather careful carelessness, "I really think we should be getting on to India, otherwise I shall have no time left to spend there."

"Good heavens, why?" I asked, having entirely forgotten that our journey could have a time limit.

"Well, I've promised Michael that I'd be in England in another six weeks."

There was a rather long pause before Faubion said, "I must say, it makes a very neat ending."

Clare said, "It's certainly not an ending for me."

Faubion said, "I meant The Trip. C'est tout, c'est fini." Then Faubion made a little speech which is as good a thing as any to finish with. He said, "We may not have seen very much, and we may not have learned very much, but I do know that I've been left with a lot of questions. Why is there, in the West, such an extraordinary ignorance about Asia? Why is no Asian history taught in schools except as advanced and optional courses?

"Why is it that foreigners who come to Asia, except for a few students and researchers, never see fit to learn any Oriental language? Not that language is the end of one's problems, but one can scarcely begin on an understanding until something of the language is mastered. As Alit used to tell us, we are surrounded by a miasma of fears about Asia—of unpredictable violence from colored races, of. a different standard of honesty, an uncomfortable distrust of their motives and loyalties.

"If an American goes to France, he knows at least the names of French historical figures, even if he remembers nothing of their story. But in Asia he has none of that half-conscious familiarity with names and places. You people," he said, turning to me, "account for half the world's population, thousands of years of the world's civilized history, yet most of the other half of the world knows nothing about you except a few incoherent and inaccurate fantasies." He stopped abruptly. "The world," he said, parodying his previous tone, "is growing bigger every day."

DATE DUE

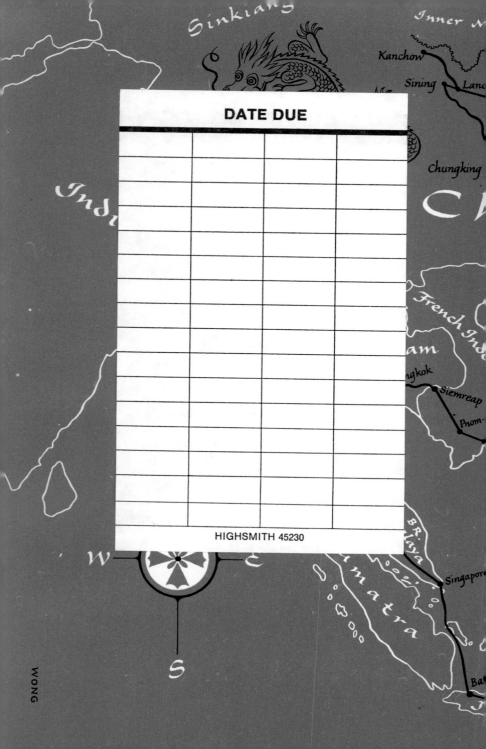

DATE DUE

HIGHSMITH 45230